Africa in the Contemporary Spanish Novel, 1990–2010

Africa in the Contemporary Spanish Novel, 1990–2010

Mahan L. Ellison

LEXINGTON BOOKS
Lanham • Boulder • New York • London

Published by Lexington Books
An imprint of The Rowman & Littlefield Publishing Group, Inc.
4501 Forbes Boulevard, Suite 200, Lanham, Maryland 20706
www.rowman.com

86-90 Paul Street, London EC2A 4NE

Copyright © 2021 by The Rowman & Littlefield Publishing Group, Inc.

All rights reserved. No part of this book may be reproduced in any form or by any electronic or mechanical means, including information storage and retrieval systems, without written permission from the publisher, except by a reviewer who may quote passages in a review.

British Library Cataloguing in Publication Information Available

Library of Congress Cataloging-in-Publication Data

Names: Ellison, Mahan L., 1981- author.
Title: Africa in the contemporary Spanish novel, 1990-2010 / Mahan L. Ellison.
Description: Lanham : Lexington Books, [2021] | Includes bibliographical references and index.
Identifiers: LCCN 2021024408 (print) | LCCN 2021024409 (ebook) | ISBN 9781793607423 (hardcover ; alk. paper) | ISBN 9781793607430 (epub) 9781793607447 (pbk)
Subjects: LCSH: Africa—In literature. | Spanish fiction—20th century—History and criticism. | Spanish fiction—21st century—History and criticism. | Other (Philosophy) in literature. | Postcolonialism in literature. | LCGFT: Literary criticism.
Classification: LCC PQ6140.A37 E55 2021 (print) | LCC PQ6140.A37 (ebook) | DDC 863/.64093586—dc23
LC record available at https://lccn.loc.gov/2021024408
LC ebook record available at https://lccn.loc.gov/2021024409

For Ashley, Dela, and Eliza

Contents

Acknowledgments	ix
Introduction	1
Chapter 1: War, Diplomacy, Decolonization, and the Other	21
Chapter 2: Gender and the Other	73
Chapter 3: Travel and the Other	121
Conclusion	177
Bibliography	181
Index	193
About the Author	201

Acknowledgments

I am grateful for the kindness of my colleagues and friends that have supported my research and encouraged me to develop it. This book would not exist without the continued support of Ana Rueda at the University of Kentucky. In addition, Debra Faszer-McMahon, Victoria L. Ketz, and N. Michelle Murray all gave me a chance to publish some of my early work that encouraged me to continue to work on this book. I have also appreciated the support of the Luso-Hispanophone Caucus of the African Literature Association, and especially from Arthur Hughes and Dorothy Odartey-Wellington.

My research would not be possible without the wonderful support of Bridgewater College's Research Support Librarian, Vickie Montigaud-Green. Her ability to get books and articles for my work is astounding. In addition, my colleagues in the World Languages & Cultures department at Bridgewater College and my division head, Betsy Hayes, have helped me to find time to focus on my research in the midst of many other responsibilities, and for that I am very grateful. I am fortunate to have some wonderful colleagues, and I thank Alma, Grace, Chris, Susan, Geraldine, Valerie, and Kara for all their support and camaraderie.

Research for this book was made possible by financial support from a grant from the Program for Cultural Cooperation Between the Spanish Ministry of Education and Culture and the United States' Universities, the Virginia Foundation for Independent Colleges Mednick Memorial Fellowship, a National Endowment for the Humanities Summer Institute, as well as more than one Bridgewater College Faculty Research Grant.

I am grateful to Ramón Mayrata, Javier Reverte, Lorenzo Silva, Donato Ndongo, Alberto Vázquez-Figueroa, Bahia Mahmud Awah, and Ebnu for their willingness to let me interview them as I began research on this project. They were patient with my questions and generous with their time. I am also grateful for the help, support, and suggestions from Abdellatif Limami, Hassan Boutakka, Mohamed Abrighach, Montserrat Abumalham, and Basilio Rodríguez Cañada.

My ability to produce a book such as this is the product of many educators, mentors, and friends, especially ones such as Ward Nicholson, Ron Friis, Gloria Pajares, and Joaquín Hita. I owe a tremendous debt of gratitude to Gloria for her patience with me; my love for language began at an early age, but Gloria instilled in me a deep love for Spanish, and especially *el andalú*. At the University of Kentucky, my interest in this field was supported by Susan Larson, Susan Carvalho, Diane King, Enrico Mario Santí, and others. I am deeply grateful for the patient educators that invested in me along the way.

My partner, Ashley Dickson, has been an understanding and sustaining companion through the eternal process of researching, writing, and publishing a book. She has read drafts, listened to ideas, offered suggestions, and endured the stresses and frustrations of life with an obsessive academic.

I owe my love for both Africa and literature to my parents, Bob and Janet Ellison, and I am thankful for the education that they gave me, from the days of homeschooling to encouraging me to study in Spain while in college. A fastidious biographer might note that the seeds of this project were sown almost thirty years ago in a small schoolhouse in Okuta, Nigeria.

A sincere thanks to the anonymous peer reviewer that provided helpful feedback for improving this book, and also to the team at Lexington Books: Emily Roderick, Trevor F. Crowell, Shelby Russell, Joseph Parry, Janice Braunstein, and all the others that work behind the scenes. I am especially appreciative of the patience that was extended to me as I worked on this manuscript during the COVID-19 pandemic.

Introduction

My intent with this project is to examine and analyze the dynamics that underlie textual distinctions of Otherness in the Spanish novel from the period of 1990 to 2010. I analyze these works—by both Peninsular and Hispanophone African authors—primarily through the work of Edward Said in *Orientalism* in order to highlight the trends that characterize the representation of Africa and the African Other in contemporary Spanish letters.

Said understood the narrative of Occident and Orient as one of cultural contestants,[1] and this critique of Orientalist discourse examines the way that writing difference in the West has traditionally been employed to maintain a supposed cultural dominance rather than as an attempt to understand and represent the Other in good faith. For Said, Orientalist discourse is a

> corporate institution [of the West] for dealing with the Orient—dealing with it by making statements about it, authorizing views of it, describing it, by teaching it, settling it, ruling over it: in short, Orientalism as a Western style for dominating, restructuring, and having authority over the Orient.[2]

This study, therefore, understands Orientalism as a discursive strategy for maintaining and affirming the assumed superiority—moral, cultural, or other—of the West by denying the humanity, moral or cultural validity, or individual agency of the contextual Other. As Orientalist discourse seeks to perpetuate a hierarchy that privileges the West over any Other, this work examines select representative examples of contemporary Spanish authors who write against this pretentious and ultimately limiting discourse, and who set aside assumptions of cultural superiority in their narration.

Writing about the Other, speaking for or representing the Other, indeed, even employing the term *Other*, is tricky business. In his 2008 collection of essays, *The Other*, Ryszard Kapuściński begins with the white, Eurocentric clarification that

> The terms 'Other' or 'Others' can be understood in all sorts of ways and used in various meanings and contexts, to distinguish gender, for example, or generation, or nationality, or religion and so on. In my case I use these terms mainly to distinguish Europeans, people from the West, whites, from those whom I call 'Others'—that is, non-Europeans, or non-whites, while fully aware that for the latter, the former are just as much 'Others.'[3]

This explanation is rather limited when considering the contemporary realities of transnational migration and the multicultural populations of many European and Western countries, not to mention the purely exterior, phenotypical markings upon which it depends. The assumption of racial homogeneity suggests that identifying an Other is an easy distinction to make. A definition such as this one might suffice for an analysis of the writing of Pedro Antonio de Alarcón in *Diario de un testigo de la Guerra de África* (1859) or Ernesto Giménez Caballero in *Notas marruecas de un soldado* (1923), but it is less useful when applied to authors that recognize alterity as nuanced and constructed. Contemporary Spanish authors are frequently re-imagining what this idea of alterity means, and the growth of a body of works by African authors writing in Spanish and publishing in Spain is further destabilizing the totemic dichotomy of Otherness as merely a racial categorization.

More useful, perhaps, is French philosopher Emmanuel Levinas's considerations of the Other. Levinas's definition is also an understanding that functions on a physical distinction between separate entities, though it is de-racialized. His Other is one stripped of "cultural signification," and simply the existential presence of an Other physical being.[4] Both interpretations are defined by the exteriority of this Other's presence. Levinas's Other is not necessarily a racial or cultural one, but simply an exterior human presence to one's self. This is an understanding of alterity that is flexible and contextual, and, as such, more relevant to an analysis of authors that re-imagine or subvert historic understandings of alterity.

Since questions of race and difference are both inherent and inevitable in a study such as this one, the American Anthropological Association's "Statement on Race" offers the reminder that

> attempt[s] to establish lines of division among biological populations [are] both arbitrary and subjective . . . the idea of 'race' has always carried more meanings than mere physical differences; indeed, physical variations in the human species have no meanings except the social ones that humans put on them.[5]

Therefore, ideas of Same and Other, as examined in this book, must be understood as contextually based and subjectively construed, and, more specifically, discursively constructed. As Levinas notes in *Humanism of the Other*, "Comprehension of the Other is therefore a hermeneutic, an exegesis."[6]

In keeping with Levinas, my use and understanding of the term *Other* builds on literary analysis and depends upon specific textual context for exact definition, but it is ultimately based upon textual presentation of *difference* or *alterity* broadly interpreted; that is, physical, cultural, linguistic, religious, ideological, or other differences that manifest as recognition between two (or more) parties of contradistinction. In the context of this book, Africa and the African are often portrayed as Spain's default Others due the historical conceptualization of Spain as a European, Catholic, Western totality.[7] The textual contexts that frame individual analyses of representation of the Other within this work not only draw upon the protagonists' interactions within plot lines but examine the very narrative that the author creates to tell the story. Descriptions—adjectives, metaphors, tone, etc.—and literary devices explicitly and implicitly mark difference. The Other that I examine is also not merely anOther person, but can, in fact, often be a totality or a geography.

When writing about an Other, even the best intentions at honesty and equitability can be problematic and hint at underlying concepts or paternalist discourse. Hélène Cixous asserts that

> everything throughout the centuries depends on the distinction between the Selfsame, the ownself . . . and that which limits it: . . . the 'other'. What is the 'Other'? If it is truly 'other', there is nothing to say; it cannot be theorized. The 'other' escapes me. It is elsewhere, outside: absolutely other.[8]

Her assertion suggests an extreme alterity that defies comprehension or representation and Said likewise criticizes the West's insistence on speaking for the Orient, just as Flaubert "spoke for and represented" his archetypal Oriental woman.[9] It is obvious that Western authors have not refrained from speaking *about* their Others; if that were the case, I would not have a book here. However, the style of narrating the Other, when analyzed, can say much about authorial assumptions, conscious or unconscious. Therefore, with a word of advice from Said, "the things to look at are style, figures of speech, setting, narrative devices, historical and social circumstances, *not* the correctness of the representation nor its fidelity to some great original."[10] When speaking about or attempting to speak for the Other, *what* is said is often only incidental, *how* it is said can be much more revealing. Levinas's statement that "comprehension of the Other is therefore a hermeneutic, an exegesis" should be directed at both the author and the critic.[11] Both should be aware of the processes of interpretation that undergird writing about any Other—the critic doubly so.

Said, while eminently useful, is not infallible. The prominence and timeliness of *Orientalism* position him as one of the most polemic and popular critical voices on discourses of West and Orient; the contributions of the insights in his tome are valuable, but, as with all theories, open to substantial critique. Daniel Varisco's *Reading Orientalism: Said and the Unsaid* (2007) offers one of the most exhaustive critiques of *Orientalism* as he examines the value of Said's work while also clearly highlighting its limitations, effectively serving as an exhortation to "move beyond the polemicized rhetoric of the binary blame game."[12] Several of the novelists that I examine here also suggest that Said's binary-based articulation of Same and Other is a limiting paradigm, while others repurpose the dichotomic structure in ways that acknowledge and subvert the power of Orientalism. While Varisco's work stands as a primary theoretical contestant to Said, other important detractors include George Landow, Bryan Turner, John MacKenzie, Ibn Warraq, Robert J. C. Young, and Bernard Lewis.[13] In short, Landow critiques Said's neglect of gender issues, Ibn Warraq criticizes the limits of Said's methods, and Young highlights the "theoretical contradictions and conflicts in Said's text."[14] As I develop my arguments and articulate my analyses in later chapters, I will return to specific criticisms of *Orientalism* as relevant.

Robert Young, in *White Mythologies* (2004), argues that Said never offered an alternative to Orientalist discourse. Some of the authors examined in this book do offer alternatives and are writing Africa and the African Other in ways that fall outside (or at least in the interstices) of the harmful dimensions of Orientalist discourse. They have developed discursive strategies that avoid the traps of Orientalism. Encounters with Others are inevitable, and to ignore the Other denies their presence, as Gayatri Spivak reminds us: "to render thought or the thinking subject transparent or invisible seems, by contrast, to hide the relentless recognition of the Other."[15] It is, therefore, incumbent upon us to analyze and understand the power and potential effects of contemporary popular discourse. We must learn from our mistakes and successes to find and challenge spaces where supposed cultural hierarchies do not recognize the humanity and validity of diverse, Other voices.

Said's *Orientalism* is immediately limiting for this project as Africa is not usually considered to be a part of "the Orient." Said does suggest similarities—"For imperialists like Balfour, or for anti-imperialists like J. A. Hobson, the Oriental, *like the African,* is a member of a subject race and not exclusively an inhabitant of a geographical area" (emphasis mine)[16]—but at the same time this comparison serves to distinguish the two. Because they are merely alike implies that they are not a unified conceptualization. The comparison does, however, realign focus on the Other from one of simple geographical difference to one of conceptual (subjective) hierarchical relationship, and in this understanding, what Said writes about Orientalism can be directly applied to the West's writing of Africa also.

Where Said's articulation of Orientalism fails to directly consider Africa, there have been others that have addressed the West's treatment of Africa. V. Y. Mudimbe's work, specifically in *The Invention of Africa* (1988) and *The Idea of Africa* (1994), is essential to understanding Europe's colonial and postcolonial interactions with Africa. Ali Mazrui notes a subtle, yet important, distinction between the theorization of Said and Mudimbe in considering that

> Edward Said's central thesis in *Orientalism* and *Culture and Imperialism* is about the invention of the Orient. V. Y. Mudimbe's central thesis in *The Invention of Africa* and *The Idea of Africa* is about the invention of Africa. But while Said insists that the Orient does not exist and has never existed outside the imagination of the West, Mudimbe is prepared to accept that the invention of Africa is a prophecy in the process of self-fulfillment.[17]

With this distinction, Mudimbe examines how Europe's conceptualization of Africa has shaped the history and present realities of Africa in significant ways.

There has been some good, recent work on Spain and its complicated history with Orientalism. Gonzalo Fernández Parrilla's work has closely examined Orientalism and postcolonial study in the Spanish case, and he notes that "Spanish Orientalism has been a practice almost limited to Arabic studies" while "Africanism was almost exclusively devoted to Morocco."[18] Susan Martin-Márquez's *Disorientations: Spanish Colonialism in Africa and the Performance of Identity* (2008) highlights some of the historical factors that complicate Orientalism in the Spanish case:

> [The] "rediscovery" of [Spain's] Andalusi past led Spaniards and foreigners alike to Orientalize the Iberian nation. While some of the Spanish elite reveled in self-exoticization, others responded anxiously by projecting their "own" alterity onto the "usual suspects" in Africa and the Middle East—but also onto other Spaniards. In this sense, Spain is a nation that is at once Orientalized and Orientalizing. The dynamic resembles a Möbius strip, calling into question the possibility of any location "outside" Orientalist discourse. For Spaniards, this positioning on both "sides" of Orientalism—as simultaneously "self" and "other"—may bring about a profound sense of "disorientation."[19]

Fernández Parrilla further explains this "Möbius strip" thus: "This dynamic of simultaneous exclusion and inclusion in the way Spain relates to its Islamic history—and in the way Spain was/is perceived from outside—is rather exceptional; in fact, as unique and ubiquitous as might be its colonial history."[20]

For all of these reasons that Martin-Márquez and Fernández Parrilla outline—Spain's unique history with the Islamic world in the European context and the limited scope of Orientalist reflections in the Spanish context—it is all the more necessary to continue to build upon the work that seeks to develop this area of study, to continue to consider how Spain's past affects its present and future and to expand it beyond a focus on Arabic and Morocco to the other areas of Africa that experienced Spanish colonialism, namely Western Sahara and Equatorial Guinea.

Fortunately, there is some recent and thoughtful academic attention being paid to the connections between Spain and Africa. Sidi M. Omar, the Saharawi academic and diplomat, has engaged with the work of Said, Bhabha, and Spivak on the issue of postcoloniality, identity, and Africa in his book *Los estudios post-coloniales: una introducción crítica* (2008).[21] And in 2019, the *Journal of Spanish Cultural Studies* published a special issue titled *Entering the Global Hispanophone* that seeks to draw attention to overlooked Hispanophone communities, ranging from Equatorial Guinea to the Philippines.[22] In the introduction to the special issue, Adolfo Campoy-Cubillo and Benita Sampedro Vizcaya conclude that

> Entering the Global Hispanophone, we contend, is not an attempt to demarcate a newly distinctive, fixed and enclosed disciplinary field, but rather an invitation to branch out beyond the traditional archives of Hispanism, engaging with some of the dispersed geographies, cultural and linguistic traditions . . . [and] It is also a determination to break away from the overarching Iberian/Latin American binary and to embrace other communities, histories, experiences and repertoires.[23]

To mark, perhaps, the institutional recognition of the growth of this field, Campoy-Cubillo and Sampedro Vizcaya note that in 2015 the Modern Language Association approved the establishment of a permanent online forum to encourage the further development of the field of study.[24] From publishing and academic trends over the past few decades, it is clear that there is a growing body of works by African authors in Spanish, and these works are receiving both popular and critical attention.[25]

Therefore, this study would not be complete without a consideration of new cultural voices that contribute to the current Spanish literary production. The promising rise in recognition of Hispano-African voices in Peninsular literature is relatively recent. These voices represent the hybridity and the growing diversity of contemporary Spain; the Equatoguinean author Donato Ndongo emphasizes this diversity by observing that "integration does not mean that we eat chorizo, but rather that the societies that take us in are sufficiently flexible to understand some of our customs."[26] The Spanish writings of authors such as Ndongo or Ahmed Daoudi contribute to the current discourse of Spanish letters, amplifying the diversity of voices within the contemporary canon.

It is also important, here, to clarify my use of the term "Hispano-African" in referring to many of these authors, especially since the term "Afro-Hispanic" is more frequently employed. When referring to African authors that write in Spanish, I prefer "Hispano-African" as a term that centers the African as the primary identity. In his dissertation, Jorge Salvo clarifies that "Hispano-African is used in contrast to Afro-Hispanic. The first represents the Hispanophone African culture of Equatorial Guinea, while the second represents the culture that has been developed by the descendants of the African slaves that were brought to Spanish America."[27] When writing about African authors that write in Spanish, I find "Hispano-African" to be more appropriate as it emphasizes the African as the primary element of literary identity. For the younger generation of authors, second generation immigrants that have grown up in Spain and are now producing works of literature, I might feel more comfortable with the more common "Afro-Hispanic."

I should also note that, among Hispanophone Moroccan authors, there is a strong resistance even to the term "Hispano-African" because it is a reminder of the often-Orientalized literature written by Spaniards about Morocco.[28] The preferred referent is "Moroccan literature expressed in Spanish."[29] In my early years of research I made the mistake of referring to Hispanophone Moroccan authors as "Hispano-African" and I was corrected quite emphatically by my Moroccan colleagues. This lesson still serves as a reminder for me to center the African/Maghrebi identity when referencing literature produced by African authors. I will often use the phrase "Hispanophone Moroccan/African literature" because it is slightly wieldier in English than the phrase "Moroccan literature expressed in Spanish," and, so far, it seems to be an acceptable substitute in many instances.

One cannot talk about African authors writing in a European language without mentioning the esteemed Ngũgĩ wa Thiong'o, and, specifically, his work *Decolonising the Mind* (1986). He would, perhaps, take issue with calling the works of these Hispanophone African authors "African literature" as he asserts that "African literatures can only be written in African languages."[30] Spanish literary production by African authors is a product of what Thiong'o calls "Colonial alienation":

> Colonial alienation takes two interlinked forms: an active (or passive) distancing of oneself from the reality around; and an active (or passive) identification with that which is most external to one's environment. It starts with a deliberate disassociation of the language of conceptualisation, of thinking, of formal education, of mental development, from the language of daily interaction in the

home and in the community. It is like separating the mind from the body so that they are occupying two unrelated linguistic spheres in the same person. On a larger scale it is like producing a society of bodiless heads and headless bodies.[31]

Thiong'o's opinion is clear and strongly expressed, but it leaves scholars and readers with the question of "how then do we understand African literature written in European languages?" My response is that we should approach Hispanophone African literatures with a critical eye to the (post-)colonial contexts that birthed them and remember that language and identity are incredibly complex dynamics. Some authors have no choice but to write in Spanish due to the underdevelopment of literacy in many regional African languages as a product of colonialism, while other authors deliberately choose to write in Spanish for questions of audience, prestige, or artistic expression.

In their 1975 book, *Kafka: Toward a Minor Literature*, Deleuze and Guattari examine the power and importance of "minor literature," defined as literature that "doesn't come from a minor language; it is rather that which a minority constructs within a major language."[32] According to Deleuze and Guattari, the work of marginalized voices writing in the the context of a major (global or colonial perhaps) language, is of revolutionary potential; these voices remind readers of the "revolutionary conditions for every literature within the heart of what is called great (or established) literature."[33] Therefore, Moroccan, Equatorial Guinean, Saharawi, and other authors that choose Spanish as their language of literary expression demonstrate the expansive possibilities of linguistic expression and deterritorialize a tradition of literary hegemony. Within a cultural paradigm that has historically privileged the West over its Other, the revolutionary potential of "minor literature" functions to destabilize persistent cultural hierarchies.

In discussing the Hispano-African literary voices, it is also important to acknowledge and address the postcolonial question. For the twenty-first century, in certain contexts, "postcolonial" is an outdated, though not irrelevant, term. This statement does not attempt to deny the pernicious and persistent relevance of postcolonial concerns; indeed, Ahmed Daoudi's *El Diablo de Yudis* (1994),[34] Concha López Sarasúa's *La llamada del almuédano* (1990),[35] and María Dueñas's *El tiempo entre costuras* (2009)[36] all directly address the Spanish colonial heritage in Africa, but I do want to emphasize that, for many contemporary Hispano-African authors, their concerns are not limited to postcolonial preoccupations; there are other pressing concerns. Ndongo, for instance, notes that exile is one for his generation; "our generation has to live with exile just as others had to live with slavery or colonialism."[37] And, while the reality of exile is very often directly linked to colonial aftereffects, it also is its own reality with unique nuances.[38] Likewise, many of the Moroccan authors writing in Spanish are choosing fewer political themes and writing narratives that focus on quotidian or genre-specific concerns. While I do not discount the role that postcolonial and subaltern themes continue to play in the representation of the Other and its concomitant analysis. I also do not want to approach these current Hispano-African authors with a theoretical framework that limits their project to a political exercise.

As examined above, Said's magnum opus, *Orientalism*, described and criticized a pattern of thought and representation that denied voice and agency to all non-Western Others. It continues to be exigent to examine the residual effect of Said's critique upon Spanish letters. One would hope that the poetic extravagances of colonial authors such as Alarcón are a thing of the past. This book begins with this hope as it focuses on the nexus of the contemporary Spanish novel and Africa. This project is primarily focused on literary analysis and does not focus on academic discourse, the media, or diplomatic writings. Instead, I consider the progress and pitfalls found in a representative selection of the fictional production in Spanish of authors from 1990 to 2010.

This is a critical and important time period. Between 1990 and 2010, Spain and Europe experienced tremendous immigration and demographic change. Literature produced in Spanish by African authors was nascent, and some of the most significant works and authors began to publish and receive attention in the 80s, 90s, and early 2000s. The two decades from 1990 to 2010 represent a crucial moment of growth and recognition for African authors writing in Spanish, and the number of authors has grown dramatically in the decade since 2010. Marvin A. Lewis published his book *An Introduction to the Literature of Equatorial Guinea* in 2007 and the following decade brought such a growth of new works by Equatoguinean authors that he followed this work up with his 2017 *Equatorial Guinean Literature in its National and Transnational Contexts*. Numerous anthologies of Moroccan literature have been published in Spanish in the past two decades,[39] and Saharawi poets maintain an active presence in Spanish literary circles.

The authors whose works I specifically analyze include Lorenzo Silva (*El nombre de los nuestros*, 2008),[40] Concha López Sarasúa (*La llamada del almuédano*, 1990),[41] Ramón Mayrata (*El imperio desierto*, 1992),[42] María Dueñas (*El tiempo entre costuras*, 2009),[43] Guillermina Mekuy (*Las tres vírgenes de Santo Tomás*, 2008),[44] Montserrat Abumalham (*¿Te acuerdas de Shahrazad?*, 2001),[45] Javier Reverte (*El médico de Ifni*, 2005),[46] Alberto Vázquez-Figueroa (*Los ojos del Tuareg*, 2005),[47] and Ahmed Daoudi (*El diablo de Yudis*, 1994).[48] These authors offer interesting, popular, critically acclaimed, and/or provocative examples of works that engage with the theme of Africa. They each approach the theme from differing angles: the war setting of *El nombre de los nuestros* contrasts directly with immigration story of *El diablo de Yudis*, just as the colonial representation in *La llamada del almuédano* differs from the decolonization process examined in *El imperio* *desierto*. Likewise, the biographies of authors such as María Dueñas and Alberto Vázquez-Figueroa or Montserrat Abumalham and Guillermina Mekuy represent differing literary backgrounds and target audiences. I have made a deliberate attempt to gather a collection of works that is varied in both theme and author in order to effectively carry out the project at hand. At the threshold of the twenty-first century, as these works looked to Africa for theme and inspiration, an analysis of these novels can highlight the strategies employed in the literary representation of Africa and the African Other in the contemporary Spanish novel.

As noted above, *Orientalism*'s focus is broad and can be applied to the literal Orient or almost any non-Western Other. I focus on the geographic region of Africa—and specifically Spain's former colonies in Morocco, Western Sahara, and Equatorial Guinea—to highlight a contemporary selection of Spanish and Hispano-African authors that are writing about Africa and the African in new and critically significant ways. In the colonial context that dominated Spain's interaction with these regions from the sixteenth to the twentieth centuries, Orientalist discourse prevailed in many writings about the African territories.[49] In looking back to the post-colonial vantage point at the threshold of the twenty-first century, I find that contemporary Spanish authors are writing about Africa in more equitable and less patronizing methods that warrant analysis, even though others continue to subtly rely on the tired tropes that characterize Orientalist discourse.

But, why Africa?

Spain's geographical proximity to Africa has been the source of a unique relationship between the continent and the country. As Mediterranean neighbors, the shores of the Iberian Peninsula and North Africa have been scenes of cultural exchange and conflict for millennia. The shared history of the two regions has unfolded through the Umayyad conquest of Hispania in 711 CE, followed by cultural coexistence on the Iberian Peninsula for over seven centuries, the *Reconquista* and eventual defeat of the Nasrid Kingdom in Granada in 1492, the colonial missions and the wars in northern Africa in the nineteenth and twentieth centuries, Spanish immigration to the African colonies in the twentieth century, and recently the influx of African immigrants into Spain. Over the centuries, Africa has left significant architectural, linguistic, and cultural impressions on Spain and Spanish culture, impressions that represent centuries of historical encounters and interactions.[50]

Throughout its history Spain has attempted to define itself not only against but also through its relationship with Africa. Africa has not, of course, been the only Other upon which Spain has constructed its cultural identity, but it cannot be denied that this particular relationship dates back into the far reaches of Spanish history, long before Spain built its glory on colonial conquest in the Americas. Whether a definition of Spanish culture has come from forcing national identity as being entirely European[51] or through Spain's attempt to recuperate its status as a colonial force after the disastrous results of the Spanish-American War in 1898,[52] the idea of Africa has served as an important Other in the Spanish psyche. For almost a century, from the 1860s to the 1950s, Spain conceived of expanding itself across the Mediterranean Sea and up to the Atlas Mountains of North Africa in an ambitious project to create an "España Transfetana."[53] Indeed, in the 1950s, 90 percent of the population in the "urban nuclei"[54] of the Spanish Protectorates of Morocco was of Spanish birth and origin.[55] The tides of immigration and settlement ventures have shifted back and forth over the Mediterranean for the last thirteen hundred years establishing connections and interactions that have profoundly shaped Spanish perceptions of Africa as an Other.

The second half of the twentieth century has only further complicated the relationship and understanding between Spain and differing regions in Africa. Long after it lost possession of its American and Pacific colonies, Spain maintained an official colonial presence in Morocco,[56] Western Sahara,[57] and Equatorial Guinea[58] up through the late seventies. The disintegration of these former colonies forced Spain to reevaluate its conception of and relationship to Africa. On the political front, new methods of engagement and understanding have needed to be employed. Old concepts of the historical "Other" have had to be reexamined. Traditional processes of political and cultural interaction have had to be reevaluated in the contemporary, globalized twenty-first century. These new political and cultural considerations have found themselves reflected and examined in the recent literary projects from Spain's contemporary authors.

As I engage with the theoretical work of Edward Said, specifically *Orientalism* (1978), to determine whether (or not) his proposed Orientalist theories still hold value for a study of the contemporary Spanish novel of thirty years later, I will also rely on works by Daniel Varisco (*Reading Orientalism: Said and the Unsaid*, 2007), Emmanuel Levinas (*Humanism of the Other*, 1972), Gil Anidjar (*The Jew, The Arab: A History of the Enemy*, 2003), Fatema Mernissi (*Scheherazade Goes West*, 2001), James C. Scott (*Seeing Like a State*, 1998), and V. Y. Mudimbe (*The Invention of Africa*, 1988 and *The Idea of Africa*, 1994), among others. These texts will serve to elucidate themes of political interaction, gender, and travel between Spain and Africa as represented in the novels. These theorists will contribute to a theoretical framework that posits the contemporary novels of Silva, López Sarasúa, Mayrata, Dueñas, Mekuy, Abumalham, Reverte, Vázquez-Figueroa, and Daoudi in their historical, cultural, and theoretical context, thereby illuminating the underlying dynamics that structure their works.

The imaginary that pertains to Africa has served such a vital role in the history and creation of modern Spain that it is revealing to examine the influences that it continues to exert on Spanish writers. Such an analysis can reveal the enduring power of the Orientalist legacy, and also the strategies that contemporary authors employ to avoid traditional literary tropes. In the last thirty years, Spain's political relationships with Africa have changed dramatically, as they have shifted from Spain's paternalistic colonial governance to differing levels of autonomy and independence. While contemporary authors seek to engage with this change, it is imperative to examine their work to evaluate the current status of the literary relationship between Spain and its historical Other so that we can understand the patterns of representation that continue to be employed in contemporary works. Also, while the novels under consideration are receiving growing critical attention, this work aspires to contribute to this growing field re-examining Spain's historical involvement with Africa by considering the status of Orientalism in contemporary Spanish fiction. These authors have made significant contributions to the contemporary literary landscape in Spain and it is imperative that the way Africa figures in their novelistic corpus be critically analyzed.

This project will engage with a variety of questions as it seeks to analyze the fate of Orientalism in contemporary Spanish fiction around three distinct but interrelated topics: (a) the political dimension, (b) gender issues, and (c) travel. The political interactions between Spain and Africa offer the opportunity to examine questions such as "How does war affect the representation of the Other?" and "How are Spanish authors re-writing historic encounters between Spain and Africa such as colonialism?" Issues of gender raise the questions of "Is Africa still a virgin land to be explored?" or "How has the representation of the erotic African Other changed?" And finally, an analysis of archetypes of travel can illuminate whether or not the North African nomad is still a romantic enigma in the popular imaginary, or how affluence affects mobility and representation in portrayals of the tourist or the immigrant. These questions, and others like them, have structured my personal approach to these novels as I have read, engaged with, and analyzed their narratives. As I selected specific texts, I also asked myself whether these novels held literary value, or whether they instead contributed to the project due to their own ambitious commercial or humanistic goals. Ultimately, I have sought to evaluate the extent to which Saidian Orientalism persists in Spanish literature, and my findings suggest a waning of influence, but also a stubborn persistence of the same.

What follows is an outline of my chapter distribution and the specific issues that I seek to address:

Chapter 1, "War, Diplomacy, Decolonization, and the Other," examines historic and contemporary engagement with and representation of the Other in a variety of encounters: war, diplomacy, and colonial motivations for interaction as portrayed in the novels of Lorenzo Silva, Concha López Sarasúa, and Ramón Mayrata. My analysis of Silva's *El nombre de los nuestros* examines the distinction between a cultural Other and the enemy combatant, and how Silva redraws lines of alterity along social class instead of cultural difference. López Sarasúa's *La llamada del almuédano* offers a view of Spanish immigration to the Moroccan Protectorate during the mid-twentieth century. This novel reconceptualizes ideas of the geographical fatherland, re-ordering the preferential hierarchy for the European peninsula. Mayrata's *El imperio desierto* takes up the issue of the decolonization of Western Sahara and the West's patronizing attempts to speak and decide for its African Other.

Chapter 2, "Gender and the Other," focuses on the use of gender and eroticized portrayals of the Other and how such depictions reflect the shifting stereotypes and motives that inspire them. Dueñas's *El tiempo entre costuras* employs colonial Morocco as a backdrop to a young woman's maturation and liberation, conferring upon Africa qualities of possibility that are unavailable in the West. Mekuy's *Las tres vírgenes de Santo Tomás* offers a provocative representation of female sexuality by an Equatoguinean author, engaging with questions of resistance, identity, and religion. And Abumalham's epistolary novel *¿Te acuerdas de Shahrazad?* invokes the literary, Oriental archetype of Shahrazad, while simultaneously deterritorializing the novel and invocation.

Finally, Chapter 3, "Travel and the Other," examines the use of travel in the novel on Africa, and specifically the representations of the archetypal figures of the tourist, the nomad, and the immigrant. The protagonist of Reverte's *El médico de Ifni* is an affluent, Spanish tourist who becomes obsessed with finding the truth about her father who died as a renegade in the Saharawi independence movement while Vázquez-Figueroa's *Los ojos del Tuareg* focuses on the lives of a small family of Tuareg nomads that must confront the Western rally car drivers that disrupt their lifestyle. Daoudi's *El diablo de Yudis* offers the story of a frustrated migrant and draws heavily on traditional Moroccan story-telling strategies. The use of each of these traveling archetypes opens for analysis distinct social and cultural representations of difference.

An analysis of these themes will articulate my thesis: contemporary Spanish authors are generally approaching Spain's former colonial enclaves in Africa (Morocco, Western Sahara, and Equatorial Guinea) with a novel understanding of their historical neighbor that is significantly more impartial in its attempt to portray a cultural and historical equal—a portrayal that consciously challenges historical inaccuracies and stereotypes that preference a cultural high ground to the Iberian peninsula. Throughout the study, as I move from war and peace to gender issues and to the displacement of travel, I will return to the central concern of whether contemporary Spanish authors are perpetuating Orientalist tendencies or if they have been able to move beyond Orientalism in their treatment of the Other.

These authors represent a diverse selection of voices in contemporary Spanish literary production. María Dueñas, Guillermina Mekuy, Alberto Vázquez-Figueroa, Lorenzo Silva, and Javier Reverte are all best-selling authors. Ahmed Daoudi, Lorenzo Silva, and Concha López Sarasúa have each received substantial critical attention from academia, and the work of each of these authors merits further analysis. María Dueñas and Montserrat Abumalham are both university professors in Spain and their works examined here are their first published works of fiction; Ahmed Daoudi's novel holds the distinction of being the first novel by a Moroccan author published in Spanish by a Spanish publisher. Abumalham is also a significant voice in recent Hispano-Moroccan literary production, and she, Dueñas, López Sarasúa, and Mekuy all contribute a feminine authorial voice to this project.

It was not an easy process to choose a limited selection of authors and novels for this work. As such, this book does not pretend to be an exhaustive examination of all relevant authors or literary works. This project does hope to highlight some trends within the contemporary Spanish literary landscape, and the authors included here should serve as a useful representative selection for such an ambition. The interest that Spanish authors have in returning to the theme of Africa must be noted. The recent literary output is staggering. Javier Reverte alone has published a trilogy of travel writings on Africa, retracing the explorations of the titans of Western exploration in Africa such as Stanley Livingstone and Mungo Park (*Caminos perdidos de África*, 2004; *Vagabundo en África*, 2005; and *El sueño de África*, 2007),[59] as well as novels on Africa (*El médico de Ifni*, 2005, and the recent *La canción de Mbama*, 2011)[60] and a collection of poetry titled *Poemas africanos* (2011).[61] Vázquez-Figueroa has repeatedly turned to Africa for inspiration in his novels such as *África llora* (2004),[62] *Tuareg* (1980), and *Arena y viento* (1953),[63] as has Lorenzo Silva in *El nombre de los nuestros* (2008)—considered in this study—and *Carta blanca* (2004),[64] as well as his non-fictional travel narrative, *Del Rif al Yebala: Viaje al sueño y la pesadilla de Marruecos* (2001).[65] Ramón Mayrata has also compiled an anthology of *Relatos del Sáhara* (2001)[66] and written a fictionalized account of Domingo Badía's eighteenth-century travels through the Maghreb in *Alí Bey El Abasí: un cristiano en La Meca* (1995).[67]

In addition to the works by authors considered in this study, there are a number of other Spanish authors employing and including Africa in their works. Lourdes Ortiz (*Fátima de los naufragios*, 1998),[68] Ignacio Martínez de Pisón (*Una guerra africana*, 2008),[69] Luis Leante (*Mira si yo te querré*, 2007),[70] Jesús Torbado (*Imperio de arena*, 1998),[71] and Bernardo Atxaga (*Siete casas en Francia*, 2009)[72] represent just a few of the authors that form a part of this focus on Africa and African themes in contemporary Spanish literature. This renewed interest is significant, and this study attempts to identify general trends in representative recent works. Questions of whether this is a commercially motivated trend or whether it is a reflection of recent immigration and political realities are largely speculative ones, but what is directly available for analysis is this question: how are these authors representing Africa and their African Other? This essential question serves as the foundation for this work, and, while I will let the chapters speak for themselves, I find that some representations move beyond the limitations of Orientalism, while others continue in its damaging tradition.

Through this work, I hope to bring attention to shifts of representation in the contemporary Spanish novel that will demonstrate the critical value of these novels while drawing attention to the contributions these authors have made to the Spanish literary field and more specifically how, in many instances, they have contributed to overturning and reevaluating long-held Orientalist stereotypes.

NOTES

1. Edward W. Said, *Orientalism* (New York: Vintage Books, 1994), 1.
2. Said, *Orientalism*, 3.
3. Ryszard Kapuściński, *The Other* (New York: Verso, 2008), 13.
4. Emmanuel Levinas, *Humanism of the Other* (Chicago: University of Illinois Press, 2003), 30.
5. "Statement on Race," American Anthropological Association, accessed May 20, 2020, https://www.americananthro.org/ConnectWithAAA/Content.aspx?ItemNumber=2583.
6. Levinas, *Humanism of the Other*, 31.
7. This essentialized vision of Spanish identity is one that was extolled during Franco's dictatorship and was built on the conceptualized unification of Spain brought about by Isabel the Catholic's expulsion of the Moors and the Jews in 1492, ignoring the incredible diversity of pre-1492 Spain.
8. Hélène Cixous and Catherine Clément, *The Newly Born Woman* (Manchester: Manchester University Press, 1986), 70.
9. Said, *Orientalism*, 6.
10. Said, *Orientalism*, 21.
11. Levinas, *Humanism of the Other*, 31.
12. Daniel Martin Varisco, *Reading Orientalism: Said and the Unsaid* (Seattle: University of Washington Press, 2007), xi.
13. See, respectively, George P. Landow's "Edward W. Said's Orientalism" (*Postcolonial Web*, 2002), Bryan Turner's *Orientalism, Postmodernism and Globalism* (Boston: Routledge, 1994), John MacKenzie's *Orientalism: History, Theory, and the Arts* (Manchester: Manchester University Press, 1995), Ibn Warraq's *Defending the West: A Critique of Edward Said's Orientalism* (New York: Prometheus Books, 2007),

Robert J. C. Young's *White Mythologies* (New York: Routledge, 2004), and Bernard Lewis, Grabar Oleg, and Edward Said's "Orientalism: An Exchange" (*New York Review of Books*, June 24, 1982).

14. Robert Young, *White Mythologies* (New York: Routledge, 2004), 180.

15. Gayatri Chakravorty Spivak, "Can the Subaltern Speak?," in *Marxism and the Interpretation of Culture*, eds. C. Nelson and L. Grossberg (Champaign: University of Illinois Press, 1988), 294.

16. Said, *Orientalism*, 92.

17. Alia A. Mazrui, "The Re-invention of Africa," *Research in African Literatures* 36, no. 3 (Fall 2005): 69.

18. Gonzalo Fernández Parrilla, "Disoriented Postcolonialities: With Edward Said in (the Labyrinth of) Al-Andalus," *Interventions* 20, no. 2 (2018): 232, 234.

19. Susan Martin-Márquez, *Disorientations: Spanish Colonialism in Africa and the Performance of Identity* (New Haven: Yale University Press, 2008), 9.

20. Fernández Parrilla, "Disoriented Postcolonialities," 234.

21. [*Post-Colonial Studies: A Critical Introduction*] Sidi M. Omar, *Los estudios post-coloniales: Una introducción crítica* (Castellón: Universitat Jaume I, 2008).

22. This special issue on the Global Hispanophone (20.1–2, 2019) follows a number of other journals that have also done special issues on Equatorial Guinea in *The Arizona Journal of Hispanic Cultural Studies* (8, 2004), *The Afro-Hispanic Review* (19.1, 2000), *Revista Debats* (123.2, 2014), and others, as well as special issues on Western Sahara in *JadMag* (1.2, 2013), *Transmodernity: Journal of Peripheral Cultural Production of the Luso-Hispanic World* (4.1, 2014), and special issues focusing on the Maghreb in the *Journal of Spanish Cultural Studies* (2011) and the *Journal of North African Studies* (24.1, 2019), among others.

23. Adolfo Campoy-Cubillo and Benita Sampedro Vizcaya, "Entering the Global Hispanophone: An Introduction," *Journal of Spanish Cultural Studies* 20, nos. 1–2 (2019): 12.

24. Campoy-Cubillo and Sampedro Vizcaya's introduction to the issue also serves as a useful summary of recent scholarship in the field. They summarize the recent book collections and special issue journals that have contributed to the development of this field.

25. Other recent and valuable works that have been useful to me in my recent research include collected editions by Dorothy Odartey-Wellington, ed., *Transafrohispanismos: Puentes culturales críticos entre África, Latinoamérica y España* (Boston: Brill Rodopi, 2018); Joanna Boampong, ed., *In and Out of Africa: Exploring Afro-Hispanic, Luso-Brazilian, and Latin American Connections* (Newcastle upon Tyne: Cambridge Scholars Publishing, 2012); and Debra Faszer-McMahon and Victoria Ketz's *African Immigrants in Contemporary Spanish Texts: Crossing the Strait* (Burlington, VT: Ashgate, 2015). As well as single-author works such as Adolfo Campoy-Cubillo's *Memories of the Maghreb* (New York: Palgrave Macmillan, 2012); Joanna Allan's *Silenced Resistance: Women, Dictatorships, and Genderwashing in Western Sahara and Equatorial Guinea* (Madison: University of Wisconsin Press, 2019); and Eric Calderwood's *Colonial al-Andalus: Spain and the Making of Modern Moroccan Culture* (Cambridge, MA: Harvard University Press, 2018), among others.

26. [la integración no significa que comamos chorizo, sino que las sociedades que nos acogen sean suficientemente flexibles para comprender algunas de nuestras costumbres.] (Unless otherwise noted, all translations from Spanish into English are my own.) Andrea Aguilar, "La integración no significa que comamos chorizo," *El País*, June 8, 2007, elpais.com/diario/2007/06/09/cultura/1181340005_850215.html.

27. [Se usa hispano africano en oposición a afro hispano. El primero representa la cultura africana de habla hispana de Guinea Ecuatorial, mientras que el segundo representa la cultura desarrollada por los descendientes de los esclavos africanos traídos a Hispanoamérica.] Jorge Salvo, "La formación de identidad en la novela hispanoafricana" (PhD diss., Florida State University, 2003), 1.

28. See Antonio Carrasco González's *Historia de la novela colonial hispanoafricana* (Madrid: Sial Ediciones, 2009) for an extensive study of this genre of works produced by Spanish authors about Africa.

29. [Literatura marroquí de expresión española]

30. Ngũgĩ wa Thiong'o, "Decolonising the Mind," *Diogenes* 184, vol. 46/4 (1998): 102.

31. Thiong'o, "Decolonising the Mind," 103.

32. Gilles Deleuze and Félix Guattari, *Kafka: Toward a Minor Literature* (Minneapolis: University of Minnesota Press, 1986), 16.

33. Deleuze and Guattari, *Kafka: Toward a Minor Literature*, 18.

34. [*The Devil in Yudis*] Ahmed Daoudi, *El diablo de Yudis* (Madrid: Ediciones VOSA, 1994).

35. [*The Call of the Muezzin*] Concha López Sarasúa, *La llamada del almuédano* (Alicante: Editorial Cálamo, 1990).

36. [*The Time in Between*] The literal translation for the title is *The Time Between the Seams* or *The Time Between Sewing*. There is an English translation that was published in 2011 and this version chose to translate the title as *The Time in Between: A Novel*. María Dueñas, *El tiempo entre costuras* (Madrid: Ediciones Temas de Hoy, 2009) and *The Time in Between: A Novel* (Madrid: Atria Books, 2011).

37. [A nuestra generación nos ha tocado vivir el exilio como a otras les tocó la esclavitud o el colonialismo.] Aguilar, "La integración no significa que comamos chorizo."

38. See Michael Ugarte's *Africans in Europe: The Culture of Exile and Emigration from Equatorial Guinea to Spain* (Chicago: University of Illinois Press, 2010) for an in-depth examination of the topic of exile in the context of Spain and Equatorial Guinea.

39. See Carmelo Pérez Beltrán's edited volume *Entre las 2 orillas* (Granada: Universidad de Granada y Fundación, 2007) or Manuel Gahete, et al.'s *Calle del Agua: Antología contemporánea de Literatura Hispanomagrebí* (Madrid: Sial Ediciones, 2008).

40. [*The Name of Ours*] Lorenzo Silva, *El nombre de los nuestros* (Barcelona: Ediciones Destino, 2008)

41. [*The Call of the Muezzin*]

42. [*The Desert Empire*] The first translation that comes to mind is that of *The Desert Empire*; however, it could also be translated as *The Deserted Empire*. Both

options are supported by the narrative. Ramón Mayrata, *El imperio desierto* (1992. Reprint, Madrid: Calamar Ediciones, 2008).

43. [*The Time in Between*]

44. [*The Three Virgins of Saint Thomas*] Guillermina Mekuy, *Las tres vírgenes de Santo Tomás* (Madrid: Suma de letras, 2008).

45. [*Do You Remember Shahrazad?*] Montserrat Abumalham Mas, *¿Te acuerdas de Shahrazad?* (Madrid: Sial Ediciones, 2001).

46. [*The Doctor from Ifni*] Javier Reverte, *El médico de Ifni* (Barcelona: Random House Mondadori, 2005).

47. [*The Eyes of the Tuareg*] Alberto Vázquez-Figueroa, *Los ojos del Tuareg* (2000. Reprint, Barcelona: DeBols!llo, 2005).

48. [*The Devil in Yudis*] To date, with the exception of Dueñas's *El tiempo entre costuras*, none of these novels have been translated into English.

49. See Carrasco González's *Historia de la novela colonial hispanoafricana* for an examination of the Orientalist tradition in the Hispano-African colonial novel, especially the section "Exotismo. Orientalismo." (11–14) or his *El reino olvidado: Cinco siglos de historia de España en África* for a broader history (Madrid: La esfera de los libros, 2012).

50. See Ángel Flores Morales *África a través del pensamiento español* (Madrid: Instituto de Estudios Africanos, 1949) for a fascinating collection of Francoist ideology regarding Africa. More contemporary texts that offer considerations of Spain and Africa's long history include *Convivencia: Jews, Muslims, and Christians in Medieval Spain,* edited by Vivian B. Mann, Thomas F. Glick, and Jerrilyn D. Dodds (New York: George Braziller, Inc., 1992); L. P. Harvey's *Islamic Spain: 1250–1500* (Chicago: The University of Chicago Press, 1992); María Rosa Menocal's *The Ornament of the World* (New York: Little, Brown and Company, 2002); and Stephen O'Shea's *Sea of Faith* (New York: Walker & Company, 2006).

51. I refer to the refrain that is most often attributed to Alexandre Dumas that "Africa begins at the Pyrenees," but can also be found repeated by such prominent Spanish voices as the writer and politician Joaquín Costa in "Los intereses de España en Marruecos" (In *África a través del pensamiento español,* ed. Ángel Flores Morales [Madrid: Instituto de estudios africanos, 1884], 141–184) or novelist Carmen Nonell in *Zoco grande* (Madrid: Colenda, 1956). (Martin-Márquez, *Disorientations*, 59, 274.)

52. As Ángel Ganivet proposes that in Africa lies "the future of Spain" [el porvenir de España]. Ángel Ganivet and Miguel de Unamuno, *El porvenir de España* (1898. Reprint, Madrid: Espasa Calpe, 2008).

53. Heriberto Cairo, "Spanish Enclaves in North Africa," in *Handbook of Global International Policy,* ed. Stuart S. Nagel (Boca Raton: CRC Press, 2000), 57–58.

54. [núcleos urbanos]

55. Vicente Gozálvez Pérez, "Descolonización y migraciones desde el África española (1956–1975)," *Investigaciones geográficas* 12 (1994): 75.

56. Morocco was officially the "Protectorado Español de Marruecos" from 1912 up to 1956, and the territory of Ifni was not returned to Morocco until 1969.

57. Western Sahara was one of the last colonial possessions of Spain. Known as the "Sáhara español" from 1884 to 1975, Spain ceded its independence in 1975.

However, due to the conflicting political interests between Western Sahara, Morocco, Mauritania, and Spain, the effective independence of the territory was never fully realized. To this day, the United Nations considers Western Sahara to be a non-decolonized territory (Tony Hodges, *Western Sahara: Roots of a Desert War*, 372).

58. Equatorial Guinea was under direct Spanish control from 1844 to 1968. It became an official Spanish protectorate in 1885 and was given colonial status in 1900.

59. [*Lost Trails of Africa, Vagabond in Africa,* and *The Dream of Africa*] Javier Reverte, *Caminos perdidos de África* (Barcelona: DeBols!llo, 2004), *Vagabundo en África* (Barcelona: DeBols!llo, 2005), and *El sueño de África: En busca de los mitos blancos del continente negro* (Barcelona: DeBols!llo, 2007).

60. [*The Song of Mbama*] Javier Reverte, *La canción de Mbama* (Madrid: Plaza & Janés, 2011).

61. [*African Poems*] Javier Reverte, *Poemas africanos* (Madrid: Reino de Cordelia, 2011).

62. [*Africa Cries*] Alberto Vázquez-Figueroa, *África llora* (1996. Reprint, Barcelona: DeBols!llo, 2004).

63. [*Sand and Wind*] Alberto Vázquez-Figueroa, *Arena y viento* (1953. Reprint, Barcelona: Plaza & Janés, 1992).

64. [*Blank Check/Carte Blanche*] Lorenzo Silva, *Carta blanca* (Madrid: Espasa, 2004).

65. [*From Rif to Yebala. Voyage to the Dream and Nightmare of Morocco*] Lorenzo Silva, *Del Rif al Yebala. Viaje al sueño y la pesadilla de Marruecos* (Barcelona: Ediciones Destino, 2001).

66. [*Tales of the Sahara*] Ramón Mayrata, editor. *Relatos del Sáhara* (Madrid: Clan, 2001).

67. [*Ali Bey the Abassid: A Christian in Mecca*] Ramón Mayrata, *Alí Bey el Abasí: Un cristiano en La Meca* (Barcelona: Planeta, 1995).

68. [*Fatima of the Shipwrecked*] Lourdes Ortiz, *Fátima de los naufragios* (Barcelona: Planeta, 1998).

69. [*An African War*] Ignacio Martínez de Pisón, *Una guerra africana* (Madrid: Ediciones SM, 2000).

70. [*See If I'll Love You*] Luis Leante, *Mira si yo te querré* (Madrid: Punto de lectura, 2008).

71. [*Empire of Sand*] Jesús Torbado, *El imperio de arena* (Barcelona, Plaza & Janés, 1998).

72. [*Seven Houses in France*] Bernardo Atxaga, *Siete casas en Francia* (Madrid: Alfaguara, 2009).

Chapter 1

War, Diplomacy, Decolonization, and the Other

Even though Spain's African colonies in Spanish Guinea and the Province of the Sahara were at the height of their status for Spain (in terms of political control, economic production, and colonial propaganda in the metropolis), in 1956 the Spanish African Empire slowly began to dismantle.[1] Spain and France recognized Moroccan independence and returned their protectorates in 1956 (minus the enclaves of Ceuta, Melilla, and Ifni); Equatorial Guinea was granted independence in 1968; Ifni was returned to Morocco in 1969, and Spain withdrew from the Spanish Sahara in 1975. In the few decades between the Spanish Civil War and the relinquishment of the colonies, there was significant emigration from Spain to Africa.[2] A census of the Spanish Sahara shows that in 1950 there were 1,320 Europeans in the colony. By 1974 that number had risen to 20,126. In Equatorial Guinea, the European population grew from 3,937 in 1950 to 9,137 in 1966. The Spanish Protectorate of Morocco experienced the highest European population; between 1935 and 1955 the expatriate population doubled from 44,379 to 90,939.[3] From the very end of the nineteenth century, with the loss of the American colonies, Spain's renewed focus on Africa brought about almost seventy-five years of intense interaction with and colonization of the Spanish African territories. These seventy-five years represent, perhaps, the most sustained and frenetic period of Spanish interest in the African continent.

At the threshold of the twenty-first century, multiple Spanish authors returned to these historical encounters that dominated much of the twentieth century, revisiting Spain's interaction with Africa. In the 1990s and early 2000s, there were a number of books that employed as a theme the fighting in Morocco, the colonies of Sidi Ifni, Spanish Sahara or the Moroccan Protectorate, and also the Spanish abandonment of the Saharan territory.[4] These works offer a valuable opportunity to examine the Spanish imaginary of Spanish-African interaction at the threshold of the twentieth century.

Among the contemporary novels looking back on recent history are Lorenzo Silva's *El nombre de los nuestros* (2008)[5] and *Carta blanca* (2004),[6] Concha López Sarasúa's *La llamada del almuédano* (1990),[7] Ramón Mayrata's *El imperio desierto* (2008)[8] and *Alí Bey El Abasí: Un cristiano en La Meca* (1995),[9] Luis Leante's *Mira si yo te querré* (2007),[10] Jesús Torbado's *El imperio de arena* (1998),[11] Ignacio Martínez de Pisón's *Una guerra africana* (2000),[12] María Dueñas's best selling *El tiempo entre costuras* (2009),[13] and Javier Reverte's *El médico de Ifni*,[14] among others.

The themes vary: Silva's novels deal primarily with the second Moroccan War[15] as does Martínez de Pisón's—their literary products paralleling Ramón Sender's *Imán* (1930) and José Díaz Fernández's *El blocao*[16] (1928). Ramón Mayrata, Javier Reverte, and Luis Leante focus on the Spanish Sahara while Concha López Sarasúa, Jesús Torbado, and María Dueñas employ Spanish emigration to the Moroccan territory as their backdrops. What links these authors together is their mining of the recent historical past for what it can offer to a fictional narrative, effectively creating a (re)imagination of the intercultural encounter brought about through war, colonization, and/or politics.

This chapter examines these representations of Spain's political and bellicose interactions with Africa from the last century. I assume the reader's familiarity with Spain's historical Moorish roots—specifically the 711 to 1492 period of Moorish/Christian coexistence on the Iberian Peninsula—focusing instead on the, at times, frenetic interest Spain held for Africa throughout much of the twentieth century.[17] After the losses of the Spanish-American War, Africa gained political interest for Spain as a continent that promised to renew the colonial prestige that was recently lost in the Americas and the Pacific. In the period immediately following this defeat, Spain reevaluated its relationship with Africa and redoubled its focus and efforts on the continent. Even though Spain had amplified its territories of Ceuta, Melilla, Tétouan, and Sidi Ifni following the first War of Africa (1859–1860), Spain's loss of Cuba and the Philippines in the Spanish-American War in 1898 caused Spain to turn its focus southward across the straits. Shortly after the turn of the twentieth century, Spain rapidly began the expansion of its African empire;[18] however, in less than seventy years, Spain would also experience the ultimate disintegration of that hoped-for African empire. This period of time represents an intense era of interaction and exchange between Spain and Africa.[19] It defined their relationship through the twentieth century and continues to influence their engagement into the twenty-first century as Spain currently deals with the influx of African immigrants into the Peninsula as well as the failure to reach a resolution on the status of the former Spanish Sahara.

The rich and abundant writings on Africa from the early nineteenth century to the early twenty-first century chart an evolution in the portrayal of the cultures of North Africa, cultures that are clearly distinct from the Iberian ones. From Domingo Badía (pseud. Ali Bey al-Abbasi), Benito Pérez Galdós and Gaspar Núñez de Arce to Ramón J. Sender, José Díaz Fernández, Isaac Muñoz, Ernesto Giménez Caballero, and Tomás Borrás and up to Javier Reverte, Ramón Mayrata, Jesús Torbado, and the other authors listed above, Africa has been portrayed through the eyes of Westerners, often revealing deep-seated cultural stereotypes that promote cultural superiority or outright colonizing intentions or, conversely, using Africa as an esperpentic lens through which to criticize Spain.[20]

In this chapter, I focus on three contemporary novels that approach the theme of Africa specifically within the contexts of war, (de)colonialism, and diplomacy as I examine how the context of engagement affects the representation of the Other. To this end, I analyze Lorenzo Silva's *El nombre de los nuestros* (2008) for its treatment of the second Moroccan War and the Disaster of Annual, Concha López Sarasúa's *La llamada del almuédano* (1990) for its viewpoint on the civilian Spanish emigration to the Moroccan Protectorate, and Ramón Mayrata's *El imperio desierto* (1992) for its focus on the Spanish withdrawal from the Saharan territory. Not only have these writers received acclaim for their works, but these three novels serve as valuable texts because they are narratives that reflect significant historical interactions between Spain and Africa in the past century. Spain fought for territory in Morocco, maintained a significant colonial presence, and lost its territories all within the boundaries of the century. An examination of these novels will consider how these interactions continue to resonate in contemporary Spanish literature.

It is worth noting that Equatorial Guinea is only tangentially and not explicitly a part of the analysis of this chapter; these works by Silva, López Sarasúa, and Mayrata focus exclusively on the North African territories. In approaching the broader themes of war, political engagement, and civilian emigration, the novels that most thoroughly develop these encounters center around the Maghreb, reflecting Spain's intense focus on North Africa, often at the expense of their West African colony. Many of the conclusions that I reach in my analysis of these novels can be transposed also to Equatorial Guinea, and, where appropriate, I will highlight such possible comparisons.

Specific to this chapter is an analysis of how methods of engagement with the Other affect literary representation. Does a war novel reflect the African Other in distinct ways from a novel about the quotidian realities of the civilian in the protectorate? What implications do methods of engagement have for maintaining or overcoming Orientalist stereotypes? The return to the past for literary inspiration highlights their engagement with the historical realities and the attempt to re-present these realities within contemporary narration.

As I examine the themes of war, colonization, and diplomacy, I highlight and analyze the efforts that Silva, López Sarasúa, and Mayrata make to present their African Other in ways that undermine traditions of Western cultural hegemony. Silva's treatment of the Rif War (1911–1927) redraws lines of Same and Other along class distinctions rather than cultural ones; López Sarasúa's novel reconceptualizes the idea of the *patria* and national belonging, decentering Western primacy, and Mayrata's work highlights how the West disenfranchised the indigenous Saharawi population while his narration attempts to recognize and value the cultural Otherness of the Saharawi. Each of these novels contributes a unique viewpoint as I will examine the dynamics of aggressive interaction, peaceful coexistence, and the intense yet (somewhat) peaceful negotiations of diplomacy and how these authors narrate the Other within these contexts. These representations are especially significant in the settings of war or diplomacy where distinctions of Same and Other and their confrontation are an essential element of the interaction. In these cases, Silva and Mayrata's efforts to redefine lines of affiliation and to represent the opposing Other equitably counter facile demarcations of Same and Other inherent in the nature of the confrontations.

In Silva's *El nombre de los nuestros,* militant conflict characterizes the encounter between the West and its African Other; in Sarasúa López's *La llamada del almuédano,* the colonial paradigm is examined in its waning, while *El imperio desierto* develops over the final months of the Spanish presence in the Saharan territory, as the protagonists work to navigate the bureaucracy and diplomacy that will establish a national sovereignty for the Saharawi. Together, these three engagements will offer considerations of the most emblematic of the encounters between cultures. These encounters function on a macro, inter*cultural* level; war, diplomacy, and colonization are encounters (or clashes) between cultures. In my examination of archetypes of travel in chapter 3, I emphasize the micro, inter*personal* encounter.

REDRAWING LINES OF ALTERITY IN LORENZO SILVA'S *EL NOMBRE DE LOS NUESTROS*

Originally trained as a lawyer, Lorenzo Silva began publishing works of fiction, literary articles, and children's literature in 1995 with the publication of *Noviembre sin violetas* (1995).[21] Since then he has published over fifteen novels that have earned him several prizes. He was a finalist for the Premio Nadal with *La flaqueza del bolchevique* (1997),[22] and he won the award for *El alquimista impaciente* in 2000.[23] He also received the Premio El Ojo Crítico in 1998 for *El lejano país de los estanques*[24] and the Premio Primavera de Novela for *Carta blanca* (2004). *La flaqueza del bolchevique* was made into a movie in 2003. Silva has been remarkably successful and prolific, and his positive reception is not limited to the general public; there has been a growing interest in Silva's work within academia in the last decade.[25]

Silva's writing is not limited to fiction; his non-fiction books include *Del Rif al Yebala: Viaje al sueño y la pesadilla de Marruecos* (2001),[26] *Y al final, la guerra: La aventura de los soldados españoles en Irak* (2006),[27] as well as various travel narratives. Pertinent to this study is his focus on Spain's interaction with North Africa in the twentieth century. Two of his fictional works, *El nombre de los nuestros* (2001) and *Carta blanca* (2004) take place in the midst of the Rif War (1911–1927). *Del Rif al Yebala* is non-fiction, recounting Silva's travels through the areas that were formerly the Spanish Protectorate in Morocco. Silva also edited and wrote a prologue and commentary for a 2001 edition of Ramón J. Sender's *Imán*. These themes are personal for Silva, as his grandfather fought in North Africa; he says about these works:

> Even though many prefer to ignore it, Morocco is the meridional neighbor of the country in which I live, Spain, intense and ancient ties of all kinds unite them also. Our history has been a common one in many moments, sometimes in a tragic form. In one of these painful episodes, the war of 1920–1927, one of my grandfathers participated. . . . For this reason, and because I also have Moroccan family members, I have not been able to look to the south with indifference.[28]

These novels are powerful indictments against Spain's military actions in Morocco, returning to the social humanism of Ramón Sender, Arturo Barea, José Antonio Balbontín, or José Díaz Fernández.[29] Silva's revision of Spain's military intervention in Africa offers a contemporary consideration of the bellicose interactions between Spain and Morocco that marked the beginning of the twentieth century.

Silva's *El nombre de los nuestros* is the focus of this section as it occurs almost entirely within the theater of war in North Africa. Developing in the midst of the Rif War, specifically June and July 1921, Silva's recounting of the weeks leading up to and the tragedy of the Disaster of Annual (July 21, 1921) offers a unique consideration of an African Other that is both culturally and strategically opposed to the Spanish forces. The war setting of the novel, developing entirely on the front lines of active battle, highlights a bellicose engagement with Moroccans. The Other is not only ethnically Other but also an enemy or fellow soldier. The umbrella term *Other* is nuanced into either a threatening aggressor or a collaborative companion, reducing emphasis on cultural *Otherness* to dynamics of hostility and friendship.

Thus, in addition to the theorists of Otherness already mentioned, central to this analysis of Silva's novel is Gil Anidjar's *The Jew, The Arab: A History of the Enemy* (2003), as Anidjar distinguishes the enemy from the Other. Emmanuel Levinas's *Humanism of the Other* (2003), and Ryszard

Kapuściński's *The Other* (2008) also provide context and insight. Articles by Ana Rueda—specifically "El enemigo 'invisible' de la Guerra de África (1859–60) y el proyecto histórico del nacionalismo español: Del Castillo, Alarcón y Landa"[30] and "Sender y otros novelistas de la guerra marroquí: humanismo social y vanguardia política"[31]—will also offer context and insight to the present study. Each of these authors engage with the question of alterity and the Other, and so contribute directly to a more complete analysis of Silva's war novel.[32] My analysis highlights how Lorenzo Silva, with *El nombre de los nuestros*, sidesteps cultural alterity and concomitant Orientalist tropes, instead emphasizing socio-economic difference over cultural difference, creating a work that highlights social inequality over cultural hierarchy.

Within *El nombre de los nuestros,* alterity is reduced to a "collective anonymity."[33] Irrespective of race or culture, all participants in the war front are exposed to the very real possibility of death and are united in their common mortality. Anidjar's theorization of the enemy proposes that

> The enemy is not the other—and the movement by which the enemy vanishes into the distance . . . is a movement that remains within the space of the same. . .
> The movement of the enemy thus has to be distinguished from that of the other who comes from afar, the neighbor or *prochain* who, before the subject, comes. Symmetrically opposed—rather than asymmetrically approaching—the enemy departs and vanishes, which is to say that the enemy also *remains* as departing and vanishing. The space within which this movement takes place is defined by Levinas as the space of the political, as the space of war.[34]

That is, the confrontation between forces—sides—jockeying for control of the same physical space or territory, refigures the dynamics of privileging Same over Other. Shared goals, relative proximity, and intense, aggressive interaction distinguish the enemy from the Other. Trajectories of parallel movement mark the relationship between opposing forces;[35] the mirroring confrontation and the dynamic instability of the war front redefine interaction with opposing forces. It is also the plurality of the opposition; *armies* or forces engage one another. The enemy is stripped of individuality—"The enemy is a thing."[36]

While Ryszard Kapuściński does not specifically distinguish the enemy from the Other, he does explicitly suggest that "conflict, collision, is just one quite unnecessary form of contact between civilisations. Another one that features even more often is exchange,"[37] and he further articulates that "the circumstances, the context . . . decide whether we see a person as an enemy or as a partner at any given moment."[38] Kapuściński is more lenient in his understanding of the Other: "The Other can be both of these [enemy or partner], and that is the basis of his changeable, elusive nature."[39] Both Anidjar and Kapuściński draw on the work of Levinas, and both seem to concur on "Levinas's assertion that war is the suspended space of indifference, where alterity has no place."[40] Indifference is a state of in-difference and the "suspension of all obligations" that form the basis of Levinas's concern for the Other.[41] The enemy may be an Other, culturally, ethnically, or otherwise, but the unique dynamics present on the battlefield—the loss of individuality, direct confrontation, and the suspension of law—are significant enough to confer extra signification upon the Other. The distinction is important: the enemy may be Other, but the Other is not necessarily an enemy. As Rueda suggests,

> the "enemy" as a discursive marker does not overlap exactly with the Other and neither with the empirical or martial enemy. Enmity has discursive specificity—military, political and even theological—in the context of war literature.[42]

It is through this "discursive specificity" that Silva is able to consciously de-emphasize alterity to find a universal ground of common humanity.

In her examination of war literature from the first War of Africa (1859–1860), Rueda proposes that, in the war setting, the enemy/Other is rendered discursively invisible for the purpose of mitigating "the horrors of the war, justified in terms of otherness, and to a certain point liberate the chronicler, and by extension the leaders of the Spanish nation, of the ethical responsibility that they contract with the Moroccan through armed action."[43] Ultimately, "the war rhetoric perpetuated two rival nationalities that were never able to assimilate."[44] The battlefield written is whitewashed palatable; difference justifies action—war is instigated to (ostensibly) civilize the Other—but the intensity of the war front is sanitized for public consumption—by dehumanizing the Other to an indistinct enemy, questions of ethical treatment of the Other are rendered null. In tracing the evolution of the treatment of the Other, Rueda also examines the progress made between the first War of Africa and the Rif War. In the literature that arose from the Rif War of 1920–1921, Rueda examines the social humanism of these works, including a consideration of Silva's work as a continuation of this project. Therefore, these articles by Rueda serve to contextualize the present study of Silva's *El nombre de los nuestros*. The literary antecedents to Silva's work highlight his efforts to discursively include not only the enemy but also the Other, and to present the horrors of the battlefield unmitigated. For Silva, war does dehumanize, but this dehumanization is not limited to the Other; each of the opposing sides is susceptible.

The plot of *El nombre de los nuestros* develops within the intense fighting of June and July 1921 in northern Morocco, specifically the military positions of Sidi Dris, Talilit, and Afrau. The narration is third person and the principal characters are the Spanish soldiers Andreu, Amador, Sergeant Molina, and the Moroccan conscript Haddú. The novel returns to the fateful unfolding of events at Annual, similar in theme to Sender's 1930 *Iman*.[45] The Riffian Harka advances upon the Spanish positions, forcing retreat to the shoreline, where a handful of soldiers are rescued but a majority are killed or captured. The chapters alternate between the positions—Sidi Dris, Afrau, and Talilit—and also include a couple of chapters on board the battleship *Laya*[46] asea off the coast, from which the generals and officers plan and give orders. The novel reaches its climax as the Spanish troops are forced to retreat, with the Harka brutally massacring many and taking some captive as prisoners of war. The last few chapters detail the experience of the prisoners of war, covering almost a year and a half between their capture and liberation—a time marked by the cruelty of their captors and the disinterested attempts by Spain to secure their release.

The friendship between Amador, Molina, Andreu, and Haddú links the geographic separation between the chapters. They are ideologically distinct: Andreu an anarchist from Barcelona, Amador a madrileño insurance salesman, sergeant Molina a veteran soldier, and Haddú a Moroccan working as a member of the indigenous police force, a significant supporting contingent for the Spanish soldiers. Yet their ideological or background differences are minimized as they face the common enemy—the Riffian Harka. Likewise, while the members of the indigenous police force are numerous, only Haddú and Hassan are named specifically. Their singular recognition is not necessarily an oversight, or a discursive erasure of the cultural Other, since within *El nombre de los nuestros* individual identity is only afforded to a select few characters. This supports an analysis of the novel as operating in the indifferent space of war—the warfront erases individuality as two opposing sides face off, and difference is subsumed within the organization engaged in conflict. That is not to say that cultural/ethnic difference is not a dynamic, yet the limited focus on Haddú and Hassan is paralleled by a similar limited focus on sergeant Molina, Amador, and Andreu. Other characters come and go but function mostly as secondary, undeveloped actors within the plot.

Even though ethnic alterity is not emphasized, as fighting intensifies it is acknowledged as a concern. The contingent cooperation between the Spanish soldiers and the indigenous police force worries the Spanish soldiers when they are forced to rely on their Moroccan counterparts. At Afrau, sergeant Molina asks Hassan "What are you all going to do, Hassan?"[47] to which Hassan responds, "I am friend, sergeant."[48] Molina considers the grammatical implications of his response:

> it's not that they were *friends*, but that they were *friendly*. In some of them it was only this, an error, but in others it hid a probable secondary meaning. One is to

be *friends* and there's nothing more to it, but *friendly* meant that they could be here today and tomorrow over there.⁴⁹

He seeks to clarify, asking again "seriously"⁵⁰ and offering to let the Moroccan conscripts leave their weapons and go home. Hassan simply replies, "'I am friend, sergeant' repeated the other."⁵¹ Whether or not it was a conscious decision on the part of Silva to close this conversation by referring to Hassan as the Other,⁵² its use fills the relationship with nuances similar to Hassan's choice of *estar* over *ser*. Possible implications include the recognition of deep-seated mistrust of the cultural Other, even when fighting on the same side, or also the more subtle distinction of Hassan as Other as distinguishing him from the enemy. Hassan is an individual who has voice and agency; Molina offers him a choice and he makes the perilous decision to stay and fight. His personal agency distinguishes him from the advancing Harka soldiers, Hassan's cultural Same. Hassan is merely Other, while the indistinct Harka are the Enemy. A third possibility is the recognition of an Other, not as culturally distinct, but as a fellow human with individual reasons for action—an Other "who is not . . . my enemy, and not my 'complement.'"⁵³ This interpretation, which focuses on the humanizing and personalizing of the Other, is supported as Hassan considers Molina's question:

> He had not interacted much with Molina but the sergeant had always been respectful with him. He wasn't like other European military types, that only saw in the indigenous soldiers some useful dogs to throw against other dogs.⁵⁴

Molina reflects on Hassan's possible motives; to Hassan's "I am friend," Molina admits, "They weren't *friends* but rather they were *friendly* . . . as the situation called for."⁵⁵ Even though Hassan accords a distinct, respectful individuality to Molina and Molina groups Hassan with the other opportunistic indigenous police, both men recognize a personal agency in the Other, that each has made a choice to be where they are. As Levinas articulates, they are not enemies, and not necessarily complements, but rather they mutually recognize personal agency.

This Moroccan Other, fighting alongside the Spanish forces, is contrasted with the Enemy, the Harka. Ethnically the Same as the indigenous police, the Harka are ideologically Other. The Harka are not described with any individuality; they are referred to consistently in the collective. This renders their individuality—their personal humanity—effectively invisible; the Harka is a faceless, threatening force. As mentioned above, Rueda notes in "El enemigo 'invisible'" that rendering the enemy invisible makes a history of the enemy impossible. Drawing on Derrida's work in *Specters of Marx*, Rueda suggests that "in the best possible scenario, it will produce a spectral history that always threatens with returning to show its face."[56] In *El nombre de los nuestros* this also rings true as the faceless mass of strategic and advancing Harka soldiers creates a menacing and threatening force that is more terrifying because of its invisibility—it is not just *unknown*; the enemy is, in this instance, *unable to be known*. It is sinister and stealthy.[57] In the very first chapter this unknown and threatening quality is planted as the Spanish soldier Pulido is terrified of his own potential death, convinced that he will die in the war.[58] Andreu attempts to comfort him, but Pulido is right and "The second night of June . . . they slit Pulido's throat with a single dagger cut in his post as sentinel."[59] They are caught off guard, unsuspecting in a scene which foreshadows the unfolding of events that form the continued plot of the novel. The stealth and surprise keep the Spanish forces on the run and on the defensive, never able to effectively hold back an attack, to their ultimate defeat and capture. In chapter 16, after the Spanish defeat and as Amador is taken captive, an indigenous woman rips off his military stripes and wears them on her head as a hat. Amador thinks back to his earlier reflection on the Harka[60]

> as something unknown and maybe nonexistent. Now the invisible monster had imposed its presence, and . . . the corporal felt that the Harka was this woman that had stripped him of his military stripes and who ridiculed him with the insolence of her ardent black eyes.[61]

The formerly invisible enemy is now face to face with Amador, personified in one individual woman. He is able to see her eyes. The invisible enemy as a threatening monster is reinforced by his reflection, and the personal encounter here only highlights the *indifference* of which Levinas speaks.[62] This woman is not an Other, she is an enemy. For Amador and the readers, her angry reaction to the captured Spanish soldier personifies and renders visible the formerly indistinct enemy. She is "symmetrically opposed—rather than asymmetrically approaching"[63] in mission, and by creating a powerful enemy, Silva gives agency to the Other. That is, what would be an Other in different contexts, is converted into a threatening force that is capable of overwhelming the Western, modern military machine within the theater of war.

This power and agency turns Orientalist tropes on their head as "Orientalism depends for its strategy on the flexible *positional* superiority, which puts the Westerner in a whole series of possible relationships with the Orient without ever losing him the relative upper hand."[64] By employing the backdrop of war—and specifically an *unsuccessful* war for the Spanish—Silva simultaneously converts the Other to a new archetype which upsets the "*positional* superiority" that undergirds Orientalist discourse. He initially employs the discursive trick of rendering the Enemy invisible that Rueda notes in Rafael del Castillo, Pedro Antonio de Alarcón, and Nicasio Landa, but instead of mitigating the horrors of war and denying the Other voice, Silva uses this phantomization of the Other to create a menacing, viable threat. Furthermore, upon coming face to face with an individual enemy, Amador recognizes the distinctly human emotion of insolence and disdain, affirming the positional superiority of the Harka in their victory. Andreu even sacrilegiously admits to Haddú that God, "If He has to be in some place. . . . He is with those over there facing us."[65] This admission denies Spain's both physical and moral superiority in addition to its (lack of) military superiority.

Silva further subverts Spanish discursive authority by emphasizing the bravery of the indigenous police force fighting alongside the more cowardly Spanish forces. In the final battle at Afrau:

> The police remained loyal, even though each time it should have been clearer to them that they were on the losing side. Hassan, the corporal, remained at the foot of the parapet, despite having been shot in the shoulder. It was the left one, he said, denying its importance and he added:
> "As long as I have a right shoulder, I have a place to support my rifle."
> The Europeans, when they were wounded, became useless. . . . If a Moor didn't get up it was because he was already dead.[66]

This description accords the indigenous forces both physical and moral stamina that is not found in the Spanish soldiers. In fact, the last resistance of the Spanish forces was from the indigenous police and "Therein was the paradox that it was them, Moors and mercenaries, who obeyed to the letter the order to defend the flag until the end, an order that only a few Europeans observed."[67] Silva denies the Spanish forces even an honorable defeat; their cowardice is highlighted by the loyalty of the indigenous police. The text further underscores the valor of their loyalty by emphasizing they are "moors and mercenaries," underscoring their cultural otherness, monetary motivation, and simultaneous allegiance to the colonizing flag. The implication is that the indigenous police force is not only more loyal than the Spanish soldiers, but they are also more honorable for keeping their word when they have less of a moral stake in the outcome.

There are brave Spanish soldiers. Sergeant Molina, Lieutenant Veiga, and Amador are each portrayed as honorable and brave men. Silva's emphasis on the bravery of the indigenous police force does not serve to deny individual bravery from participants in the battles, but rather to undermine national narratives of cultural or moral superiority of one armed force or nation against the other. It overturns the cultural hierarchy upon which Orientalist discourse depends. By recognizing individual bravery among examples both Spanish and Moroccan, Silva also avoids the trap of over-idealizing the Other. The bravery that he highlights among the indigenous police force is not limited to them and neither is it accorded to them because of their ethnicity; it is a quality that is available to any character, regardless of race, thereby emphasizing it as a personal quality rather than as a cultural one.

As Silva undermines the colonizing mantra of moral superiority, he also realigns the demarcations of Same and Other. Same and Other are reconstructed as class distinctions, not racial ones. Silva reduces war to an economic transaction, since the wealthy and powerful can literally purchase others to take their stead. With this emphasis, the hierarchy of power is reoriented from a cultural order to a socio-economic one. That is, as examined above, the cultural Other is a powerful and threatening force, able to menace the Spanish forces; the marginalized Other is a social class that transcends cultural boundaries.

Silva establishes this alignment in two specific ways: first, by examining the class distinctions at work in the Spanish army, and second, by comparing the marginalized Spanish soldiers with their Moroccan counterparts. The practice of purchasing a *substitute*[68] permeates the Spanish military forces.[69] Molina's uncle purchased a substitute for him, but his personal sense of honor would not allow him to send someone else in his stead: "No one was going to die in his place for some change."[70] Those with economic means can afford to avoid the battlefront; Amador, the outspoken socialist, points out the socio-economic injustice in saying, "I have not seen a single rich person around here."[71] Molina even finds this system of substitution recreated within his unit. When organizing a group of soldiers for an excursion, he discovers that certain soldiers are paying other soldiers to volunteer in their place. Enraged, he tells them:

> In Africa, each bullet has a name, and no bullet will make a mistake . . .
> What I want to say is that the name of the bullet cannot be bought or sold, because it will find whom it has to find and no one will carry the misfortune of another. You can buy a jacket or you can buy some shoes. But to want to buy the pain of a family is an indignity.[72]

Molina refuses to perpetuate the economic injustice that supports the entire war effort. The "otro" here is found within the Spanish forces, an economically marginalized yet culturally Same entity. Similarly, indigenous police forces fighting with Molina's men are described as "mercenaries,"[73] implying that the colonizing mission is financed by the capital of the wealthy at the expense of the alienated laborer.

Molina's fatalism can best be analyzed as a criticism of the commodification of the individual that occurs within the Spanish war effort and specifically the system of purchasing substitutes. Within this system, the soldiers are effectively reduced to "wage-labourers . . . compelled to sell [themselves]"[74] and by selling themselves, they become commodities. The human market exists to offer the financially able the opportunity to opt-out (a system in which Molina refuses to participate from the start); it converts the soldiers into commodities and in the process alienates them from themselves.[75] Within the substitution process, their lives become commodities that hold exchange-value. Molina uncovers the exploitative nature of this system by emphasizing the equal personal value of the individual. In Molina's view, no one human life is worth more or less than another; he reverses the systemic process by which "an owner of a commodity" is converted into "a commodity."[76] Molina's statement is effectively a rearticulation of Marx's description of the use-value of commodities: "Coats cannot be exchanged for coats, one use-value cannot be exchanged for another of the same kind."[77] Molina addresses the fetishism of the commodity that is occurring on the personal, human level in the war scenario. Molina's admonishment of his troops reveals the dehumanizing, de-personalizing system that characterizes this war effort. The soldiers are reminded that they are humans, not commodities to be bought and sold.

This emphasis on the individual as opposed to the assumed market value of the human-as-commodity is not limited to the Spanish. Silva does not stop at individualizing the Spanish soldier. The power of his text, and the most significant rejection of Orientalist discourse, lies in the humanization of the enemy also. In the final chapter, after the defeat at Annual and after Amador's year and a half in the prisoner-of-war camp, Molina and Amador are reunited in Melilla. Amador recounts Molina's previous speech on the name of each bullet, Molina expounds: "'Do you know what name is always on the bullet?' ... 'The name of *ours*,' said the sergeant, solemnly '*Ours* are them, those poor devils that always have it rough.... Even the Moors that we kill, if you look at it, they are *ours*. We are like them: we run, we crawl, we feel fear and no one ever helps us.'"[78] The singularity of the bullet—"*la bala*"—emphasizes the individuality of the name it metonymically carries. And yet, Molina expands this individuality to a plural and possessive communality. Not only is there a *nosotros* but it is a personal *nuestro*—and those that comprise this intimate group are the poor and disenfranchised, and not limited to the ethnic Same, but extended to the enemy also. Through Molina's voice, Silva redraws lines of Same and Other along lines of socio-economic power. The *enemy* is no longer the Harka forces that defeated the Spanish at Afrau and Sidi Dris, but rather the "four sons of bitches that are now so comfortable in Madrid"[79]—those who purchase the labor of the poor and exploit them on the colonizing battlefield. Silva emphasizes that the true battle is class warfare.

Amador is deeply affected by Molina's words and jokes that he's become a socialist too, to which Molina responds, "The hell I'm a socialist."[80] Molina's sardonic response seeks to remove political titles from the argument; for him, it is an economic injustice of which political parties are only symptoms of greater ailment. "Los nuestros" are directed and sent to war by the powerful, far away from the actual fighting (the "four sons of bitches" in Madrid). The generals and commanders make their choices distanced from the physical land they seek to dominate, aboard the battleship *Laya* offshore in the Mediterranean, or from Madrid. Silva emphasizes the unidirectional flow of power, from distanced officers and politicians to disenfranchised soldiers, in the moments leading up to the retreat. The soldiers are unable to communicate with the *Laya*, and vice versa, by radio or signs because both are using different codes that neither can understand.[81] Silva subtly inserts a communicative otherness into the Same with this twist, further fracturing the totem of the discursive Same.

For Silva, Same and Other are broader, relational terms, better constructed in socio-political or economic structures than in genetic ones. Six years after his conversation with Amador in Melilla, the war is concluded with a Spanish victory (1929). The Spanish king visits the infamous bay where the soldiers retreated. His visit marks Abd el Krim's (el Jatabi) defeat. Molina observes the ceremony of passing troops before the king and muses—in a narration that appears to be part his own and part authorial voice—that it is always the rich and powerful that send the poor to fight in wars, while those political leaders never understand the true cost of violent warfare.[82] As he critiques the colonial and war machines, he also contemplates his surroundings and his memories: "He returned, at last, to experience the fascination of those African sunsets, orange and flamboyant, over the ocean or mountains when the combatants almost forgot that they were there to kill each other and and they felt a strange immensity."[83] He appreciates his physical surroundings, validating the beauty of Africa to hold such power that it would cause him and his comrades to forget the mission they were there to fulfill. He offers to the African evenings a pacifying power that surges as a nostalgic memory. Ultimately, he moves from scenery to former enemy. In the penultimate paragraph, Molina reflects on the Harka. He remembers their indistinct, early presences, and how they proved their existence in defeating a colonial force, and yet how now they seemed once again defeated, and concludes that "the Harka would never cease to exist."[84] As the closing lines for the novel, they are powerfully evocative. The enemy is indeed a spectral presence that haunts, as Rueda suggests. Molina's reflections consider the encounter with the enemy and its continuing power to threaten. However, considered alongside Silva's re-structuring of lines of Same and Other and his effective redefinition of the enemy into a political and socio-economic enemy, this final contemplated Harka also represents the ongoing threat that the social and economically marginalized will continue to confront. The specter that haunts is not only that of the enemy Harka, but of the privileged class that sends the soldier to war. As Molina's *nuestros* encompasses even the "Moors that we killed,"[85] the menacing Others are embodied in the king and his military commanders celebrating colonial victory on the beach below.

Silva's epilogue effectively concludes a narrative that seeks to understand war and the enemy in a distinct light. The preconceived and traditional established enemy is reimagined into a more sinister and yet familiar force. The supposed positional superiority of the West is eroded, and Silva appears to be echoing Said's statement that "what we must respect and try to grasp is the sheer knitted together strength of Orientalist discourse, its very close ties to the enabling socio-economic and political institutions, and its redoubtable durability."[86] Silva has exposed these malignant forces, and it is perhaps with a certain amount of pessimism that the final line "the Harka would never cease to exist"[87] considered alongside Said's insight, refers to an enemy that takes on many forms: potentially the literal Harka or the socio-political powerful, or even a reference to the perdurability of Orientalist discourse itself. As Said suggests that Orientalist discourse is a tool of the politically powerful to achieve its own ends, Silva deconstructs that ideological paradigm to uncover the underlying dynamics at work. Silva's narrative offers an alternative conceptualization of the true enemy and the Other. Conceptualizations of Same and Other cannot be taken at face value as Silva reconstitutes understandings of Us versus Them.

This redefinition serves to powerfully destabilize official Orientalist discourse that would write Africa and the African as a distinct Other and a potential enemy. A unified conceptualization of a cultural Same is also fractured in this recapitulation; *los nuestros—ours—*becomes an identification that transcends cultural identity, and one that is not predicated on cultural uniformity. The new lines of belonging affirm a common humanity that deemphasizes phenotypic difference. Denominators such as European, Spanish, or African neither assume nor preclude individual belonging. Markers of difference instead emphasize social and economic inequality as the true forces that divide. Silva's novel effectively uncovers the insidious way in which official Orientalist discourse is employed by the powerful at the expense of the marginalized, and his novel is a forceful reconsideration of the ideological paradigm that permeates historical Western interactions with its cultural Other.

THE EXPATRIATE AND THE OTHER IN CONCHA LÓPEZ SARASÚA'S *LA LLAMADA DEL ALMUÉDANO*

Originally from Asturias, Concha López Sarasúa spent twenty years living in Morocco. She currently resides and writes in Alicante. Her writing has been positively received, and her work is the topic of a book and several articles by the Moroccan Hispanist Mohamed Abrighach. A majority of her works focus on Morocco and the Arabic world and include both fiction and travel works: *A vuelo de pájaro sobre Marruecos* (1995),[88] *La daga turca y otros relatos mediterráneos* (1996),[89] *¿Qué buscabais en Marrakech?* (2001),[90] and a children's trilogy: *Meriem y la ruta fantástica* (1991),[91] *En el país de Meriem* (1998),[92] and *Los mil y un cuentos de Meriem* (2006).[93] She has also written the novels *Cita en París* (2005)[94] and *Celanova 42: La España rural de la posguerra* (1993)[95] which was classified in the Premio de Novela Café Gijón in 1993. *¿Qué buscabais en Marrakech?* was a finalist for the Premio Café Gijón in 1999. In addition, her 1990 novel *La llamada del almuédano* was a finalist in the XXI Premio de Novela Ateneo de Sevilla. Her most recent novel is *¿Por qué tengo que emigrar?* (2009).[96]

Her focus on North Africa and her representation of it has been well received by Moroccan Hispanists such as Abrighach and others. She "confess[es] that . . . I felt my true vocation in the north of Africa, particularly in Morocco. That was undoubtedly the country that awakened my passion for the written word."[97] Abrighach notes that her work

> resuscitates the Hispanic tradition of Moors and Christians, giving place to a new literary *aljamía*[98] that flaunts a novel islamophilia. It contains, above all, a true poetics of the two shores, that is, it is a kind of poetry of diversity through which the crossed and common characteristics of the *Mare Nostrum* are exalted.[99]

Abrighach further writes that López Sarasúa's work actively strives to denounce "the imaginary border that exists between the two shores, consecrated by Hispanic amnesia."[100] This analysis clearly highlights the value of López Sarasúa's work for this study. To this end, *La llamada del almuédano* represents a distinct vision of the African Other—in this case a specifically Moroccan Other—that serves to juxtapose and complement the analyses of Silva's *El nombre de los nuestros* and Mayrata's *El imperio desierto*. As Silva's novel engages with the conflict of war and Mayrata's with the political and diplomatic interaction between the West and Africa, López Sarasúa's work offers a more pacific theme, developing within a domestic setting.

La llamada del almuédano centers on the quotidian lives of the expatriate and cosmopolitan community living in Morocco in the 1940s and early 50s. The text offers very few references to specific dates or events that could contextualize the plot within a specific year or years. Francisco Fernández arrives in 1930 and Fermín Gironés arrives in Morocco on January 20, 1946, at the end of World War II,[101] but these references are background and the amount of time that has passed since their arrival is unclear. The central character, an aging doña Natalia, has spent the majority of her adult life in Morocco and is now considering returning to Spain due to health concerns. The provision of specific dates is ultimately unnecessary as the plot is not anchored to synchronic moments, but rather to the span of time encompassing the Spanish Protectorate in Morocco,[102] up to its end in 1956.[103] This time frame reflects the waxing and waning of the international population in Morocco, in both Spanish and French controlled Protectorates. Gozálvez Pérez notes that

> By July 31st, 1955 the Spanish population in the Spanish Protectorate of Morocco was estimated to be 90,939 habitants, who represented 9.4% with respect to the natives – 963,620 –; to those indicated should be added another 25,698 Spaniards in the parts of Morocco under French administration (census from April 15th, 1951) and more than 21,500 in Tangier.[104]

Gozálvez Pérez further notes that between 1935 and 1955 the Spanish population in the Protectorate doubled.[105] This general time frame of two decades coincides with the cosmopolitan reality in which the expatriates move and go about their daily lives, and also aligns with the few specific dates that are mentioned in the text. In short, *La llamada del almuédano* traces the arc of Western presence in Morocco in the mid-twentieth century, from the frenetic Western immigration after both the Spanish Civil War and the Second World War to the slow return migration around the time of Moroccan independence.

More specifically, the novel centers on the situation of doña Natalia, a 70-year-old Spanish woman whose children are encouraging her to return to Spain so that she can receive better medical attention for her rheumatism and be closer to family. Doña Natalia spent the majority of her life in Morocco, and her husband is buried in Kenitra (formerly "Port-Lyautey") where she also has a burial site reserved. She is torn between her attachment to Morocco, the changing political situation (which only tangentially bothers her—as in the renaming of streets and the departure of friends), and her family's concerns for her. While doña Natalia is the recurring and central protagonist of the novel, the narrative is not explicitly focused on her, but rather is composed of a series of vignettes in individual chapters that include a spectrum of characters.

The novel itself is composed of thirteen chapters, each one a vignette that focuses on a specific individual or anecdote. Most chapters are titled after people—"Doña Natalia," "Rosette," "Mme. Mechbal," etc.—while some are titled after places—"Kenitra," "A Place in Africa."[106] Two chapters do not follow in this pattern; the fifth chapter is titled "Exile"[107] and the final chapter is titled "The Last Verse."[108] From this structuring of the novel, a cursory glance at the index suggests the central focal points of the work. López Sarasúa is concerned with individuals, place, the idea of exile and belonging, and the religious and cultural Other. The novel is narrated primarily in the third person, but often slips into a free indirect speech narration. The narrative is not plot driven, but rather presents a series of individual stories that paint a picture of various inhabitants of the Moroccan Protectorate.

Each of these vignettes connects in minor ways, with doña Natalia serving as the most common thread throughout them. Doña Natalia is a family friend of the Fernández Family—comprised of Francisco and Remedios and their grown daughter Rosette (María Rosa) (chapters 1, 2, and 5); she is a grandmotherly figure for Gilbert (chapter 3), confidant for María Mechbal (chapter 8), guardian and mentor for Halima (chapter 11), and herself the focus of five chapters ("Doña Natalia," "Kenitra," "Un lugar en África," "Madani, el profeta," and "La última aleya"). Some of these chapters only mention her in passing; Gilbert simply reflects that he must accompany doña Natalia and his mother to Kenitra's cemetery before lunch one day,[109] but doña Natalia's presence is subtly pervasive throughout the text.

Other characters given textual preference in specific chapters include Rosette Fernández, the daughter of a Spanish political exile from the Civil War and currently romantically involved with Rachid, a law professor at the University Mohamed V (who also warrants his own chapter); Mme. Mechbal (María) of Spanish origin and a former cabaret dancer now married to a Moroccan; Fermín Gironés, another Spanish political exile, or Halima, a Moroccan girl who works for doña Natalia and whom doña Natalia mentors. Developing action in the plot is limited, and the story line instead is primarily filled with the characters' reflections on their life choices and situations. As a whole, the cast of characters represents the variety of personages that comprise the cosmopolitan centers of mid-century Morocco. It is true that they represent a predominantly privileged class, and the politically or economically marginalized portion of Moroccan society is not given much diegetic consideration, but within this substrate the characters do also represent a spectrum of privilege and wealth. Some are political exiles while others are political elite, and some Moroccans and Spaniards are financially well off, while others are not.

The Other within the novel receives a textured and nuanced representation. For the African Other, there is the poor and unfortunate Halima, who becomes pregnant out of wedlock and is taken in by doña Natalia, and there is Rachid who is a law professor and who studied in Europe and is very westernized. Within the Spanish population, there are many political and ideological factions represented: Francisco Fernández is a self-exiled Republican while Fermín Gironés represents the radical left wing.[110] Many of the characters utter overtly racist or stereotypical comments about the African Other, and yet these exclamations are not supported by the overall tone of the narrative. Abrighach considers López Sarasúa's inclusion of such comments to be a sincere "commitment to the truth" and an attempt to demystify any accrued sense of nostalgia towards the colonial days.[111] Taken as a narrative whole, this varied cast of characters interacts and shares both the space of the Protectorate and the pages of this novel.

To analyze the Orientalism or lack thereof in López Sarasúa's text, Said continues to be a useful resource. In addition to Said's work, Mary Louise Pratt's *Imperial Eyes* is also relevant. Abrighach's book length study on the work of López Sarasúa, *Superando orillas: Lectura intercultural de la narrativa de Concha López Sarasúa* (2009), is an invaluable resource and a testament to the achievement of López Sarasúa's text. These theoretical and critical works contribute to an analysis of López Sarasúa's text that highlights how she is able to narrate a space that does not privilege the West over its African Other but rather, at times, reverses this assumed hierarchy, and consistently provides a transcultural space in which West and Orient contribute to a unique cultural reality.[112]

Since this examination follows that of Silva's *El nombre de los nuestros*, it is necessary to return to a consideration of the Other, to redefine it since it acquired significant nuances within the war setting. In *La llamada del almuédano*, the ethnic, linguistic, and/or religious Other is an acknowledged reality. As noted above, the text is filled with characters from varied backgrounds. Moreover, the narration shifts between Spanish, French, Arabic, and even occasionally English. The polyglossic nature of the text reflects the cosmopolitan reality of the Moroccan Protectorates. The narration is primarily in Spanish—such that one can reasonably follow the narrative without significant knowledge of French, Arabic, or English—but slips into the other languages without warning and without translation. Narration remains in Spanish, but dialogue contains frequent multilingual expressions. Just as the language shifts, so does the narrative viewpoint. Narrated primarily in the third-person singular, it also frequently changes to a first-person narration at points, often within a single sentence as is the case in the chapter titled "Gilbert" that alternates between the third and first person in its narration.[113] This constant shift in both language and narration creates a narrative instability that avoids privileging either language or narrative viewpoint. That is, even though Spanish is the language of the text, other linguistic realities of the plot are offered narrative space and consideration. The linguistic hybridity of the Moroccan Protectorate is recognized and represented in this narration. The fact that the non-Spanish phrases and words are presented without translation emphasizes the characters' ease of maneuverability within a linguistic setting that is presumably strange and very foreign to monolingual readers. In similar fashion, the shifting narrative viewpoint allows multiple voices the opportunity for consideration and expression.

These narrative choices serve to undermine the "flexible *positional* superiority [upon which Orientalism depends], which puts the Westerner in a whole series of possible relationships with the Orient without ever losing him the relative upper hand."[114] The language of exchange is not simply the colonial languages of French or Spanish, but rather a blending of all languages represented in the territory. The text effectively recreates a space of transculturation that goes beyond simplistic Orientalist portrayals. As Mary Louise Pratt outlines in *Imperial Eyes*, "Transculturation is a phenomenon of the contact zone."[115] The "contact zone" must be an essential consideration of this process, and Pratt defines it as "the space of colonial encounters, the space in which peoples geographically and historically separated come into contact with each other and establish ongoing relations."[116] The contact zones of *La llamada del almuédano* differ from those that Pratt examines in *Imperial Eyes* in that, for her, the "ongoing relations" that contact zones create "usually involv[e] conditions of coercion, radical inequality, and intractable conflict."[117] Her titular "imperial eyes" are ones that "passively look out and possess,"[118] whereas *La llamada del almuédano* is remarkably devoid of conflict and arrogance. Instead, it depends largely on personal, intimate story-lines for plot development, rather than adrenaline-fueled action or mystery. These contact zones are not the sites of active conquest and cultural inequality, but rather ones of interpersonal, empathetic exchange.

Even while the narrative avoids cultural hierarchy and actively decries instances of racial denigration, the contact zones that it offers are spaces of the elite and the colonial. The expatriates may be beneficent and multicultural, but they are colonial immigrants, congregating at embassy functions or colonial social clubs. As the text gives voice to the linguistic and cultural Other, it largely ignores the economically and politically marginalized Other. Abrighach contextualizes this narrative focus by suggesting that López Sarasúa "de-dramatizes the phenomenon perhaps because Spanish emigration to North Africa was not as tragic as the contemporary Moroccan voyage in *patera*."[119] Rachid, the most prominent Moroccan character, is a law professor and well versed in the Western philosophy of Socrates and Plato, Hegel, and Marx.[120] He may be ethnically Other, but he is philosophically Western. The historical context is that of the active European colonialism of Morocco, and the characters that populate the pages are the privileged class of the colony. The levels of Spanish emigration to Morocco that Gozálvez Pérez details (noted above) provide a broader context to the contact zones that the novel offers. López Sarasúa's Morocco is the cosmopolitan space of the international contact zones. She does not write the indigenous Morocco, or the culturally Other Moroccan, instead she focuses her narrative on the social space that was unique to the Protectorates. To further contextualize López Sarasúa's narrative focus, it is useful to understand that Spanish emigration to

Morocco in the mid-twentieth century was more than just a colonial venture, as Heriberto Cairo outlines:

> Naturalized geopolitics represents national destiny as dominated by nature. From the 1860s to the 1950s the geopolitical image of a Euro-African Spain was formulated in different ways. The basic argument was that there is a spatial continuity from the Pyrenees in the north to the Atlas in the south. There would be two Spains: one peninsular in the European continent and one Transfetana or Tingitana in the African continent. So the Spanish national destiny would be to achieve the unity of both Spains. Thus the incorporation of colonies in Northwest Africa or the establishment of the protectorate was not in a way an act of colonization but one of unification.[121]

Therefore, the assumption of Morocco as a geographically Other space is diminished under the conceptualization that the Protectorate is merely an extension of Spain across the Mediterranean. This consideration does not resolve any issues, but rather serves to highlight the complex ideologies, cultures, and personages that interacted in these cosmopolitan contact zones.

Doña Natalia, the novel's central protagonist, is a benevolent character, even in her status as a privileged colonial.[122] The central story-line is of her coming to terms with her imminent departure from the place that she has called home for the majority of her adult life. Morocco is her home and Spain represents for her a strange and unknown place; she is comfortable maneuvering the culturally and linguistically heterogeneous world of the Moroccan Protectorate. Her proximate departure is part of a wider trend among the expatriate Europeans living in the Protectorate; doña Natalia reflects that "little by little we're all leaving here."[123] This changing reality that comes with the newly found independence contributes to a sense of nostalgia among the remaining expatriates—"How good we used to live!"[124]—and an uneasiness at the changes such as renaming streets with Arabic names[125] or a more hostile political environment with recent crimes and aggressions against the government.[126] However, despite the characters' nostalgia for colonial glory days or the subtle exclusion of non-privileged, cultural Others, the text actively seeks to value the Moroccan Other and to present the West and its African Other equitably.

The colonial nostalgia that doña Natalia and other characters express is problematic upon analysis. The narrative indulges the characters' nostalgia, and it is not until one of the final chapters that the text offers a strong admonishment of the colonial pinings. As doña Natalia deliberates and worries about her inevitable return to Spain, she has a dream where a "Mandani, el profeta" tells her that "No one is going to notice your absence, you are just going to be one more among those that leave; you're not going to think yourself irreplaceable, are you? . . . Everything is going to continue on the same, don't you doubt it."[127] The self-assumed importance of the colonial in the Protectorate is undermined with this dream. Colonization as a *mission civilisatrice* is rendered untenable with the assertion that "the geraniums and the gladiolas in the garden will continue flowering as long as there is someone to water them."[128] And most importantly, nostalgia is negated in the assertion that she is "ilusa" or naïve.

While the multiple linguistic and narrative voices avoid a unitary viewpoint, the text also explicitly decries cultural prejudices. The clearest example is in the chapter "Mme. Mechbal." In this chapter María Mechbal, a Spaniard married to a Moroccan, visits doña Natalia for her advice on contacting the family that disowned her when she married the Moroccan Ali Mechbal. She confides in doña Natalia that her parents never forgave her for marrying "an Arab" and they have hidden her relationship from the rest of the family.[129] Doña Natalia's responds by reminding María of her happiness with her husband:

"You're happy, right?"
"You see it; I think there are things so clear that you can't hide them easily."
And she let loose with numerous details that configured the basis of her happiness; with excitement, she emphasized the virtues of that loving and kind man.[130]

For María and doña Natalia, Ali Mechbal's ethnicity is unimportant and María's parents' inability to accept her relationship is ridiculous. Her husband is described in personal qualities, not racial ones: "Ali is so good. . . . Even with a magnifying glass I don't think that I could have found another as good, and the kind man does everything I want, whether he likes it or not."[131] María shares the story of her relationship to Ali with doña Natalia, concluding by asking doña Natalia to take news to her family when she returns to Madrid so that perhaps they can "forgive her" and allow her to return with her daughter to visit. To this ultimate desire, doña Natalia responds by saying "'Let's see here, María, what is it that they have to forgive you of, my child?' This attitude infuriated her. 'Well, that's that! It's as if your husband wasn't as honorable as the best; even more, because he shows you so well, the poor man!'"[132] Doña Natalia explicitly counters any preconceptions that one culture is better than the other as she emphasizes the personal qualities over cultural difference.

Doña Natalia also emphasizes the value of the contact zone for facilitating an appreciation of the Other. In the same conversation from above, she further comforts María by recounting the first time she visited Africa, emphasizing the preconceptions that she had: "nightmares in which a Moor, black like ebony, seized one of her sons and took off with him, mounted upon a spirited steed."[133] She admits that "[l]ater, upon her arrival, she was surprised to find out that there existed Arabs with skin that was even whiter than hers, and that was saying a lot!"[134] In this admission, she suggests two things; one, that unverified preconceptions are untrustworthy—"What happens with your parents is that they don't know Morocco nor the people of this land . . . But that also happened to me before I came . . . !"[135]—and two, that her moral prejudices formed on skin color were based on absurd premises. She values the African Other through her familiarity with it, and she is confident that if María's family were to share this experience, then their preconceptions and stereotypes would be revealed as unjustified. Doña Natalia effectively emphasizes the importance of the contact zone as a space where preconceptions are replaced by appreciation.

Perhaps the most specific mention of race from doña Natalia can be found in the first chapter where she also emphasizes individual qualities over cultural generalizations: "She didn't have any complaints about the Moroccans; she found them hospitable and generous. She had been there too long not to know them; they could have their defects, but also their virtues just like the rest of the mortals."[136] Virtues and defects are shared characteristics of all humans, and generalizations cannot adequately describe entire populations or cultures.

Admittedly, there are instances where her comments are racially insensitive. For instance, during their conversation, María grabs her hands and leans to kiss them in gratitude and doña Natalia responds "Don't you see how you've become as servile as them!"[137] and this admonition—especially the specific use of *ellos*—comes across forcefully. In addition, the surprised tone of her thought "Well, madame Mechbal is plenty happy and she's married to a Moroccan!,"[138] even though it expresses a positive sentiment, it contains sarcastic undertones. That is to say, even though the narration makes specific and repeated attempts to avoid the Orientalist traps along the way, these occasional phrases that stand out in their use of divisive pronouns such as *ellos* or incredulity at the success of an interracial marriage hint at "the sheer knitted-together strength of Orientalist discourse . . . and its redoubtable durability."[139] While López Sarasúa attempts to undermine and destabilize any preconceived notions of Western "*positional* superiority" over the African Other, certain descriptions or lines remain—such as the ones above—that remind us that Orientalist portrayals still endure.

The dramatic coup over Orientalist discourse occurs in the final chapter—"The Last Verse."[140] Doña Natalia and Halima are shopping in the the street of the Consulates[141] in Rabat and decide to stop at a café for tea. They hear music and, intrigued, they go to the café from which it emanates. Doña Natalia asks what they are singing and she is told they are Andalusian songs by a waiter "in perfect Castilian, boasting about his Tetuani origin."[142] Doña Natalia is captivated by the melancholy music and further questions the waiter as to its meaning. It is in classical Arabic and so the young man must ask the musicians for clarification, but he shares with doña Natalia that it is a poem about exile by the Arabic poet Ibn Amira that was born in Valencia.[143] Surprised, doña Natalia exclaims "I'm from Valencia! Imagine that!"[144] The waiter translates the song of exile for her, and afterwards she comments to Halima:

> Do you see it, Halima? I had to come here to understand that those poets so loved my land. I didn't even know that this Ibn Amira existed. . . . The Moors were infidels, they only taught you this; infidels and invaders; but of one thing I am sure is that the one who expelled them from Valencia was named Jaume, first or second, I don't even remember! . . . Well, yes, it was Jaume the Conqueror. What an amazing coincidence . . . ![145]

Doña Natalia is deeply moved by the experience. Not only does this explanation recall the cultural diversity of Spain's past, but it also subtly evokes the diversity of contemporary Spain by employing the Catalan/Valencian spelling of "Jaume el Conqueridor."[146] The café becomes a contact zone where the Spanish, Arabic, and Catalan presences are all evoked and entwined. With few substantial changes, a similar scene can be imagined occurring in Valencia in the early thirteenth century. Her preference of the Catalan term over the Spanish "Conquistador" subtly hints at the cultural diversity that permeates Spanish identity and unites Spain and North Africa.

This scene is a revelation for the elderly doña Natalia. In the final pages of the novel, she prepares to leave and reflects on "How much had she learned this afternoon! It would never have occurred to her to think that those verses had been inspired by Valencia, her own land, how great was her ignorance! and how inhumane was exile!"[147] The poem comforts her as she feels she is about to embark on her own personal exile in moving back to Spain, and the novel closes as she listens to the muezzin calling to prayer: "Allāh akbar! Allāh akbar! From the peak of Oukaimeden a muezzin led the call to prayer."[148] She has a new understanding of exile and belonging that privileges neither Spain nor the Maghreb, but rather sympathizes with the shared pain of loss.

This final chapter is not only the moment when doña Natalia comes to terms with the reality of her return to Spain, but also makes a conscious effort to connect the contemporary reality of the mass exodus of expatriates with the thirteenth century Arab reality.[149] Doña Natalia is able to emotionally connect with the exiled suffering of the poet Ibn Amira and it causes her to reevaluate what she was taught growing up.[150] She resigns herself to a return to Spain, accepting a self-imposed exile from the land she loves. López Sarasúa complicates the concept of fatherland, re-establishing it not along lines of cultural difference or indigenous heritage, but on personal connection. Doña Natalia's perception that a return to Spain will be her own exile turns on its head the very concept of "exile" as being distanced from one's "native" land, and connects her with her historical and cultural Other, the poet Ibn Amira, as she finds solace in his poem. She realizes that her exile is no different from the one experienced by the Moors who were expelled from Spain by the Catholic Kings. She also understands that the discourse of difference that has maintained the conceptualization of Spanish-versus-Moor as entirely distinct for so many centuries is a limited understanding of a complex reality.

Even with this final and emphatic re-conceptualization of Same and Other, phrases or lines remain in the narration that discomfort or appear out of place. As doña Natalia recounts the name of "Jaume el Conqueridor," her reminiscing appears to emphasize a conquering West over its vanquished Other. The use of *jactarse*[151] to describe her waiter's use of Spanish—"in perfect Castilian, boasting about his Tetuani origin"[152]—seems slightly excessive. And when she chides Mme. Mechbal for being "as servile as them,"[153] it appears to undermine any grand effort on López Sarasúa's part to completely avoid essentializing representations within the narrative. However, Mohamed Abrighach sees López Sarasúa's narration as an extreme honesty. He credits her with being objective to a fault: "It is not an ideological positioning, but rather a compromise with the truth and a de-mythification . . . a sincere form of re-thinking history."[154] Abrighach sees these phrases that irk as "satirical humor of a noticeable intellectual audacity, above all, in that is related to the paradoxical description of the immigrants . . . it is her way of facing and living with the North African and Moroccan alterity."[155] And so, in offering López Sarasúa the benefit of the doubt, she effectively reconceptualizes ideas of fatherland and exile, valorizing both Africa and the African Other while refusing to whitewash the legacy of Orientalism and Orientalist discourse.

Abrighach's insight is charitable; the narrative could be interpreted as brutally honest in its representation, but also as (unintentionally) offensive. Ultimately, the sting is removed from doña Natalia's occasional uncomfortable observations. Her age and her affectionate title of "doña" used throughout confer upon her possibly offensive words a benign antiquity. The reader understands that she cares deeply about her home in Morocco and those with whom she interacts; her offensive utterances represent a legacy of expression that her experiences in the Protectorate belie. Within this narrative context, doña Natalia's words express Orientalist tropes while her actions and interactions undermine their power. While Abrighach's interpretation excuses the use of Orientalist discourse in López Sarasúa's text, I find that López Sarasúa's narrative goes further than a mere "de-mythification"; her representation attempts an intentional subversion of Orientalism's authority. For

López Sarasúa, Orientalism is a discursive force that persists, but it is one that loses its affective power within the intercultural contact zone.

As her narrative unfolds within the colonial setting of the Moroccan Protectorates, López Sarasúa writes an intercultural contact zone that is distinct from Silva's representation of war. López Sarasúa's novel offers a complementary historical context to Silva's work; the war setting is replaced with the colony. Physical conflict is notably absent from *La llamada del almuédano*. What propels the story are the emotional ties and the affection that interpersonal contact provides. In its quotidian preoccupations, López Sarasúa's text normalizes relationships between Westerners and their African Others. Ties between individuals—or between individuals and places—are emotional, not cultural. Even while her characters may indulge in nostalgia for the glory days of the colonial Protectorates, López Sarasúa simultaneously avoids any whitewashing of the past and shows that their discourse is undermined by their experience. The characters of the novel often employ the Orientalist speech that promoted and perpetuated colonialism and stereotypes, and yet López Sarasúa's narrative ultimately focuses on the contact zones where individuals from various cultural backgrounds come together and value emotional connections over superficial, phenotypic differences. *La llamada del almuédano* suggests that the interpersonal relationship has the potential to overcome Orientalism as it shows that the African Other is nothing more than another human being; one who loves and suffers in the same ways as the Westerner.

THE LEGIBILITY OF THE OTHER IN RAMÓN MAYRATA'S *EL IMPERIO DESIERTO*

Ramón Mayrata was first a poet and only later a novelist. His first book of poetry, *Estética de las serpientes*,[156] was published in 1972 while his first novel, *El imperio desierto*, was not published until 1992. He has since continued to publish novels and collections of short stories, including *Una duda de Alicia* (1990),[157] *Si me escuchas esta noche* (1991),[158] *El sillón malva* (1994),[159] *Sin puertas* (1996),[160] *Alí Bey, el Abasí* (1995),[161] *Confín de la ciudad* (1998),[162] and *Miracielos* (2000),[163] among other works of both prose and poetry. Mayrata worked in Paris as a reporter and translator and, in addition to his fiction and poetry, also has several non-fiction books and a collection of his literary articles titled *El ojo de la arbitrariedad* (1986).[164]

Mayrata has received some recognition throughout his career. His early poetry appears in an anthology collected by Vicente Aleixandre, *Espejo del amor y de la muerte* (1971).[165] *Alí Bey, el Abasí* has been translated into Arabic and *Miracielos* was adapted for theater by Carlos Rod in 2002.[166] His critical writing on literature and art has been collected in various works and published in journals also.[167]

Most pertinent to this study is his focus and writings on Western Sahara. *El imperio desierto* will serve as the central text for this analysis and it is worth noting that it is a work of fiction that contains significant autobiographical elements. Ramón Mayrata worked as an anthropologist in the then Spanish Sahara in the mid-1970s, in the midst of the ultimately unsuccessful decolonization of the territory.[168] The plot of *El imperio desierto* mirrors this reality as Ignacio Aguirre, a young anthropologist, is sent to the Spanish Sahara to write a history of the Saharawi people. Also relevant to this work is the anthology of stories and writings about the Saharan territory compiled by Mayrata, *Relatos del Sáhara* (2001)[169] and his fictional account of the historical figure of Alí Bey/Domingo Badía in *Alí Bey, el Abasí*. Unfortunately, these latter texts will need to be explored elsewhere, and I have chosen to focus on *El imperio desierto* here as it directly confronts the issue of Western Sahara and its decolonization. Mayrata's work with the Saharawi nation and his involvement with the cause of independence have earned him great respect among many in the contemporary Saharawi refugee community.

This section will rely upon James C. Scott's *Seeing Like a State* (1998) and Edward Said's *Orientalism* to understand the ways in which the West has historically forced the colonial subject to conform to Western ideas of organization for official recognition. Scott's articulation of the concept of *legibility* specifically illuminates this Western imposition, and I argue that Mayrata recognizes this pattern of paternalism and writes a novel that values alternate cultural valorizations and legibilities. Mayrata's text highlights the problematic nature of the West's treatment of its African colonies as exemplified in the decolonization process and international diplomatic processes. *El imperio desierto* ultimately emphasizes that a culture that does not conform to Western standards of legibility is doomed to marginalization, as implied by the double entendre of the title as either *The Desert Empire* or *The Deserted Empire*.

El imperio desierto occurs over the final year of the Spanish Sahara colony. The Spanish Sahara was governed as a Spanish territory from 1884 to 1975, notably as a separate and distinct territory from the Spanish Protectorate of Morocco. As the novel opens, Spain is initializing the process of decolonization and handing autonomy over to the Saharawi populace, due to international pressure. As a brief historical context, the governments of Morocco and Mauritania simultaneously claimed sovereignty over the territory, seeking to have the Spanish Sahara divided between them before allowing Western Sahara to establish itself as an independent state, effectively contesting the legal validity of an independent Saharawi nation. Spain took the case to the International Court of Justice, which ruled in favor of the potential Saharawi state.[170] Undeterred, King Hassan II organized a peaceful demonstration that included approximately 350,000 unarmed Moroccan civilians who marched across the border into the Spanish Sahara on November 6, 1975. Spain was unwilling to become involved in a potentially large-scale conflict due to the failing health of Franco, among other reasons, and so offered little resistance to the pacific occupation of the territory. Spain withdrew shortly thereafter, leaving the territory under internationally contested Moroccan control. The Saharawi nationalists, united under the *Frente Polisario* were forced to retreat to refugee camps in Tindouf, Algeria, where they continue to subsist, seeking international recognition and restoration.[171]

El imperio desierto develops during the most contentious time of the decolonization process. A young anthropologist, Ignacio Aguirre, is hired to go to the territory and to prepare a history textbook of the Saharawi people for use in the indigenous schools that will come with the anticipated independence. At this specific time, around 1974, the Saharan territory is clouded in secrecy, due to the Law of Official Secrets of 1968[172] that prohibits news and information about the territory from reaching the general Spanish populace. The territory is administered under strict military rule, even as the process is underway for Saharawi independence in the very near future.

As the political situation deteriorates between Spain, the Saharawi, and Morocco, Ignacio's initial mission to prepare a history textbook is replaced with a charge to compile the documentation necessary to present the case for Saharawi sovereignty to the International Court of Justice. Ignacio and his Saharawi collaborators must negotiate diplomatic avenues of official recognition and documentation, at times making concessions to the Western conceptions of validity and bureaucracy, all the while working towards an anticipated independence.

Ramón Mayrata's treatment of the Other is significant in this context, because, due to the nature of Ignacio Aguirre's anthropological project, the very goal is to establish and to highlight ethnic, political, and cultural difference. The premise of national self-determination is based upon a unique, historical Saharawi identity that ethnically separates the indigenous inhabitants of the territory from their Moroccan and Mauritanian neighbors. Ignacio's project is two-fold: first, to compile from various sources and oral histories the documentation necessary to prove the unique ethnic Otherness of the Saharawi, and second, to render this indigenous documentation *legible* for the West and specifically the International Court of Justice. Mayrata's focus on this process highlights the West's belief that the subaltern cannot speak for itself. Spain's paternalistic handling of the Spanish Sahara's decolonization suggests that "in the context of colonial production, the subaltern has no history and cannot speak";[173] Ignacio's job is to literally create a Saharawi history and to speak for the colonial subjects before the Western world.

The term *legible* is adapted from James C. Scott's use of the term in *Seeing Like a State*. This book is apropos to the Saharawi situation, as Scott examines modernity and the concomitant sedentarization of people with increased state apparatus. In Scott's words, "the state has always seemed to be the enemy of 'people who move around.'"[174] Even though Scott's use of "enemy" is not the theorized bellicose enemy of Anidjar, this articulation does highlight the fact that the Saharawi's tradition of nomadism hinders their ability to form a state that is *legible* as such to the Western world. Scott explains the concept of legibility within diplomacy as one emerging

> as a central problem in statecraft. The premodern state was, in many crucial respects, partially blind; it knew precious little about its subjects, their wealth, their landholdings and yields, their location, their very identity. It lacked anything like a detailed "map" of its terrain and its people. It lacked, for the most part, a measure, a metric, that would allow it to "translate" what it knew into a common standard necessary for a synoptic view.[175]

In Scott's view, organization, sedentarization, and standardization allow states to control their populace and also create an organized aesthetic that contributes to a consolidated national identity, distinguishable from other states. Organization and standardization effectively render a state legible.

This theorization is pertinent to the Saharawi example in *El imperio desierto* in that the Saharawi are only partially sedentarized. The infrastructure present in the Spanish Sahara colony is a Spanish infrastructure, governed by Spaniards. The nomadic heritage of the Saharawi is not legible to the international community due to its difference and the misleading appearance of a lack of national unity. Conversely, Morocco's legible (read modern, bureaucratic) state apparatus gives its claims to sovereignty a certain degree of international validity, even though the International Court of Justice ruled in favor of the Saharawi. The Western aesthetic favors a government structure that offers a clear hierarchy, where "lines of influence and command are exclusively from the center to the periphery."[176] King Hassan II's Morocco reflects this modern conceptualization of the state much more accurately than the leaderless independence movement of the Polisario in *El imperio desierto*.

Another important hurdle for the Saharawi of *El imperio desierto* is their historical reliance on the oral transmission of history. Scott offers five characteristics in the process of "State simplifications," of which two are directly relevant here: first, that "they are . . . nearly always written (verbal or numerical) *documentary* facts" and second, that "most stylized state facts are also *aggregated* facts. Aggregate facts may be impersonal . . . or simply a collection of facts about individuals."[177] The Saharawi cultural history is neither textually documented nor proximately aggregated. Prior to the Spanish decolonization of the territory, the Saharawi had relied on oral transmission of their history, and the documents that were available were dispersed throughout the families of the territory, uncatalogued and unorganized. The dispersal of the familial and historical information limits the Saharawi's ability to document and prove their traditional independence from the Moroccan sultanate. Therefore, in order to earn viability in the West's consideration, the Saharawi must gather and document their history in a manner that is legible to the West. As mentioned above, this is Ignacio Aguirre's project in the territory. To accomplish this task, Ignacio forms a team composed of Saharawi men who help him to gather scarce historical documents from families and to document family histories.[178] Ignacio's team faces significant resistance from the Spanish police force in the Saharan territory as they believe that he is aiding the popular uprising of the *Frente Polisario*. Ignacio and his colleagues also encounter reluctance from the local Saharawi populace who are hesitant to entrust their important documents to a cultural outsider. However, once Ignacio convinces his team members and the local patriarchs of his sincerity, they are able to persuade the disparate families of the territory to loan them over eight thousand pages of documents for research and archiving.[179] Ignacio succeeds in aggregating official documentation, a step towards rendering Saharawi history legible to the West.

The novel is split into five sections, of which Ignacio Aguirre is the primary focus. It maintains a third-person omniscient narration throughout, and traces the history of Ignacio's involvement with the project. The first section begins in Madrid with Ignacio as a recently graduated anthropology student; he is contacted by the Spanish government and asked to undertake this project in the Saharan territory. Sections two and three detail his arrival and research work, and in section four he returns to Madrid to present his research, but he is kidnapped in the Canary Islands by the police Comandante García Ramos from El Aaiun and held captive. He is eventually released and returns to Madrid to pass along his findings to the government.[180] In section five, Ignacio returns to the territory in the midst of the most chaotic moments of the Spanish withdrawal. He is injured in a bomb blast and later put on a plane out of the country at which point the novel ends. The plot follows many of the generic conventions of the adventure novel in its action-packed sequences, plot surprises, and romantic relationships, but it is also a serious consideration of the problems and consequences associated with Spain's botched withdrawal from the Spanish Sahara.

El imperio desierto ultimately humanizes the Saharawi Other and sympathizes with this Other that is condemned to operate within a cultural paradigm that is not their own. Mayrata represents the Saharawi Other in three specific ways that undermine and depart from traditional Orientalist discourse. These three points are: (1) Mayrata's emphasis on how the West (i.e., European

Colonial Powers, the praxis of diplomacy, and archival of knowledge) dominates all interactions; (2) the ways in which Mayrata humanizes the Saharawi and consciously avoids idolizing his cultural Other; and (3) the narrative attention to the cultural differences that disadvantage the Saharawi in a world that operates according to the Western paradigm. Through these three representational strategies, Mayrata's work offers a vision of the Saharawi Other that is sympathetic without being paternalistic, and which also recognizes cultural difference without exoticizing.

I have already alluded above to the Western domination; this is initially evident in Ignacio's official charge to write a history textbook for the Saharawi. His new job is explained to him as such:

> It appears that they are firmly decided on giving independence to the territory. . . . But they've found that there is not any existing textbook that covers the history of the Sahara. In an independent country they have to study their own history in the schools. And that is what they want you to do. A history of the territory for the new Saharans.
> —I believe that they're called Saharawis.[181]

The third-person plural of "they are firmly decided" refers to the Spanish government, subtly emphasizing that the possibility of independence is something that the colonizers offer, not something that the colonized have agency to demand for themselves. Furthermore, Ignacio is a young, inexperienced anthropologist who knows very little about the territory, and yet he is the one chosen to document the complete history of the territory and its inhabitants. His inexperience and lack of knowledge, however, is contrasted with the inexcusable ignorance of those who offer him the job, as he corrects "Saharans" with the correct nomenclature. In addition, the paternalistic use of "the new Saharans" emphasizes a nonchalant dismissal of a people group that has existed for centuries; the officials' words imply that the Spanish deserve credit for creating a new national identity. The Saharawi are not offered the opportunity to write their own history. Ignacio is privileged over potential Saharawi authors for his status as a Westerner, despite his uninspiring credentials.

For this assignment, Ignacio must serve as an intermediary, to "translate" the oral history of the Saharawi into a format that is acceptable in Western diplomatic circles, to render it legible to the West. What begins as an educational goal for his project—to create a history textbook for use in independent Saharawi schools—becomes a much higher-stakes game as Morocco and Mauritania threaten invasion and contest the presumed independence of the territory. Ignacio, therefore, becomes an official representative for the Saharawi before the International Court of Justice and the wider, Western diplomatic community. His position as such highlights the fact that the Saharawi of the novel do not have their own voice in international diplomatic circles; they must find help through their (paternalistic) colonizers who will accompany them on the pathway to self-determination. Ignacio is charged with documenting and archiving the totality of Saharawi history and warned that it will be an extremely difficult task. In fact, the West's mania for official bureaucratic documentation is subtly ridiculed when Ignacio learns during his interview with the current President of the Government that he will have virtually no oversight since no one in the Spanish government knows much of anything about the history of the territory.[182] He is assigned an official commission that validates his work, and the commissioning official notes its bureaucratic arbitrariness. And Ignacio's value stems largely from his title:

> You are not a functionary, Aguirre. You have to have a title. We have named you Director of the Commission. If you didn't have the title, you'd be lost to the Administration. All of these things have their importance. At a thousand and something kilometers of distance, you wouldn't exist for us.[183]

This admission by the President of the Government offers two important interpretations. First, the Spanish colonial government knows and/or cares very little about the Saharan territory and yet it decides and implements the decolonization process without indigenous input. Second, this passage subtly emphasizes, and perhaps ridicules, the West's obsession with official titles and bureaucracy, suggesting that Ignacio would "cease to exist" if he did not have an official title that secured his continued recognition. In between the lines of this passage is the possibility of a third interpretation: that the Saharawi are not recognized because their societal structures do not conform to legible Western paradigms.

To further emphasize the Saharawi's plight as completely unknown by the West,[184] before he leaves for his new job, Ignacio meets with one of his best friends, Jaime Barnet. As students, Jaime and Ignacio had participated in various leftist political groups, with Ignacio eventually falling in love and leaving aside his political actions, while Jaime became a fervent member of the Communist Federation.[185] As Ignacio tells Jaime about his new project, Jaime insists that he get in touch with "el Morehob," the independence movement that Trotsky's Fourth International supports:

> "Apparently, the Fourth International supports a group called Morehob."
> "What does this acronym stand for?"
> "Something like the Movement of the Blue Men."
> "It's a beautiful name."
> "It's directed by some Eduardo Moha from Algeria."

"From Algeria? Are they pro-Algerian? And the Fourth International supports them?"

"Well, we're not talking about comrades, clearly. They are very far from our positions. But there is not any other organized group in the territory. I suppose that this will be one of those movements for national liberation somewhat vague and confused, that is made up of a little bit of everything. In this is our opportunity, precisely. You understand?"[186]

Jaime's "our opportunity" belies his concern for the Morehob and/or Saharawi. Not only does neither he nor the Fourth International have any information about what the actual situation is in the Spanish Sahara (much less that there already exists an independence movement, the Polisario), but also the Fourth International hopes to use any potential independence movement for the development of their own political ends.[187] The selfish interests of Jaime, representative of the Spanish left, together with the paternalism and disinterest of the governing right further emphasize the Saharawi's marginalized position at the mercy of a manipulative West. With this scene, Mayrata sidesteps specific political accusations against the left or right, instead insinuating that both sides share blame. At the root of both Jaime's and the Spanish government's motives is the idea that the Saharawi, like Said's "Oriental" "is irrational, . . . childlike, 'different'; thus the European is rational, virtuous, mature, 'normal.'"[188] Mayrata subtly recognizes the cultural discourse that privileges the West over its Other, regardless of political orientation.

Said's articulation further contributes to this consideration, complementing Scott's idea of *legibility*:

> the way of enlivening the relationship [between the West and the Orient] was everywhere to stress the fact that the Oriental lived in a different but thoroughly organized world of his own, a world with its own national, cultural, and epistemological boundaries and principles of internal coherence. Yet what gave the Oriental's world its intelligibility and identity was not the result of his own efforts but rather the whole complex series of knowledgeable manipulations by which the Orient was identified by the West.[189]

In the case of the Saharawi and the Spanish Sahara, there is very little knowledge that the Spanish colonizers have gathered (or cared to gather). At the moment when this knowledge of the Saharawi Other is needed, Ignacio is contracted to gather the information and render it intelligible/legible. What before was simple indifference is now shown to be also extremely paternalistic. And the Saharawi are never offered the opportunity to speak directly for themselves, their voice must be "*contained* and *represented* by dominating frameworks,"[190] i.e., the voice of the naïve Western anthropologist Ignacio Aguirre.

To Ignacio's and Mayrata's credit, though, Ignacio is not only sympathetic to the Saharawi cause, but also values the differences between Western and Saharawi conceptions of knowledge and history. He finds comparisons between Spain and the Saharawi without waxing nostalgic. At the start of his career as an anthropologist, before the Sahara offer, he reflects: "For an anthropologist, Spain was a tempting country. You could still see ancestral forms of living, ones that were reduced to memory in the rest of Europe."[191] He deeply values the oral tradition that is not only a Saharawi characteristic, but one in which his grandmother took part. He used to read French novels to her, and he recognizes the value that that oral transmission of stories had for his grandmother and his relationship to her.[192] The written word, the written history, is shown to be the valued and legible documentation format in the contemporary West. Ignacio's memories of his grandmother and his reasons for becoming an anthropologist emphasize that the value placed on oral history within Spain has diminished in recent history. Memory is not valued as a legitimate or a legible documentation source for international mediation purposes.[193] The memories of Ignacio's grandmother are alluded to when the Saharawi Lieutenant Mohamed Fadel introduces him to the other indigenous guards:

> Soldiers of the Sahara! This man that you see here has come to write our history. . . . We know this history, *because we have heard it on the lips of our fathers and our grandfathers.* But there are many peoples that do not know who the Saharawi are, how they have lived up to now and the things they have done. . . . When he writes the truth, *the whisper of the voice of our ancestors* will extend throughout the world like the wind and no one will doubt that we must be an independent nation. (Emphasis mine)[194]

Ignacio shares an appreciation for the oral tradition from his own grandmother. Implicit in this excerpt is also his forthcoming documentation of that tradition: "When he *writes* the truth." Mohamed Fadel views Ignacio's future transcription of the oral history as one that will allow it to be understood and appreciated beyond the territory's borders, a transcribed version that will be acceptable for the West's logocentric favoring of the written over the oral. Fadel believes that Ignacio's written history of the Saharawi has the potential to accurately transcribe and reflect the literal voice of the Saharawi ancestors. While this documentary format is not traditionally valued by the Saharawi, Fadel recognizes that they must employ the written word to express the value of their oral history to the West.

Ignacio quickly proves himself able to manipulate written language in an effective manner. When Ignacio first arrives in the Spanish Sahara and immediately after Mohamed Fadel's introduction, the commanding secretary general Fernández-Hoz gives him twenty-four hours to prepare an initial draft that will convince him that Ignacio is the appropriate person for the job. As Ignacio struggles with his approach, he chooses to employ poetic imagery over scientific jargon, relying on the affective power of his text to convince.[195] He gives the draft to the secretary general and later attends a meeting where Fernández-Hoz addresses members of the Saharawi elders and Spanish administrators. Ignacio is suprised to discover that the secretary general's passionate speech copied his report almost word for word.[196] It is this experience that also confirms for him the power that the written word can have to influence, and it is his blending of oral descriptions with scientific documentation that allows him to achieve this effect.

Conversely, the power of the written word is also clearly understood and valued by the Saharawi; Fadel emphasizes that "the Saharawi venerates words and gives them more value than any other precious object."[197] This is specifically evident in the case of the political prisoner Basiri, captured by the Spanish and whose current presence or status is unknown. Basiri was the original founder of the Frente Polisario; he was detained four years earlier— in 1970—by the Spanish Legion and no one knows where he is kept or if he is still alive. However, his memory continues to live and inspire, not only through his previous actions, but also through a scrap of paper, written in blue pen and somehow smuggled out of his prison, that represents his last testament.[198] He effectively continues to live through his words, adding example to the affirmation by Buhe—one of Ignacio's collaborators—that the conservation and documentation of history preserves the power of their culture and ancestors.[199] Even though Basiri never appears as a physical presence in the narrative, he is a spectral character that forms an essential part of the plot through the power of his written word.

Ultimately, the Saharawi are presented as flexible and capable individuals who value their oral tradition but understand the need to cater to the Western values of documentation. It is the West that is unable to understand the African Other or cultural values and conceptualizations that differ from the Western paradigm. While this could be interpreted as Europe articulating the Orient,[200] forcing the African Other to conform to standards and practices that are defined by the West, Mayrata instead presents the Saharawi as recognizing the differences and making concessions for official recognition but not abandoning the qualities and traditions that distinguish them. Mayrata's presentation of the Saharawi is a nuanced one; it recognizes the power of Orientalism as a dominant paradigm yet suggests that the Saharawi collaborate but do not compromise with the West in its strict conceptions of what is considered "official documentation." Mayrata's text does, however, emphasize the West's overbearing paternalism and disenfranchisement of the Other.

As Mayrata outlines the West's attempts to speak for the Saharawi and the concomitant paternalism of the West for its colonized Other, he simultaneously makes an effort not to exoticize or idolize/idealize his portrayal of the Saharawi. Even though, at times, the prose waxes poetic about the exotic attraction of the desert ("The desert is another planet"[201]), Mayrata makes specific efforts to humanize the Saharawi as well as to admit the West's difficulty in understanding and speaking for its Other.

The cruelty of colonialism is an obvious component of the Spanish control of the territory. The text alludes to the Legionnaire's massacre of a group of Saharawi on July 17, 1970—the protest that led to the detention of Basiri. Comandate García Ramos, of the Territorial Police, is also a ruthless figure in his control of the city. Ignacio is, in fact, kidnapped by García Ramos and his men in the Canary Islands, and he is brutally tortured and detained. However, the Saharawi independence movement is not without its own brutality. Mayrata avoids the facile trap of idealizing their fight by showing that even sympathetic characters such as Ignacio's collaborator, Buhe, can be as cruel as the malevolent García Ramos, or even more so. At one point, Ignacio is clandestinely taken to meet with Buhe and other members of the Polisario. In a gruesome description, Buhe and the other Polisario members show Ignacio the severed head of Mahayub, another of Ignacio's collaborators and also an agent of the Moroccan crown who had recently detonated a bomb in Laayoune. The cold stoicism of Buhe and his comrades stuns Ignacio. He finds that his friends are capable of atrocities that he did not expect, and that now Buhe expresses himself "like a soldier."[202] This acknowledgement by Ignacio does shift the discourse from one of clashing cultures to one of confronting armies,[203] but it also emphasizes shared human characteristics between the West and its Other, albeit ruthless ones.

As for the West's difficulty in understanding and speaking for its Other, Mayrata first suggests this in a comical narration that comes in a letter from Manuela, Ignacio's girlfriend at the beginning of the novel. Manuela is studying anthropology in London and attends a conference. She narrates a gathering of British anthropologists clad in various cultural attires from across the world, in a scene that criticizes their cultural appropriation and their inability to appreciate cultural diversity beyond superficial markers.[204]

In their attempt to represent their studied Other, these anthropologists overcompensate. With this comical description, Mayrata subtly erodes the monolithic and the discursive power of the West's attempts to speak for the Other, effectively undermining Orientalism as a field of study. Manuela does conclude her letter with a *nota bene* by admitting that her narration is, perhaps, exaggerated, but she knows that that is the kind of thing that Ignacio would find entertaining.[205] This final addition not only admits the hyperbolic nature of her earlier narration, but also offers a meta-narrative consideration.

What is implied is that narrative exaggerations are often employed for their affective power with the reader. Ultimately, the *nota bene* admits the subjective quality of any text or attempt at representation.

Mayrata also tempers the occasional romantic tendencies of Ignacio by contrasting him with his friend Jaime. When Ignacio returns to Madrid to present his work to the government officials, he engages in a lengthy conversation with Jaime. Jaime is brutal in his pragmatism, suggesting that the Saharan territory should be handed over to Morocco for control because it contains few resources that would allow it to be a viable independent nation. In his counter-argument, Ignacio is less reasonable and relies more on eloquent and poetic opinings ("How could I explain it to you? You know that a landscape is a historical framework."[206] "The Saharawi are a miracle."[207]). Jaime warns Ignacio not to idealize the Saharawi,[208] and the ultimate effect of their back and forth is one that suggests that Ignacio may be too singular in his portrayal of the Saharawi, but Jaime is too general in his. This contrast emphasizes the difficulty of objective narration, admitting the possible faults of a Western author attempting to represent his African Other, while the text is literally about a Westerner writing the history of his African Other. The salient phrase that seeks to overcome the limitations of a textual representation comes from Ignacio: "Only when you are able to enter into a relationship with its inhabitants, does the desert stop being an inhospitable, inhuman place, and converts into the land of some men who, thanks to an adequate culture, have made it miraculously habitable."[209] Ignacio emphasizes the importance of the face-to-face encounter and the personal exchange between individuals that can contribute to understanding the Other, in this, Ignacio seems to be offering the same advice as doña Natalia in *La llamada del almuédano*. In this, the novel aligns with Kapuściński's assertion that "an encounter with Others is not a simple, automatic thing, but involves will and an effort that not everyone is always ready to undertake."[210] The Other may be different, but that difference should not serve as an impediment to mutual appreciation.

As a final point, Mayrata emphasizes the cultural differences that disadvantage the Saharawi in a world that operates within the Western paradigm. Ignacio's position as a translator, as one who will render legible the Saharawi Other to the West has been examined above. The Saharawi preference for the oral tradition over the written one also marginalizes their voice on the international stage. In addition, the very idea of what constitutes a society, a state, is conceptually different for the Saharawi. I refer specifically to infrastructure (or lack thereof). If the state "has always seemed to be the enemy of 'people who move around,'"[211] what does a state of indigenous nomads look like? The text suggests that the infrastructure present in the Spanish Sahara is of almost purely colonial construction as Ignacio's friend, the German archeologist Dr. Koller, explains to him that: "The cities are actually a colonial creation.

Almost a mirage. An illusion sustained by the motherland."[212] However, Dr. Koller does not deny that the Saharawi have their own conceptualization of "organization," it is merely one that does not adhere to the Western paradigm, she notes that "for a European, the absence of signs of the State provokes a sentiment of strangeness and neglect much more acute than that of the absence of vegetation."[213] In addition, one of Ignacio's research team members, Ma el Ainin, explains to him the Saharawi conceptualization of a "wandering State"[214] where sedentary settlements are only "the stone tunic with which to cover a body that already existed."[215] In these passages, and in his presentation of the Saharawi Other, Mayrata suggests that the cultural and geographical differences that mark the Saharawi also disadvantage them on the world stage. By implication, the Western models of state infrastructure and organization exclude other historical varieties that should be just as valid, if not more so because they have an earlier historical precedence. Mayrata's text attempts to give voice to this very different Other, at times also questioning his own authority to do so. This self-reflexive process admits its own flaws and values the differences of the Other it attempts to represent, forcefully rejecting facile stereotypes or Orientalist discourse.

The dreams of the Saharawi are ultimately deferred as Hassan II of Morocco organizes the Green March and effective takeover of the territory while the Spanish simultaneously abandon the Saharawi to fate. In the text and in history, many Saharawi fled to the refugee camps in Algeria to continue their fight for recognition, a fight which continues to this day—over forty years later. In their final encounter, as Buhe prepares to depart for Algeria, he says to Ignacio: "From this moment on we will live in the desert, like snakes. I think that I will never forget the time that we spent together, when we the Saharawi could still dream about behaving like human beings."[216] This emotional parting line expresses two powerful ideas; first, that the international community's (and specifically Spain's) abandonment of the Saharawi has dehumanized them as a people, which serves as a strong condemnation of the colonial paradigm. Secondly, it serves as a reminder that, even though cultural differences abound, there is a common humanity that should not be ignored—the Saharawi have been dehumanized by the international community, but they are not essentially different and deserve justice.

Ramón Mayrata's *El imperio desierto* attempts to write the Saharawi Other in ways that consciously subvert Orientalist discourse. He values the difference of his African Other, humanizes this Other, but ultimately also erodes his own ability to objectively represent this Other. The narrative humility of Mayrata attests to an attempt not to privilege the West over its African Other, but neither does he fall into the trap of over-idealizing the African Other. Instead, it hopes to achieve a vision of coexisting, equally valued differences, and in this sense is a powerful counter-Orientalist work of fiction.

El imperio desierto contributes to the analyses of *El nombre de los nuestros* and *La llamada del Almuédano* by examining the West's diplomatic engagement with the African Other. Mayrata's vision of this engagement is of the limited paternalistic understanding that Western bureaucracy has for systems and paradigms that differ in form or conceptualization. The Saharawi are effectively doomed to statelessness because of their difference. As Mayrata engages with this injustice, he actively writes against Oriental discourses of Western superiority by emphasizing the validity of differing cultural ideologies. Ultimately, the Spanish anthropologist or the Saharawi freedom fighter are individual humans, with hopes and flaws, who are forced to navigate the bureaucratic realm of international diplomacy. Mayrata's novel effectively valorizes the Saharawi and their fight for independence, while simultaneously admitting the pitfalls that face a Western author attempting to speak for his African Other. In this lies the counter-Orientalist power and value of this work.

NOTES

1. Pablo Estévez Hernández has done some great work in examining these former colonies alongside census data from the 50s to the 70s in "El censo de 1950 en Guinea Española: la raza como categoría de recuento" (*Revista de análisis cultural* 10 [December 2017]: 533–554) and "Censos, identidad y colonialismo en el sáhara espaõl (1950–1974): la imaginación numérica de la nación española" (*Papeles de CEIC* 89 [September 2012]: 1–34).

2. I use "emigration" here to specifically emphasize the movement of Spaniards *to* the African colonies.

3. Gozálvez Pérez, "Descolonización y migraciones desde el África española," 72.

4. This focus is aligned with a recent interest in the Spanish Civil War within Spanish letters also. Indeed, Lorenzo Silva's novel *Carta blanca* (2005) opens in the fighting of the second War of Africa and closes with the fighting of the Spanish Civil War. Other novels focusing on the Spanish Civil War include Javier Cercas's *Soldados de Salamina* (2001. Reprint, Buenos Aires: Tusquets Editores, 2004), Antonio Muñoz Molina's *La noche de los tiempos* (Barcelona: Seix Barral, 2009), and Dulce Chacón's *La voz dormida* (Madrid: Alfaguara, 2002). Novels such as Silva's *Carta blanca* or Dueñas's *El tiempo entre costuras* emphasize how the question of the Moroccan Colonies and the Spanish Civil War are essentially intertwined realities.

5. [*The Name of Ours*]
6. [*Blank Check / Carte Blanche*]
7. [*The Call of the Muezzin*]
8. [*The Desert Empire*]
9. [*Ali Bey the Abassid: A Christian in Mecca*]
10. [*See If I'll Love You*]

11. [*The Empire of Sand*]
12. [*An African War*]
13. [*The Time in Between*]
14. [*The Doctor from Ifni*]
15. Also referred to as the Rif War and notable for the Disaster of Annual on July 22, 1921. See Leguineche, *Annual 1921: El desastre de España en el Rif* (Madrid: Extra Alfaguara, 1996).
16. A *blocao* was a small, fortified structure used by Spanish troops in the Moroccan wars. It is a prominent feature of works by Sender, Díaz Fernández, Silva, and others, and the isolation and vulnerability of the soldiers stationed at the *blocao* is a recurrent theme.
17. It cannot be denied that Africa was the object of Europe's fevered attention in the nineteenth century as well. The period referred to as the "Scramble for Africa" (roughly mid-nineteenth century to early twentieth century) represented the European nations' efforts to divide up the African continent and to consolidate colonial power. Spain came somewhat late to this "scramble," but did participate, most notably waging the first War of Africa in 1859–1860. Since contemporary authors have focused instead on Spain-Africa interactions in the twentieth century, I do not include a significant focus on this time period. One notable novelistic exception to this trend is Bernardo Atxaga's *Siete casas en Francia* [*Seven Houses in France*] that takes place in the nineteenth century Belgian Congo. For information on the Scramble for Africa, see Chamberlain, *The Scramble for Africa* (New York: Longman, 1999).
18. Up to this point, Spain had largely ignored its African colonies. Fernando Pó Island (now Bioko) in Equatorial Guinea, had been under Spanish control since 1778 and Sidi Ifni had been a Spanish enclave since 1476, called Santa Cruz de la Mar Pequeña, but, compared to the American colonies, little national interest had been placed on the African territories. See Donato Ndongo and Mariano L. de Castro Antolín's *España en Guinea* (Madrid: Sequitur, 1998), Ndongo and Alicia Campos Serrano's *De colonia a estado* (Madrid: Centro de Estudios Políticos y Constitucionales, 2002), and Tomás García Figueras's *Santa Cruz de Mar Pequeña-Ifni-Sáhara* (1941. Reprint, Barcelona: Ediciones FE, 1951) or *Marruecos: La acción de España en el Norte de África* (Barcelona: Ediciones FE, 1941) for more information about the history of these territories.
19. It must be noted that this interaction was often secretive and even silent. Spain allowed little to no information about Western Sahara to appear in the press during its rule of the territory (Hodges, *Western Sahara: The Roots of a Desert War*, 135, 146).
20. The "esperpentic lens" is drawn from Ramón del Valle-Inclán's avant-garde play *Luces de Bohemia* (1920. Reprint, Madrid: Espasa-Calpe, 1973). The *Diccionario de la Real Academia Española* defines "Esperpento" as a "Literary genre created by Ramón del Valle-Inclán, Spanish writer of the Generation of '98, in which reality is distorted, emphasizing the grotesque characteristics, and undergoing a very personal elaboration of colloquial and fractured language." [Género literario creado por Ramón del Valle-Inclán, escritor español de la generación del 98, en el que se deforma la realidad, recargando sus rasgos grotescos, sometiendo a una elaboración muy personal el lenguaje coloquial y desgarrado.] The "esperpentic lens" often serves

to create a hyperbolic representation of a contemporary reality for the purpose of critique. ("Esperpento," *Diccionario de la lengua española*, Real academia española, accessed February 25, 2020, dle.rae.es/esperpento.)

21. [*November without Violets*] Lorenzo Silva, *Noviembre sin violetas* (Barcelona: Ediciones Destino, 2008).

22. [*The Weakness of the Bolshevik*] Lorenzo Silva, *La flaqueza del bolchevique* (Barcelona: Ediciones Destino, 1997).

23. [*The Impatient Alchemist*] Lorenzo Silva, *El alquimista impaciente* (Barcelona: Ediciones Destino, 2000).

24. [*The Distant Country of the Ponds*] Lorenzo Silva, *El lejano país de los estanques* (Barcelona: Ediciones Destino, 1998).

25. See Ana Rueda, "Sender y otros novelistas de la guerra marroquí: humanismo social y vanguardia política," *Romance Quarterly* 52, no. 3 (2005): 175–196. Or see Larequi, Almarcegui, Fornieles, or Gerling's interview with the author for examples.

26. [*From Rif to Yebala: Journey to the Dream and Nightmare of Morocco*]

27. [*And at the End of it All, War: The Adventure of the Spanish Soldiers in Iraq*] Lorenzo Silva and Luis Miguel Francisco, *Y al final, la guerra: La aventura de los soldados españoles en Irak* (Madrid: La Esfera de los Libros, 2006).

28. [Aunque muchos prefieran ignorarlo, Marruecos es el vecino meridional del país en que vivo, España, al que además le unen intensos y antiguos vínculos de toda índole. Nuestra historia ha sido común en muchos momentos, a veces de forma trágica. En uno de esos episodios luctuosos, la guerra de 1920–1927, participó uno de mis abuelos. . . . Por eso, y porque además tengo familia marroquí, no he podido mirar al sur con indiferencia.] Lorenzo Silva, *Lorenzo Silva: una página personal dedicada a los lectores*, accessed May 20, 2020, www.lorenzo-silva.com/.

29. See Rueda, "Sender y otros novelistas de la guerra marroquí" for a comparison between Silva and these earlier authors.

30. ["The 'Invisible' Enemy of the War of Africa (1859–60) and the Historical Project of Spanish Nationalism: Del Castillo, Alarcón and Landa"] Ana Rueda, "El enemigo 'invisible' de la Guerra de África (1859–60) y el proyecto histórico del nacionalismo español: Del Castillo, Alarcón y Landa," *The Colorado Review of Hispanic Studies*, no. 4 (2006): 147–167.

31. ["Sender and Other Novelists of the Moroccan War: Social Humanism and Political Vanguard"] Ana Rueda, "Sender y otros novelistas de la guerra marroquí: humanismo social y vanguardia política," *Romance Quarterly* 52, no. 3 (2000): 175–196.

32. For critical works that engage directly with Silva's literary production, see Craig-Odders, García Jambrina, and Oropesa; however, these articles focus primarily on Silva's detective/crime novels. Silva has been interviewed about his war writing (see Gerling, Broeck, or Esquirol), but aside from Rueda's "Sender y otros novelistas" there has not been much written about Silva's African war novels.

33. [anonimato colectivo] Rueda, "Sender y otros novelistas," 186.

34. Gil Anidjar, *The Jew, The Arab: A History of the Enemy* (Stanford: Stanford University Press, 2003): 3.

35. I examine the dynamics of movement and travel more in depth in chapter 3.

36. Anidjar, *The Jew, The Arab*, 24.
37. Kapuściński, *The Other*, 20.
38. Kapuściński, *The Other*, 21.
39. Kapuściński, *The Other*, 21.
40. Anidjar, *The Jew, The Arab*, 5.
41. Anidjar, *The Jew, The Arab*, 5.
42. [el 'enemigo' como marcador discursivo no se solapa exactamente con el Otro ni tampoco con el enemigo empírico o marcial. La enemistad tiene una especificidad discursiva—militar, política y hasta teológica—en el contexto de la literatura de guerra] Rueda, "El enemigo 'invisible' de la Guerra de África," 147.
43. [los horrores de la guerra, justificada en términos de otredad, y hasta cierto punto libera al cronista, y por extensión a los dirigentes del pueblo español, de la responsabilidad ética que contraen con el marroquí a través de la acción armada] Rueda, "El enemigo 'invisible,'" 147. Specifically examined in this article are Rafael del Castillo's *España y Marruecos: Historia de la Guerra de África, escrita desde el campamento* (Cádiz: Imprenta de la Revista Médica, 1859), Pedro Antonio Alarcón's *Diario de un testigo de la Guerra de África* (Madrid: Imprenta y Librería Gáspar y Roig, 1859), and Nicasio Landa's *La campaña de Marruecos: Memorias de un médico militar* (Madrid: Imprenta de Manuel Álvarez, 1860).
44. [la retórica bélica perpetuó dos nacionalidades rivales que nunca llegaron a asimilarse] Rueda, "El enemigo 'invisible,'" 164.
45. These similarities are examined at length in Rueda's "Sender y otros novelistas de la guerra marroquí: humanismo social y vanguardia política."
46. The battleship *Laya* played a significant role as one of the seven battleships present at the "Desembarco de Alhucemas" [Disembarking of Alhucemas] on September 8, 1925. This decisive battle put an end to the Rif War. Miguel Primo de Rivera commanded the troops, and Francisco Franco was promoted from colonel to brigadier general for his participation. See Carrasco González's *El reino olvidado: Cinco siglos de historia de España en África*.
47. [¿Qué vais a hacer vosotros, Hassan?] Silva, *El nombre de los nuestros*, 130.
48. [Yo estar amigo, sargento] Silva, *El nombre de los nuestros*, 130. This passage is a play on the two Spanish verbs for "to be," *ser* and *estar*. A general simplification of their uses is that *ser* represents an intrinsic condition or defining characteristic, while *estar* is used for situational states. The use of "estar amigo" is agrammatical in that it is both a nonconventional usage of estar and Hassan uses its infinitive, unconjugated form.
49. [no *eran*, sino que *estaban* amigos. En algunos era sólo eso, un error, pero en otros tenía un probable segundo sentido. Uno es lo que es y eso no tiene vuelta de hoja, pero estar se puede estar hoy aquí y mañana allí.] Silva, *El nombre de los nuestros*, 130.
50. [en serio]
51. [Estar amigo, sargento—repitió el otro] Silva, *El nombre de los nuestros*, 131.
52. [el otro]
53. Levinas, *Humanism of the Other*, 29.

54. [No había tenido mucho trato con Molina pero el sargento siempre había sido respetuoso con él. No era como otros militares europeos, que sólo veían en los soldados indígenas a unos perros útiles para echarlos contra otros perros.] Silva, *El nombre de los nuestros*, 130.

55. [no *eran* sino que *estaban* amigos . . . según dictaba la oportunidad.] Silva, *El nombre de los nuestros*, 130–131.

56. [en el mejor de los casos, se producirá una historia espectral que siempre amenaza con volver a presentarse] Rueda, "El enemigo invisible," 149.

57. The difference in the portrayal of the "invisible enemy" in works from the two wars (one as faceless to mitigate war's horrors and the other as faceless and threatening), can perhaps best be understood in the context of the outcomes from the two wars. In the first African War, the triumphalist spirit endures in victory, and conversely, in the Rif War the aura of the traumatic defeat at Annual casts a threatening pall over the tone. In this sense, the threatening Enemy is not only psychically threatening but also strategically threatening in the historical context of *El nombre de los nuestros*.

58. Silva, *El nombre de los nuestros*, 12.

59. [La segunda noche de junio . . . a Pulido le degollaron de un solo tajo de gumía en su puesto de centinela.] Silva, *El nombre de los nuestros*, 13–14.

60. "Harka" or "Harca" refers to the Moroccan indigenous troops. "Harca," *Diccionario de la lengua española*, Real academia española, 2014, accessed February 25, 2020, dle.rae.es/harca.

61. [como de algo desconocido y quizá inexistente. Ahora el monstruo invisible les había impuesto su presencia, y . . . el cabo sintió que la harka era esa mujer que le había despojado de los galones y le depreciaba con la insolencia de sus fogosos ojos negros.] Silva, *El nombre de los nuestros*, 234.

62. Anidjar, *The Jew, The Arab*, 5.

63. Anidjar, *The Jew, The Arab*, 3.

64. Said, *Orientalism*, 7.

65. [Si ha de estar en alguna parte . . . está con los de ahí enfrente.] Silva, *El nombre de los nuestros*, 197.

66. [Los policías permanecían leales, aunque cada vez debía resultarles más claro que militaban en el bando perdedor. Hassan, el cabo, seguía al pie del parapeto, a pesar de haber recibido un balazo en el hombro. Era el izquierdo, decía, quitándole importancia y agregaba:

—Mientras tener hombro derecho, tener donde apoyar *fusila*.

Los europeos, cuando caían heridos, quedaban inservibles. . . . Si un moro no se levantaba era que ya estaba muerto.] Silva, *El nombre de los nuestros*, 209–210.

67. [Así se dio la paradoja de que fueran ellos, moros y mercenarios, quienes obedecieran al pie de la letra la orden de defender la bandera hasta el fin, que sólo unos pocos europeos observaban.] Silva, *El nombre de los nuestros*, 227–228.

68. [*sustituto*]

69. The "cuota militar" was a way in which wealthy individuals or families could purchase a release from obligatory military service. Established by the "ley de Reclutamiento" in 1912. In 1932 it was estimated that the Spanish government earned upwards of 15 million pesetas from this official practice. See Andrés-Gallego, et al.

for more information, specifically the chapter on "Las reformas militares," in *Historia general de España y América: La Segunda República y la Guerra* (Madrid: Ediciones Rialp, 1986), 141–174.

70. [Nadie iba a morir en su lugar por unas perras.] Silva, *El nombre de los nuestros*, 30.

71. [no he visto a ningún rico por aquí.] Silva, *El nombre de los nuestros*, 70.

72. [—En África cada bala tiene un nombre, y ninguna bala va a equivocarse. . . . Lo que quiero decir es que el nombre de la bala ni se compra ni se vende, porque será el que tenga que ser y nadie se va a llevar la desgracia de otro. Se puede comprar un abrigo o se pueden comprar unos zapatos. Pero querer comprar el dolor de una familia es una indignidad.] Silva, *El nombre de los nuestros*, 96–97.

73. [mercenarios] Silva, *El nombre de los nuestros*, 227.

74. Karl Marx, *Capital, Volume 1* (New York: Penguin Books, 1990), 932.

75. As described by Marx in *Capital*, 183.

76. Marx, *Capital*, 271.

77. Marx, *Capital*, 132.

78. [—¿Sabes qué nombre se lleva la bala siempre? . . . —El nombre de los nuestros—dijo el sargento, solemne—. Los nuestros son ellos, los infelices que siempre salen mal parados. . . . Hasta los moros a los que matamos, si lo miras, son los nuestros. Nosotros somos como ellos: corremos, nos arrastramos, pasamos miedo y nunca nos ayuda nadie.] Silva, *El nombre de los nuestros*, 275.

79. [cuatro hijos de puta que ahora están tan anchos en Madrid.] Silva, *El nombre de los nuestros*, 176.

80. [Qué coño socialista.] Silva, *El nombre de los nuestros*, 276.

81. Silva, *El nombre de los nuestros*, 163–164, 181.

82. Silva, *El nombre de los nuestros*, 284.

83. [Volvió, en fin, a experimentar la fascinación de aquellos atardeceres africanos, anaranjados y flamígeros, sobre el mar o las montañas, cuando los combatientes casi olvidaban que estaban allí para matarse unos a otros y percibían una extraña inmensidad.] Silva, *El nombre de los nuestros*, 284–285.

84. [la harka no dejaría de existir nunca.] Silva, *El nombre de los nuestros*, 285.

85. [los moros a los que matamos] Silva, *El nombre de los nuestros*, 275.

86. Said, *Orientalism*, 6.

87. [la harka no dejaría de existir nunca] Silva, *El nombre de los nuestros*, 285.

88. [*As the Bird Flies Over Morocco*] Concha López Sarasúa, *A vuelo de pájaro sobre Marruecos* (Alicante: Editorial Cálamo, 1995).

89. [*The Turkish Dagger and Other Mediterranean Stories*] Concha López Sarasúa, *La daga turca y otros relatos mediterráneos* (Alicante: Editorial Cálamo, 1996).

90. [*What Were You All Looking for in Marrakech?*] Concha López Sarasúa, *¿Qué buscabais en Marrakech?* (Alicante: Editorial Cálamo, 2001).

91. [*Meriem and the Fantastic Route*] Concha López Sarasúa, *Meriem y la ruta fantástica* (Alicante: Editorial Cálamo, 1991).

92. [*In Meriem's Country*] Concha López Sarasúa, *En el país de Meriem* (Alicante: Editorial Cálamo, 1998).

93. [*The Thousand and One Tales of Meriem*] Concha López Sarasúa, *Los mil y un cuentos de Meriem* (Alicante: Editorial Cálamo, 2003).
94. [*Date in Paris*] Concha López Sarasúa, *Cita en París* (Alicante: Editorial Cálamo, 2005).
95. [*Celanova 42: Postwar Rural Spain*] Concha López Sarasúa, *Celanova 42: La España rural de la posguerra* (Alicante: Editorial Cálamo, 1993).
96. [*Why Do I Have to Emigrate?*] Concha López Sarasúa, *¿Por qué tengo que emigrar?* (Madrid: Ibersaf, 2009).
97. "Concha López Sarasúa," *New Spanish Books*, accessed May 20, 2020, www.newspanishbooks.com/author/concha-l-pez-saras.
98. The Real Academia Española defines "aljamía" as a general term among the former Muslim inhabitants of the Spanish Peninsula for the languages of the Christian populations or also describing a text in a Romance language that is transcribed with Arabic script. The term also contains the connotation of a hybridized Castilian with Arabic characteristics. "Aljamía," *Diccionario de la lengua española*, Real academia española, accessed February 25, 2020, dle.rae.es/aljamía.
99. [resucit[a] la tradición hispánica de moros y cristianos. dando lugar a una nueva aljamía literaria que ostenta una islamofilia de nuevo cuño. Encierra, sobre todo, una verdadera poética de las dos orillas, esto es, una especie de poética de la diversidad a través de la cual se exaltan los rasgos cruzados y comunes [de] las dos riberas del *Mare Nostrum*.] Mohamed Abrighach, "Concha López Sarasúa: novelista de las dos orillas," *Espéculo: Revista electrónica cuatrimestral de estudios literarios,* no. 46 (2010): np.
100. [la frontera imaginaria que existe entre las dos orillas, consagrada por la amnesia hispánica.] Abrighach, "Concha López Sarasúa: novelista de las dos orillas."
101. López Sarasúa, *La llamada del almuédano*, 93, 163.
102. See Gozálvez Pérez for an outline of the Spanish Protectorate in Morocco and especially immigration numbers of Spaniards who relocated to the Protectorate, established in 1912 and ending when both Spain and France recognized Morocco's independence on 7 April 1956.
103. The readers can assume that many expatriates are leaving Morocco due to its independence. In the initial pages doña Natalia sees a newly renamed street sign and expresses exasperation at all of the changes. López Sarasúa, *La llamada del almuédano*, 16.
104. [a 31-XII-1955 la población española en el Protectorado [sic] español de Marruecos era «estimada» en 90.939 habitantes, que representaban el 9,4% respecto a los nativos – 963.620 –; a los indicados habría que añadir otros 25.698 españoles en el Marruecos bajo administración francesa (censo de 15-IV-1951) y más de 21.500 en Tánger.] Gozálvez Pérez, "Descolonización y migraciones desde el África española," 46.
105. Gozálvez Pérez, "Descolonización y migraciones desde el África española," 70.
106. [Un lugar en África.]
107. [Exilio]

108. [La última aleya] "Aleya" is the term for a verse from the Quran. "Aleya," *Diccionario de la Real Academia Española*, Real academia española, accessed February 25, 2020, dle.rae.es/aleya.

109. López Sarasúa, *La llamada del almuédano*, 65.

110. López Sarasúa, *La llamada del almuédano*, 91.

111. [compromiso con la verdad] Mohamed Abrighach, *Superando orillas: Lectura intercultural de la narrativa de Concha López Sarasúa* (Rabat: Imprimerie El Maarif Al Jadida, 2009), 128.

112. "Transculturation" was a term coined by Fernando Ortiz to avoid the problematic prefixes of "acculturation" and "deculturation." See Enrico Santí ("Fernando Ortiz: Counterpoint and Transculturation," in *Ciphers of History: Latin American Readings for a Cultural Age* [New York: Palgrave Macmillan, 2005], 169–218) for a useful study of Malinowski and Ortiz's development and theorization of the term, especially pages 204–210.

113. López Sarasúa, *La llamada del almuédano*, 51.

114. Said, *Orientalism*, 7.

115. Mary Louise Pratt, *Imperial Eyes: Travel Writing and Transculturation* (New York: Routledge, 1992), 6.

116. Pratt, *Imperial Eyes*, 6.

117. Pratt, *Imperial Eyes*, 6.

118. Pratt, *Imperial Eyes*, 7.

119. [desdramatiza el fenómeno tal vez porque la emigración española al Norte de África no fue tan trágica como lo es la actual travesía marroquí del Estrecho en pateras.] Abrighach, *Superando orillas*, 127.

120. López Sarasúa, *La llamada del almuédano*, 130.

121. Cairo, "Spanish Enclaves in North Africa," 64. I do not suggest that López Sarasúa advocates this particular position; I merely point out the potentially distinct ideology that encouraged Spanish emigration to the Moroccan Protectorate during this time period. This conceptualization of Spain as extending from the Pyrenees to the Atlas Mountains long predates the twentieth century's Spanish tide of immigration to North Africa. Isabel la Católica envisioned the Reconquista extending across the Strait of Gibraltar. See Flores Morales for a collection of ideological statements by prominent Spanish thinkers and politicians regarding Africa.

122. The novel does not portray her as a "privileged colonial," this assumption comes from the historical context of the plot, combined with Albert Memmi's assertion that "every colonizer is privileged." Albert Memmi, *Colonizer and the Colonized* (New York: Orion Press, 1965), 11.

123. [poco a poco nos vamos todos de aquí.] López Sarasúa, *La llamada del almuédano*, 16.

124. [¡Con lo bien que vivíamos . . . !] López Sarasúa, *La llamada del almuédano*, 16.

125. López Sarasúa, *La llamada del almuédano*, 16.

126. López Sarasúa, *La llamada del almuédano*, 17.

127. [Nadie va a notar tu falta, vas a ser uno más entre los que se van; porque no vas a creerte imprescindible, ¿eh? . . . Todo va a seguir igualito, no lo dudes.] López Sarasúa, *La llamada del almuédano*, 231.

128. López Sarasúa, *La llamada del almuédano*, 231.

129. López Sarasúa, *La llamada del almuédano*, 148.

130. [[Doña Natalia:] tú eres feliz, ¿no?

[María Mechbal:] —Ya lo ve usted; yo creo que son cosas tan claras que no pueden ocultarse fácilmente.

Y dio rienda suelta a los numerosos detalles que configuraban la base de su felicidad; realzó emocionada las virtudes de aquel hombre bondadoso y enamorado.] López Sarasúa, *La llamada del almuédano*, 148.

131. [Ali es tan bueno. . . . Ni con una lupa creo que habría encontrado a otro igual, y el buenazo sí que hace todo lo que yo quiero, le guste o no.] López Sarasúa, *La llamada del almuédano*, 152.

132. [—Pero vamos a ver, María, ¿qué es lo que tienen que perdonarte, hija mía? —Le indignaba esa actitud—. ¡Pues no faltaba más! Es como si tu marido no fuese tan honrado como el mejor; más todavía, porque ¡bien que te lo demuestra el pobre!] López Sarasúa, *La llamada del almuédano*, 155–156.

133. [pesadillas en las que un moro, negro como el ébano, le arrebataba a uno de sus hijos y se perdía con él en la lejanía montado en un brioso corcel.] López Sarasúa, *La llamada del almuédano*, 157.

134. [más tarde, a su llegada, se sorprendió al comprobar que existían árabes con la piel incluso más blanca que la suya, ¡que ya era decir!] López Sarasúa, *La llamada del almuédano*, 157.

135. [Lo que ocurre a tus padres es que no conocen Marruecos ni a las gentes de esta tierra. . . ¡Pero si me ocurrió a mí también antes de venirme. . . !] López Sarasúa, *La llamada del almuédano*, 156.

136. [No tenía queja de los marroquíes; los encontraba hospitalarios y dadivosos. Eran muchos años los que llevaba allí para no conocerlos; tendrían sus defectos, pero también sus virtudes como el resto de los mortales.] López Sarasúa, *La llamada del almuédano*, 25.

137. [¡Ves como te has vuelto tan servil como ellos!] López Sarasúa, *La llamada del almuédano*, 156.

138. [¡Pues no es poco feliz madame Mechbal y está casada con un marroquí!] López Sarasúa, *La llamada del almuédano*, 21–22.

139. Said, *Orientalism*, 6.

140. [La última aleya]

141. [calle de los Cónsules]

142. [en perfecto castellano, jactándose de su procedencia tetuaní.] López Sarasúa, *La llamada del almuédano*, 249.

143. López Sarasúa, *La llamada del almuédano*, 250. Abū-l-Mutarrif Ibn Amira (~1184 to ~1270) was a poet born in Valencia or Alcira and forced into exile when James I reconquered Valencia. Ibn Amira went to Tunisia in exile. See Margarita Lachica, "Poetas árabes del País Valenciano," *Anales de la Universidad de Alicante, Historia Medieval* 9 (1992–1993): 17–37.

144. [De Valencia soy yo, ¡fíjese!] López Sarasúa, *La llamada del almuédano*, 251.

145. [¿Has visto, Halima?, he tenido que venir aquí para enterarme de que aquellos poetas querían tanto a mi tierra. Ni sabía que hubiese existido este Ibn Amira. . . . Los moros eran infieles, sólo te enseñaban eso; infieles e invasores; de lo que sí estoy segura es que el que los expulsó de Valencia se llamaba Jaume, primero o segundo, ¡ya ni me acuerdo! . . . Bueno, sí, era Jaume el Conqueridor. ¡Lo que son las cosas. . . !] López Sarasúa, *La llamada del almuédano*, 251.

146. James I the Conqueror, Jaime I de Aragón, (1208–1276) was responsible for the "reconquest" of the Balearic Islands between 1229 and 1235 and Valencia in 1238. See Harvey's *Islamic Spain* for more information on James I.

147. [¡Cuánto había aprendido esa tarde! Nunca se le habría ocurrido pensar que aquellos versos los había inspirado Valencia, su propia tierra, ¡cuán grande era su ignorancia!, ¡y qué inhumano el exilio!] López Sarasúa, *La llamada del almuédano*, 254.

148. [Allāh akbar! Allāh akbar! Desde la cumbre del Oukaimeden un almuédano llamaba a la plegaria.] López Sarasúa, *La llamada del almuédano*, 255.

149. "The reconquest of Spain" contained many battles and exiles before the final date of 1492. *Jaume el Conqueridor* successfully wrested the Kingdom of Valencia from Moorish control in the thirteenth century. See Harvey, *Islamic Spain*.

150. López Sarasúa, *La llamada del almuédano*, 251.

151. [To boast, to brag.] López Sarasúa, *La llamada del almuédano*, 249.

152. [en perfecto castellano, jactándose de su procedencia tetuaní] López Sarasúa, *La llamada del almuédano*, 249.

153. [tan servil como ellos] López Sarasúa, *La llamada del almuédano*, 156.

154. [No es un posicionamiento ideológico, sino un compromiso con la verdad y una desmitificación . . . una sincera forma de repensar la historia] Abrighach, *Superando orillas*, 128.

155. [humor satírico de notable audacia intelectual, sobre todo, en lo relacionado con la descripción de la paradoja de los inmigrantes . . . en su forma de encarar y convivir con la alteridad norteafricana y marroquí.] Abrighach, *Superando orillas*, 127.

156. [*Aesthetic of the Serpents*] Ramón Mayrata, *Estética de las serpientes* (Madrid: Azur, 1972).

157. [*Alicia's Doubt*] Ramón Mayrata, *Una duda de Alicia* (Madrid: Frakson D. L., 1990).

158. [*If You Listen to Me Tonight*] Ramón Mayrata, *Si me escuchas esta noche* (Madrid: Mondadori, 1991).

159. [*The Mauve Chair*] Ramón Mayrata, *El sillón malva* (Barcelona: Planeta, 1994).

160. [*Without Doors*] Ramón Mayrata, *Sin puertas: Poemas, 1990–1991* (Valencia: Pre-Textos, 1996).

161. [*Ali Bey, al Abbasi*]

162. [*Border of the City*] Ramón Mayrata, *Confín de la ciudad: El olivar de Castillejo* (Madrid: Los Libros de la Galera Sol, 1998).

163. Ramón Mayrata, *Miracielos* (Barcelona: Muchnik Editores, 2000).

164. [*The Eye of Arbitrariness*] Ramón Mayrata, *El ojo de la arbitrariedad* (Madrid: Ediciones Libertarias, 1986).

165. [*Mirror of Love and of Death*] Vicente Aleixandre, ed., *Espejo del amor y de la muerte: antología de poesía española última* (Madrid: Azur, 1971).

166. Ramón Mayrata, *Miracielos: Adaptación Teatral de Carlos Rod.* Cádiz: XVII Festival Iberoamericano de Teatro de Cádiz, 2002.

167. See his articles "El hombre del ojo blanco y opaco," *Suplemento literario la nación* (1994): 8, "La perplejidad el arte moderno," in *Los espectáculos del arte: Instituciones y funciones del arte contemporáneo*, edited by F. Calvo Serraller (Barcelona: Tusquets, 1993), 111–134, "El esplendor de la Tierra Pura," *Album, letras, artes*, no. 53 (1997): 67–78, or *Viaje por Egipto y Asia menor* with Jesús Tablate (Madrid: Álbum letras artes, 1996).

168. See Hodges, *Western Sahara: The Roots of a Desert War*, for an extensive consideration of the Spanish presence and decolonization in the Western Sahara, or Jacob Mundy and Stephen Zunes, *Western Sahara: War, Nationalism, and Conflict Resolution* (Syracuse: Syracuse University Press, 2010), and Sampedro Vizcaya, "Transiting Western Sahara," (*Journal of Spanish Cultural Studies* 20, nos. 1–2 [2019]: 17–38) for more recent studies.

169. [*Stories from the Sahara*]

170. See "Western Sahara: Advisory Opinion of 16 October 1975" for the International Court of Justice's ruling (accessed May 20, 2020, www.icj-cij.org/files/case-related/61/6197.pdf).

171. For more information about the Spanish withdrawal from the Sahara territory, see Hodges, Mundy & Zunes, or Sampedro Vizcaya.

172. [*Ley de Secretos Oficiales*] See *Noticias jurídicas*, "Ley 9/1968, de 5 de abril, reguladora de los Secretos Oficiales" (accessed May 25, 2020, noticias.juridicas.com/base_datos/Admin/l9-1968.html) for the full content of the law passed in 1968. See also Carreras Serra, *Las normas jurídicas de los periodistas* (Barcelona: UOC, 2008), for an explanation and a contextualization of the law, especially chapter 20 "Los secretos oficiales" (281–286).

173. Spivak, "Can the Subaltern Speak?," 287.

174. James C. Scott, *Seeing Like a State: How Certain Schemes to Improve the Human Condition Have Failed* (New Haven: Yale University Press, 1998), 1.

175. Scott, *Seeing Like a State*, 2.

176. Scott, *Seeing Like a State*, 112.

177. Scott, *Seeing Like a State*, 80.

178. The 2008 edition of *El imperio desierto* is followed by the short story "Aquel mendigo de la Plaza Esbehiheh" [That Beggar from the Plaza Esbehiheh] that examines more in depth the difficulties that the protagonist (one very similar to Ignacio Aguirre) faces in convincing the Saharawi to commit their oral traditions to written format. In *El imperio desierto* (Madrid: Calamar Ediciones, 2008), 369–390.

179. Mayrata, *El imperio desierto*, 153.

180. The specific ministry to which Ignacio reports is never explicitly mentioned. The effect of this omission within the text is one of general culpability upon all branches of the Spanish government, instead of any singular agency.

181. [Parece que están firmemente decididos a dar la independencia al territorio. . . . Pero se han encontrado con que no existe ningún libro de texto que recoja la historia

del Sáhara. En un país independiente tienen que estudiar su propia historia en las escuelas. Y eso es lo que quieren que tú hagas. Una historia del territorio para uso de los nuevos saharianos.]
[Ignacio:]—Me parece que se llaman saharauis.] Mayrata, *El imperio desierto*, 20.

182. Mayrata, *El imperio desierto*, 36.

183.[—Usted no es funcionario, Aguirre. Tiene que tener un nombre. Le hemos nombrado director de la Comisión. De otro modo se perdería para la Administración. Todas estas cosas tienen su importancia. A mil y pico kilómetros de distancia, usted no existiría para nosotros.] Mayrata, *El imperio desierto*, 36.

184. The reason largely being the Spanish *Ley de Secretos Oficiales* that prohibited information about the territory from being reported.

185. Mayrata, *El imperio desierto*, 42.

186. [[Jaime:] — Por lo visto, la IV Internacional apoya a un grupo que se llama el Morehob.
[Ignacio:] — ¿Qué significan esas siglas?
— Algo así como Movimiento de los Hombres Azules.
— Es un hermoso nombre.
— Lo dirige un tal Eduardo Moha desde Argel.
— ¿Desde Argel? ¿Son proargelinos? ¿Y la IV Internacional les apoya?
— Bueno, no se trata de camaradas, claro. Están muy lejos de nuestras posiciones. Pero no existe ningún otro grupo organizado en el territorio. Yo supongo que será uno de esos movimientos de liberación nacional un poco vagos y confusos, en los que cabe todo. En eso consiste nuestra oportunidad, precisamente. ¿Comprendes?] Mayrata, *El imperio desierto*, 43.

187. Mayrata, *El imperio desierto*, 43.

188. Said, *Orientalism*, 40.

189. Said, *Orientalism*, 40.

190. Said, *Orientalism*, 40.

191. [Para un antropólogo, España era un país tentador. Aún podía apreciarse formas de vida ancestrales, reducidas al recuerdo en el resto de Europa] Mayrata, *El imperio desierto*, 13.

192. Mayrata, *El imperio desierto*, 34.

193. The West's obsession with the written word as more valued than the spoken word has been theorized extensively. Derrida's "Plato's Pharmacy," in *Dissemination* (1972. Reprint, New York: Continuum Books, 2004), 67–186, and *Of Grammatology* (1974. Reprint, Baltimore: The Johns Hopkins University Press, 1998) being two of the most often referenced. Walter Ong, in *Orality and Literacy* (New York: Methuen, 1982), suggests that, at the very least, "writing from the beginning did not reduce orality but enhanced it, making it possible to organize 'principles' or constituents of oratory into a scientific 'art,' a sequentially ordered body of explanation that showed how and why oratory achieved and could be made to achieve its various specific effects" (9). That is, the written word is, at minimum, a marked improvement upon the purely oral communicative format.

194. [—¡Soldados del Sáhara! Este hombre que veis aquí ha venido a escribir nuestra historia. . . . Nosotros la conocemos, *porque la hemos escuchado de los labios*

de nuestros padres y abuelos. Pero hay muchas gentes que no saben quiénes son los saharauis, cómo han vivido hasta ahora y las cosas que han hecho. . . . Cuando él escriba la verdad, *el susurro de la voz de nuestros mayores* se extenderá por el mundo como el viento y nadie pondrá en duda que hemos de ser un pueblo independiente.] Mayrata, *El imperio desierto*, 69–70.

195. Mayrata, *El imperio desierto*, 85.
196. Mayrata, *El imperio desierto*, 88.
197. [el saharaui venera las palabras y les concede mayor valor que a los objetos más preciados.] Mayrata, *El imperio desierto*, 70.
198. Mayrata, *El imperio desierto*, 172.
199. Mayrata, *El imperio desierto*, 172.
200. Said, *Orientalism*, 57.
201. [El desierto es otro planeta.] Mayrata, *El imperio desierto*, 305.
202. [como un militar] Mayrata, *El imperio desierto*, 237.
203. See the first section of this chapter on *El nombre de los nuestros* for an examination of the difference between the Other and the enemy.
204. Mayrata, *El imperio desierto*, 46.
205. Mayrata, *El imperio desierto*, 47.
206. [¿Cómo lograría explicártelo? Tú sabes que un paisaje es un marco histórico.] Mayrata, *El imperio desierto*, 304.
207. [Los saharauis son un milagro] Mayrata, *El imperio desierto*, 305.
208. Mayrata, *El imperio desierto*, 305.
209. [Sólo cuando consigues entrar en relación con sus habitantes, el desierto deja de ser un paraje inhóspito, inhumano, para convertirse en la tierra de unos hombres que gracias a una cultura adecuada lo han hecho milagrosamente habitable.] Mayrata, *El imperio desierto*, 305.
210. Kapuściński, *The Other*, 31.
211. Scott, *Seeing Like a State*, 1.
212. [Las ciudades actuales son una creación colonial. Casi un espejismo. Una ilusión sostenida por la metrópoli.] Mayrata, *El imperio desierto*, 63.
213. [para un europeo, la ausencia de rastros del Estado provoca un sentimiento de extrañeza y desamparo mucho más vivo que la ausencia de vegetación.] Mayrata, *El imperio desierto*, 78.
214. [Estado errante] Mayrata, *El imperio desierto*, 109.
215. [la túnica de piedra con la que cubrir un cuerpo que ya existía] Mayrata, *El imperio desierto*, 109.
216. [A partir de ahora viviremos en el desierto, como culebras. Creo que nunca olvidaré el tiempo que pasamos juntos, cuando los saharauis aún podíamos soñar con comportarnos como seres humanos.] Mayrata, *El imperio desierto*, 360.

Chapter 2

Gender and the Other

In *Diario de un testigo de la Guerra de África* (1856),[1] Pedro Antonio de Alarcón describes his arrival on the coast of Ceuta by invoking the mythological characterization of Africa:

> Mythology, always revealing, has represented Africa for us as a strikingly beautiful woman, of Oriental demeanor, almost nude, seated on an elephant (symbol of her unending deserts), holding in one hand the cornucopia, to remind us of her bright and opulent vegetation, and a scorpion in the other, to signify that in her all of the gifts of Nature, rather than producing life, give death, and that her air, her land, her water, her sun, and her inhabitants, all is harmful, frightening, and venomous— . . . in her resides the new, the fearful, the strange, the unknown.[2]

Alarcón goes on to paraphrase the Roman general Scipio Africanus by declaring: "upon planting my foot on this part of the world . . . I could do nothing less than bend my knee, putting my thoughts to my God and my motherland, and exclaim . . . —*Africa, now you are mine!*"[3] Alarcón's passionate descriptions gender an entire continent, reducing it to a discursive construct that is emphatically possessed by the Westerner.

As Alarcón makes of Africa a fevered, female subject that is desired and possessed by the Western male, likewise do many of the paintings of Mariano Fortuny i Marsal[4]—such as the "Odalisque" (1861)—sexualize the Oriental woman, splaying the nude female body in lush tones for a Western audience.[5] The image of the Odalisque is conflated with that of Africa as the two express "the new, the fearful, the strange, the unknown."[6] Throughout Spanish letters, Africa has served as a gendered Other and its inhabitants eroticized. Spanish colonialism operated under the impetus of glory for the "patria"—the fatherland—while Africa was virgin territory to be conquered and ravished. The West effectively stands before "the entire Orient . . . prone, like a lounging odalisque," prepared for a colonial "penetration."[7] This image of the reclining Odalisque as well as Jean-Léon Gérôme's *The Snake Charmer* which graces the cover of the first edition of Said's theoretical work clearly reflect the "stark thesis of *Orientalism* . . . replicated in . . . image."[8]

The blatant Orientalism of Alarcón and Fortuny has persisted in differing levels of force since the first War of Africa. Indeed, the seductive and sensual "morita"[9] is such a recurring figure in the works by authors from the two Hispano-African Wars, that it can almost be considered an exception to encounter a work that does not have a young and beautiful "Aixa"[10] whose gaze intrigues and whose innocence seduces the young Spanish soldier. In *El blocao* (1928), José Díaz Fernández describes his Aixa as

> indecisive and trembling, filtering herself like a bit of light through the green wall of rose bushes. If Aixa were a European girl, she would remember me as an idiot; so cowardly, inexpressive and immobile I imagine myself in that moment. I had the great luck that Aixa was not a little girl from high society, accustomed to weighing the timidity of her suitors, rather a *morita* of barely 15 years. . . . She was unveiled and was like a recently bought sweet that had just been unwrapped from its silk paper. Dark. But the darkness of a peach that is not very ripe, with the soft fuzz that makes the skin of the fruit so similar to that of a woman.[11]

Díaz Fernández's Aixa is clearly Other and his narrator notes that this Otherness offers him a chance to escape the timidity that normally would plague him in front of a Western female. The trope of the veil attempts to represent her as she is, but instead reveals more about the Western narrator mesmerized by her dark and fruit-like skin. Both Aixa and Africa seduce and are seduced by the Western author, and these are tropes that continue to play out in contemporary Spanish literature.

This chapter examines contemporary representations of the Other that are explicitly or subtly gendered or eroticized. While chapter 1 focused on how methods of engagement affect literary representation, here I examine the broader implications that an eroticized literary representation suggests, and in so doing I essentially invert my point of critical observation as I continue to examine how the Orientalist tendency is reflected, maintained, or rejected in the Spanish novel. This combined process of examination will contribute to a more complete analysis of the portrayal of Africa in the contemporary Spanish novel.

In the Western tradition, Western culture has been valued over any Other, and this assumed authority has lent itself (completely) to the colonizing mission. One of the relationships that must be considered in this study is how positions of cultural or political superiority and authority have shifted in their literary representations. If there has indeed been a shift in this assumption in the contemporary Spanish novel, then this would be a valuable indication of the need to reevaluate theories of Orientalism to see if they can be applied to the new novel on Africa. An essential component of my analysis of the valorization of the Other will be investigating specifically gendered portrayals of the African Other in this chapter. I do this by examining three works, María Dueñas's 2009 *El tiempo entre costuras*,[12] Guillermina Mekuy's 2008 *Las tres vírgenes de Santo Tomás*,[13] and Montserrat Abumalham's 2001 *¿Te acuerdas de Shahrazad?*[14] Each of these novels contributes a specific angle to the discussion of gender and Africa. Dueñas's novel relies on the romantic idea of Africa as a land of opportunity where a young Spanish woman can rebuild her life; Mekuy's novel presents a provocative re-envisioning of Equatorial Guinean female sexuality, and Abumalham's epistolary novel gives voice to the literary, Oriental archetype of Shahrazad. While Mekuy's work is the most explicitly erotic of the three, Dueñas's narrative implies the seductive qualities that Africa is able to confer upon her protagonist and Abumalham draws on the narrative seduction of the historical, literary archetype of Shahrazad.

These authors represent a variety of viewpoints and approaches to the question and representation of a gendered Africa and its ability to seduce. Dueñas's protagonist benefits from the romantic qualities that experience in Africa provides to her. Mekuy's work offers an opportunity to examine the auto-conceptualization of sexuality by an Equatorial Guinean female author. Abumalham, as a female Hispano-Maghrebi author, contributes an Other voice as she draws on Oriental literary traditions and merges them with Spanish ones, creating a work in Spanish with an Othered narrator who seduces through the epistolary genre. They also represent a range of style and target audience. *El tiempo entre costuras* was a runaway best-seller and *Las tres vírgenes de Santo Tomás* is sometimes classified as a popular, erotic novel. The representation of Africa and the African in these novels is a significant element for their commercial success.[15] *¿Te acuerdas de Shahrazad?* is a short epistolary novel, more philosophical in its prose than the gripping page-turners of Dueñas and Mekuy.

In the section on *El tiempo entre costuras*, I examine the use of Africa as a land of possibility, liberating a young Spanish woman to recreate her life and identity. Africa contributes both cultural and erotic capital to Sira Quiroga as she is literally turned into Arish Agoriuq, International Spy. My consideration of *Las tres vírgenes de Santo Tomás* examines how Mekuy employs traditional Equatorial Guinean strategies of resistance in order to re-conceptualize her oppressed sexuality. The final section of this chapter, examining *¿Te acuerdas de Shahrazad?*, analyzes the way Abumalham writes this culturally Other voice in ways that circumvent Orientalist discursive tendencies.

As noted above in the poetic prose of Alarcón, Africa has long been gendered and eroticized in the Western imagination.[16] In *Travel as Metaphor*, Abbeele astutely elaborates that there has traditionally been a "phallocentrism whereby the 'law of the home' (*oikonomia*) organizes a set of gender determinations."[17] The same gender determinations that perpetuate perceived hierarchies of male privilege are repeated geographically to render Africa analogous to the marginalized female. Africa has so often been portrayed as "'virgin' territories to be conquered, 'dark continents' to be explored,"[18] imbuing the continent with gender-laden metaphors. These gendered representations of place highlight underlying conceptions of Same and Other while strengthening paradigms of Western, male power.

The metaphorical gendering of the African geography contributes to the concomitant eroticization of the African. The odalisque, the morita, the harem, and the virile African male are often deeply embedded with sensual connotations in the Western literary tradition. Alarcón, Fortuny i Marsal, and Díaz Fernández represent just a few of the Western artists that relied on these tropes in their work. Fatema Mernissi's book *Scheherazade Goes West: Different Cultures, Different Harems* (2001) examines in detail the West's fascination with the sensual possibilities of an erotic Other, writing that the emblematic Scheherazade achieved "what the Muslims who had fought the Crusaders failed to do: She ravished the Christians. . . . The translations [of *The Arabian Nights*] opened up the gates to an Orient where sexuality was boldly explored."[19] Contemporary authors are not immune to the temptation to hyper-sexualize Africa and the African, and even when not blatant, there often persists a reliance on tired erotic tropes of the continent and its inhabitants.

The effect of this gendering is most often to perpetuate Orientalist stereotypes and the subtle assumption of Western (and masculine) dominance. These tropes prove difficult to dislodge and continue to survive in contemporary Spanish letters. They may be more subtle or nuanced, but Africa and the African are still heavily gendered and eroticized in many works, including some of the ones under consideration here. These sexually powerful stereotypes do have the potential to undermine Orientalist discourse, and by examining the ways in which Dueñas, Mekuy, and Abumalham narrate questions of gender and alterity we can find the nexus between the writing of gender and the status of Orientalist discourse in the contemporary Spanish novel.

Juan Goytisolo used Africa as an eroticized and liberated Other from which to criticize Spanish sexual and political conservatism. For Goytisolo, the eroticization of the African Other served as a controversial juxtaposition to an impotent and deflated Spanish virility. This contentious provocation is being replaced by new gendered representations in the contemporary Spanish novel. Each of the authors examined in this chapter represents a unique take on Africa and the African Other that implicates questions of gender and alterity. For Dueñas's Sira Quiroga, Africa literally offers her cultural and seductive capital that allow her to recreate her life. Mekuy employs traditions of resistance from Equatorial Guinea in order to provoke and resist the control of her narrator's sexuality by Western moral codes. And Abumalham's Shahrazad is an Othered voice that speaks with poetry and strength but avoids totalizing discourse or ultimate authority.

As is examined in other chapters in this study, authors as distinct as Javier Reverte and Ahmed Daoudi—as well as the three authors of this chapter—are writing Africa in ways that differ from the project of Goytisolo, Alarcón, or Fortuny. Transcultural gender interactions reflect changing social and moral mores; portrayals of interracial marriage and LGBT relationships have distinct functions in the contemporary novel from Goytisolo's provocative manifestos, and the image of Africa as a reclining Odalisque is being reimagined in fascinating ways. Ultimately, in this chapter I analyze how gendered portrayals of the Other have contributed to Orientalist stereotypes, or been used to overturn them, and how these contemporary Spanish authors are employing such gendered portrayals with new motives. The ultimate question will be: Do these new representations perpetuate gendered conceptualizations of the Other that maintain Western prominence or do new erotic portrayals of the Other serve distinct functions in the contemporary novel that potentially overturn the traditions of Orientalist discourse on Africa? Unfortunately, the answers are not all emancipating; it appears that gendering Africa and eroticizing the African Other prove to be the easiest traps for Western writers, the most tempting metaphors and imagery. Alarcón's invocation of Africa as a woman concludes with the portentous affirmation that "in this manner, Africa will always be the magnet of the burning imaginations,"[20] and his words still ring true. However, that is not to say that contemporary authors are writing under the same Orientalist paradigm of Alarcón, Díaz Fernández, or even Goytisolo. At the threshold of the twenty-first century, it is necessary to examine the intersections of gender, representation, and Africa in the contemporary Spanish novel so that we can identify and move beyond discursive constructions that privilege one geography or gender over another.

REFASHIONING SELF IN MARÍA DUEÑAS'S
EL TIEMPO ENTRE COSTURAS

María Dueñas's 2009 novel *El tiempo entre costuras* was a runaway bestseller. It is listed as one of the most requested books in Spanish libraries[21] with over a million copies sold and the translation and publication rights granted to over 27 countries.[22] It is Dueñas's first work of fiction; she wrote it while a professor of Philology at the University of Murcia, where she also completed her PhD in English. She holds a master's degree in Romance and

Classical Languages from Michigan State University and throughout her career has taught at a number of other universities including the University of Castilla-La Mancha, the Universidad Nacional de Educación a Distancia, and West Virginia University. She has since published three, well-received novels. In 2012 she published *Misión olvido*,[23] in 2015 *La Templanza*,[24] and in 2018 *Las Hijas del Capitán*.[25]

The editorial reviews of *El tiempo entre costuras* offer glowing endorsements from authors such as the Nobel laureate Mario Vargas Llosa, Esmeralda Santiago, and Kate Morton. It was adapted for a mini-series on Antena 3 which debuted in fall 2012.[26] The book is indeed a page-turner, full of cliffhangers and shocking twists. The prose is accessible without diluting the quality of its literary expression. Its structure and plot development are such that it is not surprising that it lends itself to the medium of television and also shares much in common with the serial novels of the late nineteenth and early twentieth centuries, such as Clarín's *La Regenta*. It is an impressive and captivating work for a first novel, developing over 600 pages.

The historical setting is what is initially pertinent to this study. Colonial Tétouan, that is the Tétouan of the Spanish Protectorate in Morocco, is the backdrop for a significant portion of the plot.[27] María Dueñas is admittedly fascinated by Spain's colonial presence in Morocco. Her training as an academic led her to close her fictional text with a bibliography of historical works that helped her to recreate her historical fiction narrative, and she prefaces the bibliography by stating that "The conventions of academic life to which I have been committed for more than twenty years demand that authors recognize their sources in an organized and rigorous manner."[28] There is, therefore, a stated attempt at a historic fidelity and a certain "academic rigor," and yet she also states on her blog for the book that:

> To recreate with fidelity the settings of Tangier and Tétouan, I have relied on, above all, the testimonies of those who lived in this environment and this time firsthand: some of the members of the Association The Medina and, above all, my own maternal family, residents for decades of the Protectorate. Thanks to the memories charged with nostalgia of all of them, the characters of the novel have been able to travel the streets, the corners and the heartbeat of our colonial past in the north of Africa, a context almost disappeared from our collective memory and hardly ever evoked in the contemporary Spanish narrative.[29]

This statement is revealing in the use of the phrase "memories charged with nostalgia,"[30] perhaps inadvertently uncovering a collective mourning for the lost African colony. It is also a reminder that, as well researched and documented as Dueñas attempts to be when recreating this past, from the vantage point of the twenty-first century this is an impossible task to accomplish objectively. Thus, it is perhaps most appropriate to highlight at this point what the novel accomplishes and what are its limitations as relevant to the examination of Orientalism in the contemporary Spanish novel.

The plot of *El tiempo entre costuras* develops within the colonial circles of Tétouan and Tangier. The characters are predominantly European, with only an occasional "morita"[31] who works as a servant. The African Other is a marginal figure within the novel, and this is striking in that the plot develops in Africa and also in that the book is dedicated "To all the former residents of the Spanish Protectorate in Morocco and to the Moroccans that lived alongside them."[32] There is little interaction between European and African; the colonial cities of Tétouan (Spanish) and Tangier (International Zone) are frenetic cosmopolitan zones where Europeans come to live and play and only infrequently interact with the indigenous population. Therefore, this analysis of *El tiempo entre costuras* does not focus on Dueñas's representation of the African Other, but rather on Africa itself as a place of colonial possibility. To paraphrase Ana Rueda, rendering the Other discursively invisible effectively mitigates the horrors of colonization, liberating the writer and the Spanish public from the ethical responsibility towards the Other.[33] The Moroccan Other does not form a part of the essential plot line, and by focusing almost exclusively on the comings and goings of the European inhabitants, Dueñas does not need to address the issues of economic, social, or political inequality that undergird the colonial paradigm.[34]

Therefore, my analysis here does not focus on the African within the novel, but rather on Africa as a place "charged with nostalgia"[35] for the Spanish collective memory. If the African is rendered textually invisible, then one must ask the question *why Africa*? If the primary characters of the story are Portuguese, French, British, or Spanish, why could the novel not have taken place in France, Spain, or Portugal? Again, the colonial paradigm contains the answer to this question; the opportunity available in a colony[36] combined with the exoticism of Africa within the discourse of Western Orientalism confers upon the colonial territory a certain cultural capital, an exotic value, which is not available from European geographical counterparts. I will return to these questions below, by examining them more in depth within the text, but my examination of this novel does warrant this initial explanation of the potential shortcomings and choices of the author. This novel is pertinent to this study not for its representation of the African Other, but for its representation of Africa as a playground for the European colonial powers and the exotic imagery of Africa as a transformative space for the European.

This consideration of *El tiempo entre costuras* focuses on the portrayal of Dueñas's protagonist, Sira Quiroga, as she leaves Spain for Morocco and establishes a successful sewing business in Tétouan. Africa serves as a stage where Sira is able to rebuild her life after a series of disasters, and when she later returns to Spain under an assumed, Arabized name, the exotic flair that she adopts—effectively a Europeanized Africanness that is palatable to the upper echelons of European society—confers upon her an exotic cultural capital that she is able to convert into literal capital through the success of her haute couture sewing shop. As a theoretical framework to this approach, I will rely on contemporary feminist theory by theorists such as Chandra Mohanty, Linda McDowell, and Kristyn Gorton. Alongside *Orientalism*, I also use Daniel Varisco's *Reading Orientalism: Said and the Unsaid* (2007) to contribute to my analysis of the Orientalism of the novel. These critics will help to illuminate my thesis that Dueñas's Africa is a space where an unprivileged, poor Spanish girl can find opportunity unavailable to her in her homeland; Africa is a transformative space where the European can find tremendous opportunity.

The novel is narrated in the first-person voice of the protagonist, the singular Sira Quiroga. The story traces her life from a young girl in a poor neighborhood in Madrid, to Tangier and Tétouan immediately before, during, and after the Spanish Civil War, to a return to Madrid and Lisbon in the time leading up to World War II. She tells of her misfortunes and fortunes as she witnesses and participates in some of the most dramatic moments for Spain and Europe in the twentieth century. From her youth in Madrid, Sira elopes to Tangier with a charming man who soon leaves her pregnant and robs her of all her money. She flees to Tétouan, destitute, and miscarries. As the Civil War breaks out in Spain, the local police commissioner takes her passport and forces her to pay the pending debts of her disappeared lover from Tangier. With the help of friends, she is eventually able to open a high-fashion boutique serving the wealthy expatriates who are trapped in the Moroccan territory due to the war in Spain. Sira's skills as a seamstress allow her business to flourish and she becomes the premier *modiste* of the Moroccan territory. She is eventually able to get her mother out of Madrid to join her in Tétouan where they begin to work together.

In the years leading up to World War II, Sira is contacted by the British Secret Intelligence Service and recruited to work for them in Madrid. She agrees, leaving her shop in Tétouan to her mother and returning to Madrid to open a shop that would service the wives of Spanish and German military and political leaders. In order to return to Spain, she adopts an assumed identity with a Moroccan passport and an alias, "Arish Agoriuq"—

> It wasn't by any means an Arabic name, but it sounded strange and wouldn't be suspicious in Madrid, where no one had any idea what people went by over there in Moorish lands.[37]

She finds great success as a *modista* and as a spy and is sent on a mission to Lisbon to obtain information about a Portuguese merchant who is suspected of making deals with the Germans that work against the British. She runs into a British reporter, Marcus Logan, whom she originally had met in Tétouan, finds out that the Portuguese merchant wants him dead and alerts him. She gathers all of the information needed and as she is returning to Madrid by train discovers that a hit squad is after her and on her train. Marcus Logan shows up and they escape the train and return to Madrid by car. In Madrid again, when Sira/Arish discovers that Marcus is also a spy for the British and not a reporter, she rekindles her relationship with him and she makes a conscious decision to take charge of her life and control her own future. In the epilogue, Sira narrates what became of her many companions throughout the novel.

As a narrative that reads well—as is obvious from its commercial success and television adaptation—an analysis of the novel highlights its limitations. It is clearly a Eurocentric plot, despite the fact that it develops largely within North Africa. While questions of European colonialism are ignored, questions of gender are nevertheless pertinent; Sira develops from a young naïf into a strong and independent woman, even though Dueñas chooses to end the novel with the fairy tale happy ending of her being rescued by the British spy Marcus Logan and becoming romantically involved with him.

Indeed, the "feminist" qualities of the narrative are ones more associated with second wave feminism—"financial autonomy, a successful career, sexual freedom"[38]—than of the more global, postcolonial concerns of contemporary feminist theory. Sira is a successful capitalist; her business flourishes, as she is literally able to profit from the initial investment of capital. This is significant to emphasize that while Dueñas may be promoting a feminist agenda (consciously or not), it is not the third wave one of theorists such as Chandra Mohanty who seeks an "anticapitalist critique" and a solidarity with the experience of the marginalized, feminine Other.[39] Dueñas's rags-to-riches story is one clearly bearing the "authorizing signature of Western humanist discourse."[40] Sira begins as an oppressed young woman who is taken advantage of by an older man, and she eventually becomes a mature and forceful woman who consciously decides to control her own future.

This transformation should not be considered in isolation. It is relevant to this project because it occurs in the narrative and historical space of the Spanish Protectorate in Morocco. In her article "Place and Space," Linda McDowell suggests that "[t]he mapping of a place or location onto gender identities has been a key part of the establishment and maintenance of women's position and is reflected in both the materiality and the symbolic representation of women's lives."[41] Therefore, the geographical space of Africa—written as the European Protectorates—contributes to the dynamics at work within the plot. Africa offers a significant convergence of place and gender that reflects long-held Western conceptualizations of the continent as a "zone of potential loss or profit."[42] Sira discovers that, for her, Africa becomes a territory of opportunity and self-discovery, of literal profit. Her position of privilege as a colonizer enables her to re-create herself, or perhaps more appropriately *refashion* herself.

The conflux of gender and Africa in this work is only pertinent to this study in what we can analyze as the contemporary representation of Africa in the Spanish novel. To this end, it is useful to compare analogies of male:female::West:Africa.[43] By showing that the traditional male/female hierarchy is upset through Sira's personal success it can perhaps be extrapolated that a simultaneous upset occurs in the West/Africa dichotomy, privileging Africa over a European West that is war-ridden and financially exhausted. Despite the colonial setting, and the nostalgia for that time period, Dueñas inverts the "*positional* superiority" of the West over Orient—and upon which Orientalism depends—through a representation of Africa that is perhaps idealized in nostalgia, but nonetheless reconfigures the traditionally superordinate hierarchy of West over Africa.[44]

However, just as Dueñas's feminism seems to be drawn from the sixties and seventies second wave movement, so is the image of Africa also anchored in the colonial nostalgia. But while initially problematic, it is also nuanced and still critically significant. In early thirties Spain, the country is plunged into chaos and Sira is called to come and meet her estranged father for the first time. Sensing the impending fall of the Second Republic and the outbreak of war, he gives to Sira her inheritance and advises: "To Morocco; go to the Protectorate, it's a good place to live. A tranquil place where, since the end of the war with the Moors, nothing ever happens. Begin a new life far from this crazy country, because on the least expected day something big is going to explode and no one will be left alive."[45] Europe is unstable and dangerous, in Africa lies opportunity and tranquility that contrast sharply with a crumbling West as the New York Stock Market crumbles.[46] The image of West as rational and ordered versus Africa as savage and dangerous is overturned in this moment of Western history. Ironically, the "Protectorate" becomes a refuge that protects the colonizers from their own instability.

Dueñas's counter-Orientalism is subtle, but present. As Sira begins to settle into life in Tétouan, her neighbor and friend Félix Aranda teaches her about why Spain is in Morocco. She learns about the Rif War and the steady immigration of Spanish families to the territory and Sira's reflections on this knowledge are blatantly patronizing:

> In exchange for their imposed presence . . . Spain had provided Morocco advances in equipment, health, and infrastructure, and the first steps towards

a moderate improvement in agricultural exploitation. And a school of arts and traditional works. And all that the natives were able to obtain as a benefit in the activities destined to satisfy the colonizing population: power lines, potable water, schools and academies, businesses, public transport, clinics and hospitals, the train that united Tétouan with Ceuta, the one that even went to the beach at Río Martín. Spain from Morocco, in material terms, had received very little.[47]

The list of colonial "gifts" to Morocco is long and posits Spain's beneficent and patronizing role as colonizer. However, Dueñas closes the history lesson with a somber reminder of what Spain did receive from its African territory:

In human terms . . . yes, something important had been obtained for one of the sides of the civil contest: thousands of soldiers from the Moroccan indigenous force that in those days fought like beasts on the other side of the Strait for the foreign cause of the revolting army.[48]

Dueñas highlights the manipulative and exploitative colonial relationship, unearthing the dark secret of Spain's relationship with the Protectorate and of the Nationalist's mercenary support. Spain's presupposed moral high ground is eroded by this assertion.

Dueñas further undermines any moral high ground of colonial Spain through her fictionalized account of historical figures such as Serrano Suñer[49] and Johannes Bernhardt.[50] They are manipulative and underhanded politicians who are morally corrupt and seek to exploit the mineral resources of Morocco and Spain. On the other hand, Juan Luis Beigbeder y Atienza—first the High Commissary of Spain in Morocco[51] and later a Minister of Foreign Affairs[52]—is portrayed as genuinely interested in Moroccan life and culture.[53] He learns Arabic, meets with tribal leaders regularly, is respected by the local population, and keeps a Koran open on his desk: he is considered "an illustrious Africanist and a profound scholar of Islam."[54] Even though Beigbeder is close to Franco (in the novel), he is also distrusted by the caudillo for initially unknown reasons. However, the reader eventually discovers that Franco's distrust is a result of his jealousy for Beigbeder's linguistic skills. Beigbeder explains to Sira that Franco, despite his reputation, neither speaks Arabic nor holds the support of the Moroccan public.[55] Franco is presented as a failure in this representation, such that the Moroccan public does not care for him at all, and Spain's colonial mission in Africa is reduced to a petty attempt to achieve a level of colonial power, even though it would not rival the African territories of France and England.[56] In these descriptions, both Franco and Spain are impotent colonialists, ultimately manipulated by Hitler's Germany. These subtle additions counterbalance the nostalgic idealization of the colonial Protectorates.

For better or for worse, as mentioned above, Spain's Moroccan territories serve as the backdrop for Sira's transformation from a shy young naïf into an independent and strong woman. When Sira arrives in Tétuoan, recently abandoned by her lover, sick and miscarrying and in debt to creditors in Tangier, she is at rock bottom. She has nothing to her name and is alone in an unknown city in a foreign country, unable to return to Madrid because war has broken out. As she is questioned by the local commissary Claudio Vázquez, she thinks to herself how she has always been dependent on others.[57] But as the days pass, Sira learns to adapt and to live alone[58] as she finds an interior strength that she had not previously recognized.[59] She rediscovers her sewing skills, ones her mother taught her as a child but which she had not used in years, and establishes her business, serving the wealthiest and most powerful in the Protectorate. She only much later confesses the sordid tales of her youthful misfortunes to her friend Rosalinda, who responds to her humble and tragic history with "to whom the hell does it matter where you come from when you are the best *modista* in all of Morocco."[60] Her business acumen brings her financial success, and she is soon able to pay off her creditors and begin saving to bring her mother out of Spain to join her in Tétouan.

Sira soon discovers a new self-confidence and a strength that she previously did not possess. She attends a party with the British journalist/spy, Marcus Logan, and he asks her for her help in uncovering some information from Serrano Suñer and Johannes Bernhardt. She agrees to help, but she also negotiates her own conditions that Logan will also find out some information for her. Sira holds up her end of the agreement and discovers more information about secret agreements between Bernhardt and Suñer than Logan expected. Sira's poise and confidence in navigating the situation hint at a developing personal strength and agency.

It is true that Sira's personal maturation could have occurred in Spain, the Americas, or some other Western backdrop, but Africa does contribute in specific ways to this process, and not just for Sira. Her closest friend Rosalinda, a British expatriate who is romantically involved with Beigbeder, has also found in the Spanish Protectorate a place to escape from her past and to recreate a new life. For the wealthy colonials, Morocco offers them everything from their homeland, plus a degree of anonymity.[61] Africa reveals its mystique when Sira is contacted by the British Special Intelligence Service to move back to Madrid and open up another shop, with the purpose of spying upon the wealthy and powerful wives. As noted above, she is given a new, assumed identity, that of "Arish Agoriuq"—an affected Arabic-sounding name. At this point, she is, in effect, a completely distinct person from the young girl who left Madrid several years before.

When she returns to Madrid, she relies on her exotic, Orientalist narrative to find financial success and to stand out. For the decor of her new shop,

"Arish" describes that she decorated her shop with Moroccan handicrafts "with the intention of giving my shop in Madrid an exotic atmosphere in concordance with my new name and my supposed past as a prestigious Tangerian dressmaker. . . . A small piece of Africa in the center of the map of the exhausted Spain."[62] She teaches her assistants to prepare and serve tea "in the Moorish fashion,"[63] how to "paint their eyes with khol,"[64] and she even sews a caftan "to give her appearance an exotic air."[65] Sira/Arish openly admits that it is a "false exoticism,"[66] but it functions not only to increase her perceived cultural capital among Madrid's elite, but also to give her personal strength; she is "protected by the armor of my false exoticism."[67] She questions what led her to agree to return to Madrid as a spy and *moaísta*, wondering if she did it for loyalty to Rosalinda[68] or out of familial and patriotic duty,[69] and she ultimately considers that "Maybe I didn't do it for anyone or maybe just for myself."[70] She finds her sense of personal agency strengthened by her experience in Morocco, and this identity serves her as a personal "armor."[71]

Such an appropriation is problematic. Sira exploits another culture for her own benefit. As she assumes a Moroccan passport and affects an exotic air, Sira creates a Moroccan "alias" that has little to do with the reality. Said suggests that, in *Itinéraire de Paris à Jérusalem*,[72] Chateaubriand "attempts to *consume* the Orient. He not only appropriates it, he represents and speaks for it,"[73] and a similar argument can be made for Sira except that she attempts to *sell* the Orient rather than *consume* it. Arish employs her exotic persona to achieve financial success in her shop and to gain the confidence of the political elite in Madrid. Said's further analysis of the work of Chateaubriand, Lamartine, Renan, and Sacy, also serves to understand Dueñas's and Sira's use of Africa; by including Dueñas in the list of authors above, it can be said that

> their Orient was not so much grasped, appropriated, reduced, or codified as lived in, exploited aesthetically and imaginatively as a roomy place full of possibility. What mattered to them was the structure of their work as an independent, aesthetic, and personal fact, and not the ways by which, if one wanted to, one could effectively dominate or set down the Orient graphically. Their egos never absorbed the Orient, nor totally identified the Orient with documentary and textual knowledge of it (with official Orientalism, in short).[74]

Said seems to suggest that the Orientalism of Chateaubriand, Lamartine, Renan, and Sacy (and one could include Dueñas) is an *orientalism*—without the capital "O"—that is more benign than the official, academic narrative against which he writes. He appears to insinuate that it functions on similar principles but lacks the rigor and force of the academic project of Orientalism. Said essentially gives these authors a pass; their work lacks the political support that undergird Orientalism as a destructive force.

Indeed, Daniel Varisco, in *Reading Orientalism*, takes issue with Said's dismissal of this Orientalism-*lite*. Varisco contests that "Said's suggestion that Orientalism is a 'style'"[75] is too narrowly defined by Said:

> Consider the various ways any given individual could appropriate the Orient as a pilgrim, crusader, hardened mercenary, merchant, missionary, colonial administrator, poet, novelist, satirist, artist, mystic, tourist. It is precisely this tinker-tailor-candlestickmaker hetero-genus-ness in discourse that is obscured in the argument of *Orientalism*.[76]

Varisco's assertion does not dismiss the purely "aesthetic" or "imaginative" use of Africa/the Orient as a benign project, but rather highlights the pervasiveness of Orientalist discourse across a range of genres and "styles."

Varisco's reminder underscores the problems of Dueñas's novel. While Sira is able to parlay debt and ruin in Africa to personal fortune and independence by appropriating a culture that is not her own, the representation of Africa is mired in a tradition of representation that leaves it as a land of possibility for the Westerner, almost devoid of indigenous inhabitants. Therefore, it is useful to return to my previous suggestion that what may be at work is an analogous relationship of male:female::West:Africa. As Sira upsets the traditional male/female hierarchy by gaining control of the direction of her life,[77] is there a concurrent upset of the West and Africa's relationship of Western dominance?

It is clear that Sira finds the strength to be independent through Africa, and yet the representation of Africa—even though positive—does not diverge from a narrative of colonial nostalgia. Within the text Morocco is not a land of Moroccans, but of Europeans. When Sira/Arish meets Manuel da Silva in Lisbon for the first time, they share the following exchange:

> [Sira/Arish:] "You've never been in Morocco?"
>
> [Manuel da Silva:] "No. And I lament it; above all if all of the Moroccan women are like yourself."
>
> "It is a fascinating country of marvelous people, but I am afraid that it would be difficult to find many women like myself there. I am an atypical Moroccan because my mother is Spanish. I am not Muslim and my maternal language is not Arabic, but rather Spanish. But I adore Morocco."[78]

Africa—Morocco—is reduced to little more than an imagined, exotic geographical space. The qualities that do not serve her are discarded: she is *not* Muslim, she does *not* speak Arabic, but she does pepper her speech with words and phrases in both French and Arabic: "possibly in the latter a little non-sensical, given that I often repeated simple expressions retained from overhearing them in the streets of Tangier and Tétouan, but whose exact meaning and use I did not know."[79] Her false exoticism enables her to overcome the *"positional* superiority" of the male/female paradigm, but it does little for Africa's unequal, colonial relationship with the West.

Africa does occupy a favored and favorable position within the text, and so it would be relatively easy to affirm the benign nature of the representation as Said appears to do with Chateaubriand, Lamartine, Renan, and Sacy. But such a reading would overlook the fact that, while *El tiempo entre costuras* does not offer a negative representation of Africa, neither does it depart from a pattern of representation that appropriates Africa for Western purposes. *El tiempo entre costuras* is a novel that—as V. Y. Mudimbe suggests in *The Idea of Africa*—"exploit[s] the exotic representations and categories of Africa as illustrated, say, in English or French literature, and . . . marginalize[s] Africa" and continues "a tradition which, for centuries, has conveyed this exotic idea of Africa."[80] It is, ultimately, ethnocentric and Eurocentric, despite a large portion of the plot developing within the geographical space of Africa. And while it is perhaps Orientalism-*lite*, it does not depart from the Western paradigm of representation that appropriates Africa for its own ends.

Neither is the feminism of this novel particularly contemporary. Sira's maturation is powerful and inspiring as she maneuvers and manipulates her passage to personal agency. But this is a Western feminism, anchored in second-wave feminist ideas of financial, professional, and sexual equality for women. Sira's story and the novel's commercial success show that "women's 'liberation' is a marketable commodity."[81] This is not a feminism concerned with questions of "decolonization, anticapitalist critique, and solidarity."[82] Dueñas's tale of female liberation posits one archetype and does not address the diversity of contemporary feminism. Mohanty's critique of such a position is telling for this study:

> [in such an instance] power is automatically defined in binary terms: people who have it (read: men) and people who do not (read: women). Men exploit, women are exploited. Such simplistic formulations are historically reductive; they are also ineffectual in designing strategies to combat oppressions. All they do is reinforce binary divisions between men and women.[83]

Dueñas does upend the binary hierarchy of powerful men and impotent women in Sira's story, but Sira only becomes a co-exploiter. Sira is the one who exploits Africa, and I would hold that this ultimate, insidious interpretation suggests that, hidden between the seams of this novel, are surviving remnants of Orientalist discourse, alive and well.

SEX, VIRGINITY, AND RESISTANCE IN GUILLERMINA MEKUY'S *LAS TRES VÍRGENES DE SANTO TOMÁS*

Guillermina Mekuy Mba Obono was born in Evinayong, on mainland Equatorial Guinea, in 1982; she is ethnically Fang.[84] At the age of five, her family moved to Madrid, Spain where she grew up and studied Law and Political Science at the Autonomous University of Madrid. She has published three novels, in addition to serving as the General Director of Libraries and Museums, Secretary of State Head of Culture, Minister of Culture and Tourism, and Minister of Culture and Artisanal Promotion in Equatorial Guinea. Currently, she resides in Spain with her family. In 2013 she founded the cultural magazine Meik, and, in 2016, the publishing house Mk Ediciones that seeks to publish emerging female authors.

Her first novel, *El llanto de la perra*,[85] was written when she was seventeen and published by Plaza & Janés in 2005.[86] This was followed by *Las tres vírgenes de Santo Tomás*,[87] published by Suma de Letras in 2008, and *Tres almas para un corazón*[88] from Grupo Planeta in 2011. As a part of the growing number of Hispano-African voices that were published in the 1990s and early 2000s, her work has received some critical analysis, mostly focusing on her works' (questionable) engagements with feminism,[89] but it is important to recognize, as Marta Sofía López Rodríguez notes, that Mekuy should be contextualized as one of the literary "'daughters,' or now almost 'granddaughters'"[90] of the Hispano-Equatoguinean literary matriarch María Nsué Angüe. Selena Nobile describes Mekuy as an example of the second-generation immigrant author,[91] and López Rodríguez situates her with other authors such as Chimamanda Ngozi Adichie, Sefi Atta, Doreen Baingana, or Leila Aboulela as

> female authors that have notably amplified the stylistic and thematic horizon created by their ancestors, including matters such as the progressive urbanization of the continent, the addition of global and transnational perspectives on politics and the African economy, the explicit defense of feminist principles that their elders embraced with more reticence, the open discussion of sexual questions, or the deepening of the intersections between the public and private spheres in their nations of origin, placing special emphasis on denouncing the structures of domination and tyrannical power that equally affect society as a whole and the individuals that make it up.[92]

López Rodríguez goes on to lament the lack of many other female voices in Hispano-Equatoguinean literature,[93] and Marvin Lewis emphasizes that Mekuy's work "provide[s] a window of opportunity to explore further the roles of Equatorial Guinean women at home and abroad as they seek to establish themselves in a post-colonial, independent society."[94]

Therefore, Mekuy's writing offers an important opportunity to examine the representation of gender and the African Other from the perspective of a female/Equatoguinean/postcolonial narrative voice. For this analysis, I focus on Mekuy's second book *Las tres vírgenes de Santo Tomás* for its exploration of the erotic awakening of its female, African protagonist. The novel is a *bildungsroman*, narrated in the first-person voice by María Fátima, the middle of three sisters and the daughter of the Equatoguinean Tomás Ondó Mikó and his Spanish wife Teresa. As the protagonist develops her empowered sense of sexuality, her resistance to external control echoes Fang patterns of resistance from colonial Spanish Guinea, and her approach de-centers patriarchal power structures.[95]

The first four chapters take place in Equatorial Guinea, in the interior mainland, Fang region of Evinayong. When María Fátima is nine years old, the family moves to Madrid and the two younger daughters are immediately sent to a convent so that they can "pray for the sins of the world, maintaining the purity of your sex out of the reach of men."[96] During her teen years, María Fátima experiences the development of sexual curiosity, and, together with two friends, escapes the convent so that she can experience "the real world."[97] The rest of the novel narrates her journey of erotic discovery as she meets new people, pursues studies and a career in law, rekindles her relationships with her sisters, and, eventually, reconciles with her disapproving parents.

Central to the development of the narrative is the religious fervor of María Fátima's parents. Her father is devoutly religious, to the extreme that he believes himself to be an incarnation of the Catholic saint Thomas Aquinas. Her Spanish mother, the daughter of "some colonists like the many that had arrived to our land,"[98] is a supportive wife, but also a powerful animist priestess—"the great white sorceress"[99]—that feels a deep, spiritual connection to Equatorial Guinea. The father, disappointed that he had three daughters instead of sons, is singularly preoccupied with the virginity of his daughters, hence the novel's title. Despite this patriarchal obsession, each of the three daughters mature into a sexually satisfied sense of self-confidence, while maintaining their "virginities" in the narrowest understanding of the term.

The question of virginity is, perhaps, the most problematic theme of the novel. On its surface, it is so because the narrative is preoccupied with a definition of virginity that is uniquely heteronormative and phallocentric; that is, in the novel, the only "threat" to the daughters' virginity is phallic penetration of the vagina. Each of the three daughters engages in various sexual activities but maintain their self-identification as "virgins" because they have not engaged in the specific sexual act of penis-in-vagina intercourse. This limited definition also appears to diminish the validity of the satisfying sexual relationship that María Fátima's oldest sister, María Inmaculada, experiences with her female partner. Because they are both women, María Inmaculada's virginity is never threatened. This is a very reductive understanding of sex and sexuality, however, the manner in which Mekuy explores this limited conceptualization in the novel functions as a powerful subversion of religion, colonialism, and identity, and echoes the resistance of Fang women in colonial Spanish Guinea. Through its exploration of sexuality and identity, Mekuy effectively de-centers paradigms of power and privilege, opening a new space of expression and existence.

This representation is not without problematic elements. As María Fátima embarks on her journey of sexual discovery, she engages in transactional sex work that presents these interactions as powerful moments of female empowerment and agency without considering the risks or broader socio-economic realities that make this her only option for subsistence. As her confidence grows, Fátima and her friends begin a monthly auction of their sexual services, and, since she is technically a virgin, she is the prize that commands the highest bids. One of the sharpest critiques of *El llanto de la perra* is also directly applicable to *Las tres vírgenes de Santo Tomás*. Marta Sofía López Rodríguez writes that

> Given the enormous collective efforts that African, Afro-Caribbean, and Afro-American women have invested and continue investing in dignifying the black woman, the priceless example of their collective resistance in the face of all kinds of exploitation, including the exploitation of their bodies, the attitude of submission of the narrator in *El llanto de la perra* comes across as profoundly offensive. The notion of "sexual slavery" assumed voluntarily, from a victimist and self-complacent position, should make the bones of Nora Zeale Hurston, Bessie Head, Mariama Bâ, and so many other warriors for the dignity of black women turn over in their tombs.[100]

López Rodríguez concludes that Mekuy is

> literarily orphaned, an apocryphal daughter of exile, and her novel has been born out of this motherlessness: disconnected from the literary tradition of black women, from the culture of origin of the author, from African orality and also the written narratives from the continent and the diaspora, and indifferent to the tragic history of Equatorial Guinea.[101]

And it is hard to disagree with this analysis. These scenes seem designed to titillate the reader without engaging with the struggles that historically preface them, but where López Rodríguez emphasizes the work's disconnection with its supposed literary heritage, I understand this rupture as a deliberate act of resistance that draws power through provocation.

At various points, Mekuy's text deliberately rejects cultural and familial inheritances as its protagonist asserts her own autonomy and agency. Joanna Boampong notes that "Mekuy's female African protagonist does break the mold in which African women have traditionally been cast,"[102] and one way to understand Mekuy's narrative is that it creates a new, "in-between" space, as Homi Bhabha describes in *The Location of Culture*; a space that "provide[s] the terrain for elaborating strategies of selfhood . . . that initiate new signs of identity, and innovative sites of collaboration, and contestation."[103] As López Ródriguez notes, Mekuy's new "in-between" space is dislocated from history in that it is not directly informed by it, nor a direct contestant to it, but, in drawing on Bhabha's engagement with Fanon and Hall, this novel demonstrates that "the meaning and symbols of culture have no primordial unity or fixity; that even the same signs can be appropriated, translated, rehistoricized and read anew."[104] It is helpful to note Edwards Soja's reminder that it is not "a simple additive or 'in-between' positioning that can be marked with dogmatic assurity. It is instead an invitation to continuous deconstruction and reconstitution, to a constant effort to move beyond the established limits of our understanding of the world."[105] Mekuy's explicit and unorthodox treatment of sex "desecrat[es] the sacred subject of sex and the erotic that most African writers feel obliged to avoid,"[106] and through this "desecration" her protagonists create new "signs of identity . . . and contestation."[107]

Upon arrival in Spain, the two younger sisters, María Fátima and María Lourdes, are sent to a convent with her father's reasoning that he wishes to maintain "the purity of your sex out of the reach of men."[108] In an attempt to control their sexuality, the young girls are literally placed in the margins, cloistered behind walls to protect them from the corrupting influence of the male phallus. But it is soon revealed that this protected space is not, in fact, impenetrable. As Fátima plots her escape with her friends Nela and Selung, they reveal that they both lost their virginity to the gardener's son inside the convent. It is later uncovered that Fátima's younger sister, Lourdes, begins a sexual relationship with Father Andrew, the convent's priest, even as she prepares to take on the role of Mother Superior at the convent. The walled, physical space of the convent, employed to control their sexuality, is shown to be ineffective. In spite of the physical obstacles, the characters exert their personal autonomy as they pursue their desires.

The convent is the physical space that attempts to contain them, but its existence is predicated on the religious ideology that Thomas Aquinas elaborated in the thirteenth century. While the walls of the convent are the physical manifestation of Aquinas's moral limits, the broader ideology structures each of the three daughter's life. The novel outlines this ideology describing Aquinas as "A friar that lived in the thirteenth century and considered women to be biologically inferior to men."[109] The father's obsession with Aquinas establishes the phallocentric focus on sexuality. Mekuy prefaces various chapters of the book with direct quotes from Aquinas: "The masculine seed contains the power of reproduction, and the mother only contributes a womb that gives nourishment to this seed,"[110] and "As an individual, woman is a weak and flawed being."[111] These quotes structure and inform the daughters' first engagements with sexuality, and their reactions are to initially engage in sexual activities, but to maintain their virginity by denying phallic penetration. This brings to mind Judith Butler's consideration that "if there is no radical repudiation of a culturally constructed sexuality, what is left is the question of how to acknowledge and 'do' the construction one is invariably in."[112] The young women choose to obey the letter of the law, as they subvert the control that it holds over them. At the same time, the three sisters' development of empowering sexual identities under this paradigm is also a strong negation of the phallus as the source of feminine pleasure. They appropriate the prohibitions on their sexuality by denying the phallus as a source of sexual satisfaction.

For the sisters, pleasure comes from being desired and touched, and is not dependent on that phallus. María Fátima derives a sense of power over her sexuality through this approach; as she considers her escape from the convent and her new path in search of her desires, she reflects that

> In that moment, I saw the open heavens. Not the seraphic place that my mother talked about, but instead the possibility of being free, that possibility of, in the name of I don't know what revelation or sudden love from Teresa, definitively escaping. And what's more, to convert myself into a searcher of the pleasure that pulled at me and I felt that it was the only source of life and I was going to become a virgin that was touched and desired.[113]

This liberation and autonomy are not complete, however, as she promises to maintain her virginity, but her approach to sexual fulfillment de-centers the controlling power of the patriarchal obsession. Where Fátima was literally placed in the margins, she, in turn, places the phallus and her virginity in the margins of her own sexual empowerment. Fátima chooses to obey the letter of the law imposed by her parents, but she exploits a technicality that allows her to feel liberated and powerful. When Fátima seeks out her parents' blessing, her mother requests this concession:

> "I only ask you for one thing: you can offer your body to lust, emulate all of the other women that have prostituted themselves . . . but . . . you will continue being a virgin. You will be desired, caressed, licked, subjugated, but no one will penetrate in you, not even when you are in the middle of an orgy of men that want to possess you and to whom you will give everything, except one: the humid treasure of your virginity."

I agreed with a nod of my head and I thought that I owed her this for having helped to release me from my chains, again and forever. I also thought that, following her request, I could fulfill my most intimate desires, and no one would dominate me, only I would decide what would be fair game for anyone.[114]

This conflicting presentation of a freedom that is still contained within patriarchal boundaries is the primary problematic sticking point for some scholars that have written on Mekuy's work. It appears that Mekuy's idea of feminine agency is not able to get completely free from patriarchal control. However, if this example is contextualized with a look back at women's sexual freedoms in Spanish Guinea, then Mekuy's presentation makes more sense.

In her 2019 book *Silenced Resistance: Women Dictatorships, and Genderwashing in Western Sahara and Equatorial Guinea*, Joanna Allan examines the ways in which women in Spanish Guinea found ways to exert agency and navigate between traditional cultural moral structures and colonial imports. She writes:

> The Spanish import of Christianity also impacted negatively on women's sexual freedoms, especially in the Fang case. Unlike other Guinean ethnicities or Spanish citizens for whom premarital chastity was imperative for women, Fang girls were allowed to explore their sexualities before they were married. Yet the arrival of Christianity converted female sexuality into a terrible and dangerous force to be tamed in and outside of marriage.[115]

This conflict for Fátima and her sisters is, therefore, a continuation of this colonial dynamic, and on display is the friction between the pre-colonial Fang tolerance of sexual exploration for young women and the prohibitive colonial, Catholic sexual mores. Allan goes on to note that the introduction of Catholicism in Spanish Guinea did provide new powers for some women, and, in spite of the inevitable compromises, "Guinean women glimpsed opportunities at the missions and exploited them when they could. If there was empowerment, Guinean women empowered themselves."[116] Through this lens, it becomes clear that Mekuy's writing rejects the sensitivities introduced by Spanish colonial rule, and her protagonists engage in methods of resistance that parallel those of Guinean women under colonial rule.

Fátima appropriates the prohibition against phallic penetration as a way to establish power and dominance in her early relationships with men; she exerts her powers of domination over the patriarchy by subverting its powers:

> I was conscious of the fact—and I would be more so later on—that when men looked at me, when they desired to possess me, and, even so, it was this same desire that gave me power over them; it is what gave me the capacity to dominate them, to control them.[117]

Fátima effectively exploits the opportunities before her in order to find empowerment over those that would control her; she engages in a strategy of resistance that echoes that of Fang women under Spanish colonial rule.

The treatment of traditional Fang religious traditions in the novel also supports a reading of Mekuy's text as undermining colonial, Catholic, and patriarchal power structures. Fátima's mother—white, Spanish, and the daughter of colonialists Spanish Guinea—becomes an adept of Fang animism and rises to the status of "the great white sorceress."[118] While her Guinean father fervently adopts Catholicism, her Spanish mother immerses herself in the Fang religious traditions.[119] The father's religious beliefs torment him; they drive his daughters away from him and lead him to seek penitence through lashes. Mekuy does suggest that there are underlying mental issues that her father deals with, but Catholicism is the aggravating factor that structures his descent into fanaticism. On the contrary, Fang animism is a supportive force that provides community and meaning for her mother, and which her mother extends to her daughter Fátima. Mekuy's treatment of Fang traditional religious practices privileges their power, while highlighting the destructive power of Catholic fanaticism.

In addition to destabilizing the totemic primacy of Catholicism, this privileging of animism also invokes traditional Fang practices of feminine solidarity and empowerment. Allan writes that

> Some Fang women had, before Catholicization took hold, formed part of all-female religious movements. . . . Since [some were] feared by men, [they] could also serve as a counter to male abuses. Likewise, Fang Bwiti religious practices also provided spaces for women to challenge gendered systems of power: all-woman dances explicitly mocked men, while the religion served as a spiritual refuge from colonialism.[120]

In this context, animism not only undermines colonial, Catholic power, but also patriarchal power. And since the mother is a white European, it extends Fang animism into a universal feminine power that rivals the global stretch of Catholicism; that is, it cannot be written off as simply a local, African religious practice. In an interview with Elisa Rizo, Mekuy defends her use of a white European woman as a powerful animist sorceress with the explanation that

> I mix African culture with European through a white woman that lives the life of an African, because she's involved in animism, in the practicing of black magic, witchcraft, and all that. And why did I do that? Since I live in Europe, having a white woman as a protagonist in a novel where she participates in these African rites, it makes it easier for people to understand. If the whole family were black, people would say "well, that's just how things are in Africa" and my book would

just be something exotic and different. But when it's a white woman, it's much easier for people to imagine themselves as this woman because they can see something they can relate to. And then the father, since he's black, was the one who was so religious, that was meant to be a critique.[121]

Her self-analysis highlights her strategy for provoking sympathy for and legitimizing the power of traditional African religious practices, while diminishing that of Catholicism and the patriarchy. Mekuy's privileging of Fang animism builds on feminine traditions of resistance in Spanish Guinea, re-deploying their power in the postcolonial context where the same power structures continue to maintain hegemony.

María Fátima's escape from the convent can also be understood as a strategy of resistance that draws on Fang traditions. As María Nsué Angüe's 1985 novel *Ekomo*[122] explores female agency in Equatorial Guinea, it describes the tradition of *abóm*, a premarital "kidnapping" tradition that the protagonist uses "to achieve the best outcome that she can manage in . . . difficult circumstances."[123] In a traditional case of *abóm*, when faced with an undesirable arranged marriage, a woman elopes with a man of her choice, "hoping to later convince her father to consent such a union."[124] Drawing on the work of Enrique Okenve—and noting that the English and Spanish translations of *abóm* ("kidnapping" and "secuestro") deny the women agency as participants in the practice—Allan writes that Fang women "reappropriated [the] typical Fang social practice to escape coerced marriage."[125] Allan further writes that this practice developed in popularity under Spanish colonial rule as

> The clash with colonial culture illustrated to women that gender-based norms were not necessarily inevitable or "the natural way of things." Some began to rebel against the gendered practices that they disliked. Okenve finds that it became common for women to challenge coerced marriages, something that had previously been unthinkable. The *abóm*, then, was one form of women's resistance. Women rejected unwanted marriages arranged by their parents and "ran away" in the night with their lovers.[126]

According to Allan and Okenve, this practice "illustrates the resilience and subtle forms of resistance Guinean women . . . used to get their way."[127]

With this context, Fátima's escape from the convent acquires new meaning. She participates in a cultural tradition that unites her with an Equatorial Guinean matriarchy that precedes her. She exerts her own agency in determining her life plans, and she pursues her desires. While the specter of enforced virginity remains, Fátima undermines its power and re-forges it as her own source of power. James C. Scott notes the importance of such a rebellion when he considers the tools of resistance available to many marginalized groups:

foot-dragging, dissimulations, false compliance, feigned ignorance, desertion, pilfering, smuggling, poaching, arson, slander, sabotage, surreptitious assault and murder, anonymous threats, and so on. These techniques, for the most part quite prosaic, are the ordinary means of class struggle. They are the techniques of "first resort" in those common historical circumstances in which open defiance is impossible or entails mortal danger. When they are widely practiced by members of an entire class against elites or the state, they may have aggregate consequences all out of proportion to their banality when considered singly. No adequate account of class relations is possible without assessing their importance.[128]

The actions of Mekuy's protagonist, therefore, accomplish two key things. First, they connect to a tradition of anti-colonial, anti-patriarchal resistance by Equatorial Guinean women, and second, through this association, her rebellion—even within the confines established by her father—and her actions assume aggregate power through the context of collective practice.

Mekuy's text also seems to suggest that the most important element is the moment of provocation, of subversion, rather than liberation. This would support a reading of the novel as a contribution towards undermining patriarchy, even if the protagonist does not experience full liberation from it herself. As Fátima describes the power that withholding her virginity gives to her, she reflects that "I liked to play and to provoke desire, and I knew the power of provocation and the acts that weren't finalized would give me more power over men than consummated sex. I knew that the imagination was the most powerful weapon."[129] Fátima realizes that she can upset the dynamics of power from within her current sexual paradigm. She draws her own conclusion about the power of her virginity and its uses that parallels, but differs from, the morals of her father. Her sexual encounters become scenes of revolutionary power as she realizes that power lies in provocation, not consummation.

Enrique Okenve and Joanna Allan interpret the practice of *abóm* as a "tool used by women in the face of socioeconomic changes brought about by the Spanish (capitalist) intrusion."[130] With the escape from the convent, Mekuy adapts the practice of *abóm* to the context of a Hispano-Guinean girl living in contemporary Spain, and she expands her critique of socioeconomic inequalities that exist under neoliberalism. Above, I noted the problematic scenes where the teen girls auction themselves off to the highest bidder in exchange for sexual favors. To many readers, these scenes must come across as tone-deaf and ignorant of the historical tragedy of slavery, but Fátima's internal monologue insists that she sees it differently:

> what some people would consider dirty and immoral, and I saw with clarity that, even though it could be a little bit immoral for society, for me, it was better than

living in hypocrisy like so many other people, and, instead of buying bodies, they bought souls. What I did was better than those that used their power to enslave others that had nothing, these people that lived on the margins of any moral consciousness as to what was truly important: to allow the poor and ignorant to live and thrive. What we did was just innocent games in the midst of a society that converted the weak into victims and the powerful into executioners, that, instead of treating life like a diversion, they made it a market where the same people always lost.[131]

For Fátima, she has the freedom to engage in these "innocent games"[132] between consenting adults, and she finds empowerment and pleasure in these activities. She also recognizes her own privilege and suggests that critics that are concerned with her personal choices should instead focus on the injustices of a socioeconomic system that robs the vulnerable of their agency. This small reflection does little to allay questions about the tactlessness of the scene, but it is consistent with Mekuy's focus on the revolutionary power of provocation. Depending on the reader, these scenes hold the power to titillate or provoke, and both of these are strategies that Fátima deliberately uses to empower herself.

Marta Sofía López Rodríguez suggests that Mekuy's focus on the proliferous erotic escapades of her protagonists "is involuntarily reinforcing a denigrating stereotype of the insatiable sensuality of the black woman that the majority of female African authors have combatted and denounced with ferocity in their texts."[133] While it is true that the erotic themes of Mekuy's works appear disconnected from her literary and historical antecedents, Joanna Boampong notes the similarities she shares with the Cameroonian-Francophone author Calixthe Beyala and her protagonist Irene Fofo in *Femme nue, femme noire*[134] (2003).[135] And female Hispano-African authors have continued to explore sexuality more openly in the years following Mekuy's publication of her three novels. Trifonia Melibea Obono's celebrated 2016 novel *La bastarda* and O'sírimia Mota Ripeu's 2017 *El punto ciego de Cassandra* engage with many of the same sexual themes as Mekuy. In this context, the revolutionary power of Mekuy's provocations becomes more apparent; Mekuy's novels appear to have opened a space for expression that other female Hispano-African authors have since joined. To return to Joanna Boampong's desciption, Mekuy's desecration of "the sacred subject of sex"[136] is an appropriate way to characterize her provocative writing, but she desecrates more than just sex. Mekuy's writing undermines and erodes the powers that seek to control women and their sexuality. She decenters virginity and the phallus in sex and subverts the moral authority of the Catholic church.

Mekuy's writing is not as disconnected from tradition as it first appears. As noted above, the resistance to moral and social norms that María Fátima performs in the novel reflects strategies of resistance that Fang and Bubi women employed in colonial Spanish Guinea. In *Silenced Resistance*, Joanna Allan examines how the misbehavior of female students functioned to disrupt colonial control. She writes that "the increased 'bad behavior' of schoolgirls as independence approached speaks of the objects of resistance: efforts to undermine the Spanish teachers and the Falangista syllabus were as much anticolonial as antisexist."[137] Like the examples that Allan highlights in her study, Mekuy's protagonist and her two sisters participate in "bad behaviors" and, in so doing, they "subver[t] notions of the 'appropriate' role for women."[138] Their provocations reimagine what a fulfilling life could be for these women, outside of the confines of religious and patriarchal dogmatism. Therefore, Mekuy's novel should not be considered disconnected from its Equatoguinean heritage, but rather it takes the traditions of Equatoguinean feminine resistance and expands upon them.

While Mekuy does, perhaps, involuntarily reinforce a stereotype of the black woman as overtly sensual,[139] it is important to note that Fátima is not the silent, passive stereotype whose problematic representation Said criticizes in *Orientalism*. Fátima is not Flaubert's Egyptian courtesan. Mekuy writes an empowered African woman that both supports and defies stereotypes. Mekuy's protagonist supports the idiosyncratic patriarchal obsession with virginity, while undermining its power of control over her bodily autonomy. Fátima is unconcerned with what others think of her choices; she employs desire and provocation as tools of resistance and empowerment. In an interview with Elisa Rizo, Mekuy echoes this defiance:

> Sensuality continues to be some that women refrain from writing about. But when you read books written by men, they're the ones who write about it the most, but no one questions them doing so. Because they're men . . . they employ all kinds of language, but since they're men, they can be forgiven for this. But when a woman touches on a topic like this, then she's questioned about it.[140]

Mekuy essentially rejects the legacy of Orientalist and colonial tropes by repeating them and employing their power for her own ends, as Fátima does with her virginity.

In a final consideration, if we return the Orientalist/colonial trope of Africa as "'virgin' territories to be conquered, 'dark continents' to be explored,"[141] and add to it Said's repeated use/critique of the word "penetration" to describe the West's imperial expansion,[142] then this novel's singular focus on the maintenance of virginity assumes broader meanings. In *Geografías de lo exótico*,[143] Rosa Cerarols Ramírez directly connects the feminized imagery of Africa to the African woman: "The treatment of the feminine theme in Spanish Orientalist narratives emphasizes [Africa's] vulnerability in order to justify and encourage colonial penetration."[144] With this broader context, the patriarch of *Las tres vírgenes de Santo Tomás*, is not only "protecting" the virginity of his daughters, but also metaphorically resisting colonial conquest. Fátima accepts this condition and refuses to allow herself to be penetrated sexually. She rejects vulnerability and assumes power from this resistance. The Orientalist trope of territorial "penetration" is, therefore, challenged and subverted, as Mekuy writes within a symbolic paradigm and undermines its precepts.

Mekuy's novels have been the focus of some valid critiques, some of which I have noted above. In addition, the novel's colloquial registers, melodramatic elements,[145] erotic focus, and the fact that Mekuy was in her late teens and early twenties when she wrote and published them have, perhaps, hindered the reception of these works as "serious" literature. But these perceptions should not stand in the way of acknowledging some of the subtly subversive acts of resistance that this particular book accomplishes.

With her second novel, *Las tres vírgenes de Santo Tomás,* Mekuy takes the traditional Equatoguinean feminine resistance and reimagines it in the context of a young African immigrant living in contemporary Spain. Her novel subverts the power of the patriarchy and assumes power from the act of provocation. Its odd obsession with virginity is also a provocation that appears to defy concerns about patriarchal control of feminine sexuality, but as Mekuy's protagonist explores the wonders of a non-phallocentric sexuality, she builds a satisfying sexual identity that circumvents the limitations placed on her.

While at first glance it may not appear so, Mekuy's writing engages with the legacy of Orientalism, the patriarchy, and resistance. Fátima is not Flaubert's Egyptian courtesan that "never spoke of herself, . . . never represented her emotions, presence, or history";[146] she is an active agent that assumes power as a provocateur. Mekuy's provocations and her protagonist's acts of resistance serve as contestants to the powers of Orientalism and the patriarchy. Her writing is subtly connected to a tradition of female Fang resistance to authority, and through this connection, Mekuy finds an inheritance that can be re-imagined for a post-colonial, globalized world.

THE OTHER RESPONDS IN MONTSERRAT ABUMALHAM'S ¿*TE ACUERDAS DE SHAHRAZAD?*

Montserrat Abumalham Mas is of Lebanese origin, but was born in Tétouan, Morocco, and she is currently a professor emeritus of Arabic and Islamic Studies in the Philology Department at the Universidad Complutense de Madrid.[147] The novel considered here, *¿Te acuerdas de Shahrazad?* (2001),[148] is her first work of fiction; she has one other fictional work *De la ceiba y* *el quetzal*,¹⁴⁹ published in 2016. Her academic work, however, is extensive, including some thirty plus articles and the book *El Islam* (1999). Her articles focus on issues of Islam and Arabic in a variety of issues from poetry to immigration, and she has also published on Judeo-Arabic and the Arabic-Christian Bible.¹⁵⁰ Pedro Martínez Montávez, in the prologue to the novel, praises Abumalham's academic work as insightful and illuminating and her fiction as "well-conceived, organized, and composed"¹⁵¹ and drawing masterfully on the tradition of Arabic literature.

¿*Te acuerdas de Shahrazad?* reflects the academic work of Abumalham in drawing on a variety of literary traditions from the traditional tale of *The Arabian Nights* to the Egyptian writer Taufiq al-Hakim's play *Shahrazad* (1934) and contemporary Lebanese literature by authors such as Yubran Jalil Yubran, Mijail Naima, and Iliya Abu-Madi.¹⁵² The novel shares the epistolary genre with Spanish authors such as Carmen Martín Gaite's *Nubosidad variable* (1992)¹⁵³ and Olga Guirao's *Carta con diez años de retraso* (2002),¹⁵⁴ among others,¹⁵⁵ and similarities can also be seen in Abumalham's work and other contemporary Hispanophone Moroccan literature such as Ahmed Daoudi's *El diablo de Yudis* (1994),¹⁵⁶ Mohamed Bouissef Rekab's *La señora* (2006),¹⁵⁷ and Larbi el-Harti's *Después de Tánger* (2003),¹⁵⁸ the latter two of which were published after Abumalham's novel. Thematic similarities between Abumalham and these other Hispanophone Moroccan authors partially justify my analysis of her novel within this study. Though Abumalham is of Lebanese heritage, she grew up in Morocco and Spain,¹⁵⁹ and her primary language of professional and literary expression is Spanish. She represents a growing group of authors from Arabic backgrounds that choose to write in Spanish and for a predominantly Western audience.¹⁶⁰ As Abumalham draws on Arabic literary archetypes and stories, and expresses them in Spanish, her representation of this cultural (and literary) Other contributes directly to the current study.

¿*Te acuerdas de Shahrazad?* contributes to this chapter specifically in its invocation and representation of the literary archetype of Shahrazad.¹⁶¹ As the central female protagonist of the novel, and as a literary and cultural Other, this representation of the mythical Arabic storyteller will serve for an analysis of the writing of gender and the Other in Spanish letters by a Moroccan-born author. Additionally, one of the most apparent characteristics of the novel warrants a preliminary justification: this novel never explicitly locates itself geographically. Neither does Shahrazad as narrator divulge her location or telling details about her identity. This geographical ambiguity continues the literary tradition of Shahrazad as pan-Arabic rather than belonging to one specific country or people. In *Scheherazade Goes West*, Fatema Mernissi talks at length about "Scheherazade" and *The Arabian Nights*, how it has been adopted by individual storytellers throughout its history as a story passed along orally. Mernissi's grandmother, and various translations, place it as originating in Basra and Baghdad and also occurring in lands that have been interpreted as East Africa, "the land of the Amazons," the "Seychelles, Madagascar, or Malacca, and still others situate it in China or Indonesia."[162] To further contribute to the ambiguous geographicality of Shahrazad, the first editors of a written version of *The Arabian Nights* were French (1704) and the first edition in Arabic came from Calcutta, India, more than a hundred years later in 1814.[163]

Indeed, Shahrazad has, for centuries, fascinated and seduced the West.[164] As a literary archetype, she represents the erotic allure of the Muslim woman. Mernissi describes this seduction as an erotic and spiritual weapon that overcomes the West:

> Scheherazade [achieves] what the Muslims who had fought the Crusaders failed to do: She ravished the Christians, from devout Catholics to Protestants and the Greek Orthodox, using only words: "Versions . . . appeared in England, Germany, Italy, Holland, Denmark, Russia, and Belgium." . . . The subjugation of Christian souls by Scheherazade's tales was so satanically pervasive that ensuing translations . . . reached a staggering number.[165]

Shahrazad, therefore, represents, and has represented for centuries, a cultural and religious Other that has both tempted and corrupted Western hegemonic morality. As this geographically ambiguous Other, she belongs as much to the oral tradition of the Maghreb as she does to Mesopotamia and Southern Asia. Additionally, by employing the figure of Sharazad and not explicitly locating the narrator or the space within the text, Abumalham participates in a tradition common to other recent works by Hispanophone Moroccan authors. Ahmed Daoudi's novel *El diablo de Yudis* occurs in an invented land—the island of Yudis and the continent of Burwilasch and has a street storyteller at its center,[166] Mohamed Bouiseff Rekab's *La Señora* is a figure that echoes the erotic qualities of Shahrazad's tales, and Larbi el-Harti's *Después de Tánger* contains "the sensuality of The Thousand and One Nights."[167] Abumalham's text shares much in common with these other contemporary Hispanophone Moroccan authors, and represents the important distinction of also being the work of a female author. Not only does Abumalham represent a cultural Other but also a gendered Other within a canon of predominantly male voices.[168]

In returning to the idea of Shahrazad as a Maghrebi literary archetype, the question of the ambiguous geographical location within the novel and also its timelessness becomes relevant to this study for its very quality of ambiguity. *¿Te acuerdas de Shahrazad?* contributes specifically to this study on works about Africa as a work by a Hispanophone Maghrebi author invoking Arabic literary archetypes, writing in Spanish, and de-emphasizing the specific geography of the plot.[169] The Maghreb, Spain, Europe, and the Middle East are all implicitly invoked while none is privileged. Arabic literary ideas written in a European language merge Same and Other into a single narrative. This singularity makes Abumalham's novel a necessary inclusion in this study. *¿Te acuerdas de Shahrazad?* is a novel that overturns the hegemony of Orientalist discourse; the Western and the Oriental are melded into a masterful, intercultural text that gives voice to the cultural Other and speaks to a Western public.

In its short 65 pages, the archetype of Shahrazad is the (almost) sole narrative voice. It is an epistolary novel and comprised of 46 letters written by the presumed Shahrazad. These letters are prefaced by a two-page narration that recounts in brief the story of Shahrazad as found in *The Arabian Nights* and offers context for the letters that follow. The recipient of the letters is described as "a man who was not a king, but lived in a kingdom as far away as the final mists of the human soul."[170] He is sad, lonely, lovelorn, desperate, and, one day, finds a letter from an unknown writer in his mailbox.[171] At first, he is unsure of what to do with these letters from an unknown writer; they are neither provocative nor remarkably comforting:

> It was neither a long nor a short letter. Neither was it concise nor protracted. Neither was it respectful nor daring. Nor extravagant nor vulgar. He didn't know what to think about that letter that was neither anonymous nor from known signature. At the end of the text appeared only a name: Shahrazad.[172]

The letters that comprise the novel are only those of Shahrazad; the man's responses—if he wrote any—are not included. The unnamed narrator employs the first person in the final paragraph of this introduction, as is common with the epistolary genre, to take credit for the organization of the text,[173] and this editorial voice asserts an attempt at fidelity.[174] The first of these semi-anonymous letters is dated April 27 and they are dated approximately eight days apart each, covering a year and five months with the penultimate letter dated September 8 and the final letter "undated."[175] These unrequested letters become very meaningful to the recipient, even as he is unable to respond because there is no return address included.

The choice of the epistolary genre contributes to the narrative's effect in a number of ways. It contributes a sense of intimacy to the narration—the letters are ostensibly meant for the eyes of the "sad man" alone. As Rueda notes, in "El poder de la carta privada,"[176] "epistolary production problematizes the dichotomies between fiction and reality, private and public space, truth and falsity, past and present, character and author."[177] In addition, the very concept of a text composed of letters implies a sense of distance between letter-writer and recipient, what Rueda calls "epistolary distance."[178] Abumalham appears cognizant of these generic qualities, and exploits their potential actively. In the initial chapter introducing the letters, she begins retelling the story of Shahrazad with the line referencing a kingdom as far away as "the most profound folds of the human heart."[179] A couple of paragraphs later, as the narrator describes the sad man who receives the letters, he is depicted as living in a kingdom as far away as "the final mists of the human soul."[180] Shahrazad's first letter emphasizes that "Your kingdom is too far away,"[181] and her letters repeatedly employ adjectives of distance, both literal and metaphorical.

Abumalham's narration is ambiguous, as the epistolary genre is also in its false intimacy, reality, etc. It contains descriptions that are full of neither-nor constructions: "neither serious nor laughing out loud"[182] or unimportant conjecture: "Each one can put the excuse that seems best to them; he was timid and did not dare to say anything to her . . . or a thousand and one other possibilities."[183] And in the second paragraph of the first letter, Shahrazad writes that "There are always differences between reality and fiction."[184] Past and present become confused as Shahrazad retells memories from her childhood, and as the diegetic editor of the text admits that complete fidelity to the order of the letters is impossible due to their lack of the year. Montserrat Abumalham effectively exploits the characteristics of the epistolary genre to establish a narrative ambiguity and to imbue the text with a sense of geographical distance and personal solitude.

This imbued sense of distance also subtly implicates Otherness within the text. Shahrazad is an Other literary archetype, emblematic of the Orient. Abumalham's Shahrazad makes allusions that invoke non-European characteristics or sources. She casually mentions wearing a veil in her youth,[185] she tells the tale of a woman "as black as the night" (18),[186] and she references "the Oriental poets."[187] Her emphasis on the distance that separates her from the sad man also implies that he is Other, from a different "kingdom." The description of his kingdom as being "as far away as the final mists of the human soul"[188] juxtaposes an indecipherability from obscuring mists and also an emphasis on shared human qualities in the soul. The reader can assume that Shahrazad is Other, but there is no way to know exactly from where she writes. Neither is the identity of the man clear aside from his residence in a "faraway kingdom." This absence of explicit geographical referents avoids privileging one culture over its Other, while admitting that Otherness is an element of this interchange. While there are hints that Shahrazad is Oriental or African, the reader cannot know with certainty.

In fact, by employing Shahrazad as the main narrator, Abumalham effects a subtle coup over the hegemonic paradigm of West/Other. The tale of the mythical/traditional Shahrazad is fraught with nuances, and Mernissi describes one such "subversive," nuanced coup that her tale implies:

If we admit that Shahrayar and Scheherazade represent the cosmic conflict between Day (the masculine as objective order, the realm of the law) and Night (the feminine as subjective order, the realm of desire), then the fact that the King does not kill the queen leaves Muslim men in unbearable uncertainty regarding the outcome of battle. "By allowing Scheherazade to stay alive, the King suspends the law he established himself," writes [Abdesslam] Cheddadi. Paradoxically, it is Shahrayar, the male, who becomes paralyzed, by granting Scheherazade the right to live, speak, and thrive.[189]

The traditional Shahrazad has been analyzed as a powerful figure that subverts male hegemonic power and overturns the male/female hierarchy through her cunning manipulation of Shahrayar. Abumalham's Shahrazad also beguiles a male subject—not only is he her gendered Other, he is also her cultural Other, an inhabitant of the faraway kingdom.

In addition, Mernissi's dichotomy of "the masculine as objective order, the realm of law" and "the feminine as subjective order, the realm of desire" echoes Orientalist discourse of the "Oriental character" as one defined by "Oriental despotism, Oriental sensuality, and the like" contrasted to the rationalism of the West.[190] Mernissi's dichotomy can easily be paraphrased as "the *West* as objective order, the realm of law" and "the *Orient* as subjective order, the realm of desire," and this platitude is found repeatedly in Said's *Orientalism*:

> On the one hand there are Westerners, and on the other there are Arab-Orientals; the former are (in no particular order) rational, peaceful, liberal, logical, capable of holding real values, without natural suspicion; the latter are none of these things.[191]

Abumalham effectively extends the discourse for Otherness from one of gender relations to one of cultural Otherness. Just as the Shahrazad of *The Arabian Nights* threatens hegemonic masculinity through subtle feminine agency, so does Shahrazad of *¿Te acuerdas de Shahrazad?* speak as a cultural Other, displacing the narrative authority of the West.

The power of Shahrazad's voice is amplified through the generic convention of the epistolary novel. The sad man has no voice; his letters are not included, and the geographical anonymity of Shahrazad also robs him of his opportunity to respond. This narrative dominance, however, is unassuming and subtle. The effect is that this voice of the Other does not wish to silence response, but rather create its own space for expression. The narrator of the first chapter, after mentioning that the sad man did not have an address to which respond, also suggests that this did not, perhaps, stop the man from responding.[192] In addition, while the letters do not leave textual space for a response, the narrator—Shahrazad—leaves temporal space for a response by invoking the nightly stories of the original Shahrazad. Each letter concludes with a variation of "It dawns and I should be quiet. If my lord esteems it appropriate, I will continue tomorrow."[193] As Mernissi notes, in the quotation above, the night is Shahrazad's and the day is left for a response. This allusion to the original Shahrazad also emphasizes that this process of expression, writing the letters, is a matter of extreme importance—as the original Shahrazad employed her story-telling to delay her own execution. As for Abumalham's Shahrazad, she also lives through her words, and it is not a desire to silence her Other, but to assert her own existence. The final letter and the novel itself concludes with the following lines:

> However, I have lived and I have died various times. But, above all, I have lived. My life has been full and it has been thanks to you. I started these letters thinking about giving you life, what a vanity of mine! and life you have given to me. While I breathe, my breath of life will always be yours, because mine is the word, the only reason for life, and because yours is silence and, without silence, the word does not exist.
>
> Now it is not important if there are other dawns, now Shahrazad does not have to fight to save her life, she has won. Shahrazad is alive, even if she dies.[194]

Shahrazad's opportunity to speak to her Other validates her efforts. Her words gave her a "razón de vida" and they were deeply meaningful to the sad man who died holding her written words close. It is also significant that she abandons the first-person voice, emphasizing that the process of letter writing ensures survival by suggesting that Shahrazad will live forever, or at the very least outlive the epistolographer.

Indeed, the novel functions as a call for attention, to hear the voice of this cultural Other. From the title, which is a direct question, to the repetition of "¿Te acuerdas de Shahrazad?" in the initial chapter and as the first line of the first letter, the text asks for recognition of this Oriental archetype from its Western, Spanish-speaking audience. The first letter even gives the sad man directions on how to read the letter and what to expect: "But you should be patient and constant. You should not skip over lines. You should read each one of the letters, because there are no idle letters."[195] It offers a gentle, coaxing voice that offers to guide rather than forcefully demanding recognition. The letters also question the authenticity of this Other voice:

> Am I my name, am I a name? If you call me tree, will I be a tree or will I keep being a woman? If I am Shahrazad, am I a woman, a voice, a word, a dream, a figment of your imagination? Am I the one who writes to you or is it yourself that pretends to write a letter and later reads it as if it came from afar, forcing me with your fiction to be, without me actually existing?
>
> Is this literature?[196]

The text self-referentially questions whether it is an authentic voice of this cultural Other, or another creation of the Orient by the West. By questioning the authenticity of its own voice, the novel avoids the trap of making this specific representation authoritative. Its self-questioning both speaks for the Orient, and subtly suggests that the process of representation is problematic and authenticity is difficult to achieve and/or verify.

This narrative humility, and daily self-silencing is a subtle power play. Shahrazad's demure narration is also a strategy of seduction. By ending each letter *in media res*, she employs the same element of suspense that the historical literary Shahrazad used to prolong her life. In this sense, her feigned humility represents the personal agency and affective power of the narrator over her audience. Strategic use of seduction and suspense functions to engage the narrator's target audience. In this, Abumalham draws directly on the example of the original Shahrazad.

These two narrative characteristics also leave (metaphorical) space for an Other to speak, and they refrain the text from serving as an authoritative view of an essentialized Other. Primarily, they serve to counterbalance the geographical non-specificity of the novel, which could be interpreted as a universalized representation of the West's Other. By not specifying Shahrazad's location or origin, there is the danger that she comes to represent and speak for a more generalized population. The functioning dynamic of such an interpretation would therefore be an essentialized binary between the West and the Orient, or, drawing on the analyses of *The Arabian Nights*, the binary of men and women. Chandra Mohanty notes the problematic nature of such reductive reasoning in gender studies, as Daniel Varisco does in Said's work, and both agree that such "simplistic formulations are historically reductive. . . . All they do is reinforce binary divisions between men and women [or the West and its Other]."[197] However, Abumalham and her Shahrazad both seem to be aware of these dangers and therefore take steps to avoid a totalizing narrative. Just as Shahrazad questions who the true diegetic author of the letters is, so does she continually recognize inconsistencies and Others within herself: "Maybe one day, I will have the strength to . . . recognize the person that I was or that lived inside of me. / . . . Maybe you are always someone different from who you are before you, and you are used to co-existing with an other different I that acts autonomously."[198] She recognizes the Other within herself, and furthermore, questions the very constructions of West and Orient: "The children of the West dream that the Magi from the East fill them with gifts. Meanwhile, what do the children of the East dream? . . . In short, a key question: where is the Orient, if in each land, that lives ignorant of the other lands, there is an East and a West?"[199] Shahrazad individualizes conceptualizations of the West and the Orient. Even though Shahrazad as an archetype invokes generalizations of the emblematic and seductive storyteller, reductively representing the Orient, and the geographic non-specificity of the novel also universalizes the potential representative power of her voice, Abumalham's Shahrazad is conscious of the subjective nature of such representations and addresses them directly.

Just as the traditional Shahrazad both embodies and subverts hegemonic binary divisions—on the one hand by employing the seductive female archetype and on the other by simultaneously breaking the "law of the father" (the king) in liberating all women from their death—so does Abumalham's narrator assume a role yet nuances its implementation. Abumalham's Shahrazad questions her own existence—"Am I the one who writes to you or is it yourself that pretends to write a letter and later reads it?"[200]—she also questions the existence of the recipient of her letters: "Man or ghost of my imagination? . . . / It is possible that you are my invention and for that I love you as I love myself."[201] This "ghost"[202] seduces her in one of her letters and she revels in "the creative grace of the word."[203] Just as her literary predecessor, this Shahrazad understands the power of words. For this reason, she fills her narration with ambiguity and self-reflection, constantly questioning her own authenticity and authority to represent.

Abumalham's Shahrazad is Other in both gender and culture, and yet the external reader is left unknowing whether she is an authentic spokeswoman for these Others, or whether she is a creation of the Western mind. The generic convention of the epistolary novel promises intimacy and confession, and what is subtly confessed is an inability to write objectively. Words are powerful tools; for the original Shahrazad, they hold the power of life and death. For this Shahrazad, they are potent tools of creation that must be wielded with caution. Abumalham's text invokes many things—questions of gender, culture, interpersonal relationships, the act of writing—but it maintains a tone of ambiguity that rejects supreme authority over any grand narrative.

As a novel by a Hispano-Libano-Moroccan—a Maghrebi—author, *¿Te acuerdas de Shahrazad?* does represent the voice of a cultural Other speaking to a Western audience. Abumalham's Shahrazad does not assume this task lightly. The use of letters as a novelistic format inherently leaves open the possibility for response, for communication and exchange between cultures and individuals. But this is Shahrazad's opportunity to speak (more specifically, in this case to write), and her words do not seek to merely create a "simple *inversion* of what exists" by establishing predominance over the Other.[204] Instead, Shahrazad opens a nuanced "dialogue" that privileges neither and is cautious in its own assumptions. The reader is introduced to the text through a question—*¿Te acuerdas de Shahrazad?*—and at the end the question remains unresolved. The Western reader is presented with a complex, compassionate, and unassuming Other that speaks forcefully and carefully. Abumalham's text is masterful in its nuance, effectively undermining the power of Orientalist discourse by giving written, and therefore legible and enduring, voice to Shahrazad and by avoiding the pitfalls of a potential reverse Orientalism.

NOTES

1. [*Diary of a Witness of the War of Africa*]
2. [La Mitología, siempre reveladora, nos la representa en una mujer bizarra, de porte oriental, casi desnuda, sentada sobre un elefante (símbolo de sus interminables desiertos), teniendo en una mano el cuerno de la abundancia, como recordando su vivaz y opulenta vegetación, y un escorpión en la otra, para significar que en ella todos los dones de la Naturaleza, lejos de producir la vida, dan la muerte, y que su aire, su tierra, su agua, su sol y sus habitantes, todo es nocivo, espantable y ponzoñoso— . . . en ella reside lo nuevo, lo temeroso, lo estraño, lo desconocido.] Alarcón, *Diario de un testigo*, 11.
3. [al asentar mi planta en esta parte del Mundo . . . no puedo menos de doblar la rodilla, poniendo el pensamiento en mi Dios y en mi madre patria, y exclamar. . . . —¡*África, ya eres mía!*] Alarcón, *Diario de un testigo*, 11.
4. Mariano Fortuny i Marsal (1838–1874) was a Spanish painter whose work was both largely Romantic and Orientalist in composition. In the first War of Africa, he was charged with painting the Spanish campaigns in Morocco. For more information, see James Thompson and David Scott's work *The East Imagined, Experienced, Remembered: Orientalist Nineteenth Century Paintings* (Dublin: National Gallery of Ireland, 1988).
5. In *Disorientations*, Martin-Márquez suggests that the composition of Fortuny's odalisque paintings "serves to entrap and immobilize the imperialist viewer. Thus, Fortuny's odalisques consistently function to destabilize the racialized and gendered power structures that were so essential to Orientalist works of the period" (371). While this dynamic may be true, Fortuny does deliberately employ the trope of Oriental sensuality as a marketable quality for a Western audience.
6. [lo nuevo, lo temeroso, lo estraño, lo desconocido] Alarcón, *Diario de un testigo*, 11.
7. Varisco, *Reading Orientalism*, 55.
8. Varisco, *Reading Orientalism*, 25.
9. "Morita" is the diminutive for "mora," a female "moor."
10. Aixa is a common Muslim name. Aisha bint Abu Bakr (612–678) was one of Muhammed's wives. It is also often transcribed as A'ishah, Aisyah, Ayesha, A'isha, Aishat, Aishah, or Aisha. See Denise Spellberg's *Politics, Gender, and the Islamic Past: The Legacy of A'isha Bint Abi Bakr* (New York: Columbia University Press, 1994).
11. [Indecisa y trémula, filtrándose como un poco de luz por el verde tabique de los rosales. Si Aixa fuera una muchacha europea me recordaría como un tonto; tan acobardado, inexpresivo e inmóvil me figuro a mí mismo en aquel momento. Tuve la gran suerte de que Aixa no fuese una señorita de la buena sociedad, acostumbrada a medir la timidez de sus pretendientes, sino una morita de apenas quince años. . .

. Estaba sin velos y era como una chuchería recién comprada a la que acababan de quitar la envoltura de papel de seda. Morena. Pero una morenez de melocotón no muy maduro, con esa pelusa que hace la piel de la fruta tan parecida a piel de mujer.] Díaz Fernández, *El blocao* (1928. Reprint, Madrid: Viamonte, 1998), 24–25.

12. [*The Time in Between*]

13. [*The Three Virgins of Saint Thomas*]

14. [*Do You Remember Shahrazad?*]

15. See the beginning of the specific sections on these works for a brief summary of their editorial success.

16. See Reina Lewis *Gendering Orientalism: Race, Femininity, and Representation* (New York: Routledge, 1996) or Barbara Hodgson *Dreaming of East: Western Women and the Exotic Allure of the Orient* (Berkeley: Greystone Books, 2005) for works dealing with gender and the Orient.

17. Georges Van den Abbeele, *Travel as Metaphor* (Minneapolis: University of Minneapolis Press, 1992), xxv.

18. Abbeele, *Travel as Metaphor*, xxv.

19. Fatema Mernissi, *Scheherazade Goes West: Different Cultures, Different Harems* (New York: Washington Square Press, 2001), 61–64.

20. [De esta manera, África será siempre el imán de las imaginaciones ardientes] Alarcón, *Diario de un testigo*, 11.

21. Marta Eulalia Martí, "Pasión por la lectura en su año internacional," *Granadadigital.com*, April 25, 2012.

22. *María Dueñas*, Ediciones Planeta Madrid, S.A., 2020, accessed April 16, 2020, www.mariaduenas.es.

23. The English translation of *Misión olvido* (Madrid: Atria Books, 2014) is titled *The Heart Has Its Reasons* (Farmington Hills, Michigan: Thorndike Press, 2014).

24. The English translation of *La Templanza* (Madrid: Atria Books, 2015) is titled *The Vineyard* (New York: Washington Square Press, 2018).

25. [*The Captain's Daughters*] María Dueñas, *Las hijas del capitán* (New York: Harper Collins Español, 2019).

26. Dueñas, screenplay for *El tiempo entre costuras*, Antena 3 Televisión, 2012.

27. The Spanish Protectorate of Morocco was officially established in 1912 by the Treaty of Fez and ended with the recognition of Moroccan independence in 1956. See Villanova's *El Protectorado de España en Marruecos: Organización política y territorial* (Barcelona: Edicions Bellaterra, 2004) for more information.

28. [Las convenciones de la vida académica a la que llevo vinculada más de veinte años exigen a los autores reconocer sus fuentes de manera ordenada y rigurosa.] Dueñas, *El tiempo entre costuras*, 633.

29. [Para recomponer con fidelidad los escenarios de Tánger y Tetuán en esos días, he recurrido sobre todo de los testimonios de aquellos que vivieron ese entorno y ese tiempo en primera persona: algunos de los miembros de la Asociación La Medina y, sobre todo, mi propia familia materna, residente durante décadas en el Protectorado. Gracias a los recuerdos cargados de nostalgia de todos ellos, los personajes de la novela han podido recorrer las calles, los rincones y el pálpito de nuestro pasado colonial en el norte de África, un contexto casi desvanecido de la memoria colectiva

y apenas evocado en la narrativa española contemporánea.] María Dueñas, "El tiempo entre costuras—María Dueñas," accessed April 29, 2020, *eltiempoentrecosturas. blogspot.com.*

30. [recuerdos cargados de nostalgia] Dueñas, *eltiempoentrecosturas.blogspot.com*

31. Here the term is not as sexualized as in the context of Díaz Fernández's *El blocao*, but rather refers to a young, unmarried Moroccan girl.

32. [A todos los antiguos residentes del Protectorado español en Marruecos y a los marroquíes que con ellos convivieron.] Dueñas, *El tiempo entre costuras*, 9.

33. As already examined in chapter 1, and as articulated by Rueda in "El enemigo 'invisible' de la Guerra de África," 147.

34. Memmi's seminal *The Colonizer and the Colonized* (1965) examines the ways in which "every colonizer is privileged" over the indigenous inhabitants within the colonial sphere (11). Therefore, to clarify, even though the protagonist Sira Quiroga is initially a poor and helpless individual, her mere status as a European offers her opportunity not available to the Moroccan colonial population. Dueñas focuses primarily on the social and economic divisions among Europeans, but it is important to consider the relativity of such a representation in the colonial context.

35. [cargado de nostalgia]

36. In discussing the colonizer, Memmi suggests that "leaving for a colony is not a choice sought because of its uncertain dangers, nor is it a desire of one tempted by adventure. It is simply a voyage towards an easier life" (*The Colonizer and the Colonized*, 3), and offers the "best possible definition of a colony: a place where one earns more and spends less" (4). This opportunity is so lucrative that Memmi believes that "the colonialist knows that in his own country he would be nothing; he would go back to being a mediocre man" (61).

37. [No era un nombre árabe en absoluto, pero sonaba extraño y no resultaría sospechoso en Madrid, donde nadie tenía idea de cómo se llamaba la gente allá por la tierra mora.] Dueñas, *El tiempo entre costuras*, 388.

38. Kristyn Gorton, "(Un)fashionable Feminists: The Media and Ally McBeal," in *Third Wave Feminism: A Critical Exploration*, eds. Stacy Gillis, Gillian Howie, and Rebecca Mumford (New York: Palgrave Macmillan, 2007), 212.

39. Chandra Talpade Mohanty, *Feminism Without Borders: Decolonizing Theory, Practicing Solidarity* (Durham, North Carolina: Duke University Press, 2003), 8.

40. Mohanty, *Feminism Without Borders*, 19

41. Linda McDowell, "Place and Space," in *A Concise Companion to Feminist Theory*, ed. Mary Eagleton (Blackwell Publishing Ltd, 2003), 13.

42. Abbeele, *Travel as Metaphor*, xvi.

43. Mohanty examines the subordinate categories of nature:culture::female:male further in *Feminism Without Borders*, 36.

44. Said, *Orientalism*, 7.

45. [A Marruecos; iros al Protectorado, es un buen sitio para vivir. Un sitio tranquilo donde, desde el final de la guerra con los moros, nunca pasa nada. Empezad una vida nueva lejos de este país enloquecido, porque el día menos pensado va a estallar algo tremendo y aquí no va a quedar nadie vivo.] Dueñas, *El tiempo entre costuras*, 52.

46. Dueñas, *El tiempo entre costuras*, 56.

47. [A cambio de su impuesta presencia . . . España había proporcionado a Marruecos avances en equipamientos, sanidad y obras, y los primeros pasos hacia una moderada mejora de la explotación agrícola. Y una escuela de artes y oficios tradicionales. Y todo aquello que los nativos pudieran obtener de beneficio en las actividades destinadas a satisfacer a la población colonizadora: el tendido eléctrico, el agua potable, escuelas y academias, comercios, el transporte público, dispensarios y hospitales, el tren que unía Tetuán con Ceuta, el que aún llevaba a la playa de Río Martín. España de Marruecos, en términos materiales, había conseguido muy poco.] Dueñas, *El tiempo entre costuras*, 201.

48. [En términos humanos . . . sí había obtenido algo importante para uno de los dos bandos de la contienda civil: miles de soldados de las fuerzas indígenas marroquíes que en aquellos días luchaban como fieras al otro lado del Estrecho por la causa ajena del ejército sublevado.] Dueñas, *El tiempo entre costuras*, 201.

49. Ramón Serrano Suñer, "el Cuñadíssimo" [the exalted brother-in-law], was the Interior and Foreign Affairs Minister and the President of the Falangist caucus (Falange Española Tradicionalista de las JONS) under Francisco Franco. He was brother-in-law to Franco as they both married sisters. He was pro-Third Reich before and during World War II. See Ignacio Merino, *Serrano Suñer: Conciencia y poder* (Madrid: Algaba Ediciones, 2004), for a biography and Wayne H. Bowen, *Spaniards and Nazi Germany: Collaboration in the New Order* (Columbia, Missouri: University of Missouri Press, 2000), for an examination of Spain's collaboration with Nazi Germany.

50. Johannes Berhardt was the head of a German mining consortium in Spain, seeking to obtain mining rights for tungsten, used in making missiles. See Stanley G. Payne, *Franco and Hitler: Spain, Germany, and World War II* (New Haven: Yale University Press, 2008) for a detailed history of the German-Spanish relations of World War II, specifically the chapter "Neutrality by Compulsion," 236–252.

51. Dueñas, *El tiempo entre costuras*, 226.

52. Dueñas, *El tiempo entre costuras*, 351.

53. See Payne, 47 or Charles R. Halstead, "A 'Somewhat Machiavellian' Face: Colonel Juan Beigbeder as High Commissioner in Spanish Morocco, 1937–1939" (*Historian* 37, no. 1 [1974]: 46–66).

54. [ilustre africanista y profundo conocedor del islam] Dueñas, *El tiempo entre costuras*, 352.

55. Dueñas, *El tiempo entre costuras*, 436.

56. Dueñas, *El tiempo entre costuras*, 200.

57. Dueñas, *El tiempo entre costuras*, 88.

58. Dueñas, *El tiempo entre costuras*, 104.

59. Dueñas, *El tiempo entre costuras*, 133.

60. [a quién demonios importa de dónde vienes cuando eres la mejor modista de todo Marruecos.] Dueñas, *El tiempo entre costuras*, 264.

61. Dueñas, *El tiempo entre costuras*, 339.

62. [con la ilusión de dar a mi taller madrileño un aire exótico en concordancia con mi nuevo nombre y mi supuesto pasado de prestigiosa modista tangerina. . . . Un

pedacito de África en el centro del mapa de la exhausta España.] Dueñas, *El tiempo entre costuras*, 415.

63. [a la manera moruna] Dueñas, *El tiempo entre costuras*, 419.
64. [pintarse los ojos con khol] Dueñas, *El tiempo entre costuras*, 419.
65. [para dar a su presencia un aire exótico] Dueñas, *El tiempo entre costuras*, 419.
66. [falso exotismo] Dueñas, *El tiempo entre costuras*, 419.
67. [protegida por la armadura de mi falso exotismo.] Dueñas, *El tiempo entre costuras*, 419.
68. Dueñas, *El tiempo entre costuras*, 416.
69. Dueñas, *El tiempo entre costuras*, 416.
70. [Quizá no lo hice por nadie o tan sólo por mí misma] Dueñas, *El tiempo entre costuras*, 416.
71. [armadura] Dueñas, *El tiempo entre costuras*, 419.
72. [Record of a Journey from Paris to Jerusalem]
73. Said, *Orientalism*, 174.
74. Said, *Orientalism*, 182.
75. Varisco, *Reading Orientalism*, 297.
76. Varisco, *Reading Orientalism*, 298.
77. Dueñas, *El tiempo entre costuras*, 605.
78. [—¿No ha estado nunca en Marruecos?

—No. Y lo lamento; sobre todo si todas las marroquíes son como usted.

—Es un país fascinante de gente maravillosa, pero me temo que le sería difícil encontrar allí muchas mujeres como yo. Soy una marroquí atípica porque mi madre es española. No soy musulmana y mi lengua materna no es el árabe, sino el español. Pero adoro Marruecos.] Dueñas, *El tiempo entre costuras*, 512.

79. [posiblemente decía en esta lengua bastantes sandeces, habida cuenta de que a menudo repetía simples expresiones retenidas a fuerza de haberlas oído en las calles de Tánger y Tetuán, pero cuyo sentido y uso exacto desconocía.] Dueñas, *El tiempo entre costuras*, 419.
80. V. Y. Mudimbe, *The Idea of Africa* (Indianapolis: Indiana University Press, 1994), xi.
81. Gorton, "(Un)fashionable Feminists," 212.
82. Mohanty, *Feminism Without Borders*, 3.
83. Mohanty, *Feminism Without Borders*, 31.
84. The Fang ethnic group represents almost 85% of the total population of Equatorial Guinea, and signifcant Fang populations can also be found in Cameroon and Gabon. The Fang comprise the majority ethnic group on mainland Equatorial Guinea, while the Bubi primarily inhabit Bioko Island, Equatorial Guinea (Young, "Bubi," 206–207 and "Fang," 460. In *The Encyclopedia of Africa, Vol. 1*, eds. Anthony Appiah and Henry Louis Gates [Oxford: Oxford University Press, 2010]). Eric Young writes in the *Encyclopedia of Africa* that "In Spanish Guinea, colonial officials favored the Bubi and perpetuated the myth of Fang primitivism. . . . Some Fang resisted outright the European intrusion and in 1926 formed the Elarayong movement in Cameroon to create unity within the Fang nation" (460).

85. [*The Cry of the Bitch*] Guillermina Mekuy, *El llanto de la perra* (Barcelona: Random House Mondadori, 2005).
86. Elisa G. Rizo, "Entrevista a Guillermina Mekuy Mba Obono," *Revista Iberoamericana* LXXX, nos. 248–249 (2014): 1134.
87. [*The Three Virgins of Saint Thomas*]
88. [*Three Souls for a Heart*] Guillermina Mekuy, *Tres almas para un corazón* (Madrid: Grupo Planeta, 2011).
89. Marvin Lewis, *An Introduction to the Literature of Equatorial Guinea* (Columbia, Missouri, University of Missouri Press, 2007), 109 and Marta Sofía López Rodríguez, "(Des)Madres e hijas: De *Ekomo* a *El llanto de la perra*," *Afroeuropa* 2, no. 2 (2008): 9.
90. ['hijas,' o ya casi 'las nietas'] López Rodríguez, "(Des)Madres e hijas," 1.
91. Nobile, "María Nsué Angüe y Guillermina Mekuy De la escritura femenina en Guinea Ecuatorial a la construcción de una matria migrante," In the proceedings of the XXXVIII Congreso Internacional del Instituto International de Literatura Iberoamericana, Georgetown University, June 9–12, 2010.
92. [autoras (que) han ampliado notablemente el horizonte temático y estilístico creado por sus antecesoras, incluyendo asuntos como la experiencia de la progresiva urbanización del continente, la aportación de perspectivas globales y transnacionales sobre la política y la economía africanas, la defensa explícita del ideario mujerista y/o feminista que sus mayores abrazaban con más reticencias, el tratamiento abierto de cuestiones sexuales o la profundización en las intersecciones entre el ámbito de lo público y lo privado en sus naciones de origen, poniendo especial énfasis en denunciar las estructuras de dominación y poder tiránico que afectan por igual al conjunto de la sociedad y a los individuos que la componen.] López Rodríguez, "(Des)Madres e hijas," 2.
93. Recent years have brought some new additions to this list. Victoria Evita Ika's *Kanga: La tierra de los sueños* [*Kanga: The Land of Dreams*] (Madrid: Sial Ediciones, 2016) and *Mokámbo: Aromas de libertad* [*Mokámbo: Aromas of Freedom*] (Majadahonda: Creativa, 2010), Trifonia Melibea Obono's *La bastarda* [*The Bastard*] (2016. Reprint, Madrid: Flores Raras, 2018) and *Las mujeres hablan mucho y mal* [*Women Talk a lot and Badly*] (Madrid: Sial Ediciones, 2018), and O'sírima Mota Ripeu's *El punto ciego de Cassandra* [*Cassandra's Blindspot*] (Madrid: Sial Ediciones, 2017). This is, of course, only a partial list and does not represent the totality of contemporary female authors from Equatorial Guinea. López Rodríguez, "(Des)Madres e hijas," 2.
94. Lewis, *An Introduction to the Literature of Equatorial Guinea*, 109.
95. Joanna Allan's 2019 book *Silenced Resistance: Women Dictatorships, and Genderwashing in Western Sahara and Equatorial Guinea* examines these historical resistances in depth.
96. [reza(r) por los pecados del mundo, manteniendo la pureza de vuestros sexos al margen de los hombres.] Mekuy, *Las tres vírgenes de Santo Tomás*, 19.
97. [el mundo de verdad] Mekuy, *Las tres vírgenes de Santo Tomás*, 83.
98. [unos colonos de los muchos que habían llegado a nuestro pueblo] Mekuy, *Las tres vírgenes de Santo Tomás*, 209.

114   Chapter 2

99. [la gran hechicera blanca] Mekuy, *Las tres vírgenes de Santo Tomás*, 210.

100. [Dado el enorme esfuerzo colectivo que las mujeres africanas, afro-caribeñas y afro-americanas han invertido y continúan invirtiendo en la dignificación de la mujer negra, y el impagable ejemplo de su resistencia común frente a todo tipo de explotación, incluida la explotación de sus cuerpos, resulta profundamente ofensiva esta actitud de sumisión en la narradora de *El llanto de la perra*. La noción de una "esclavitud sexual" asumida de forma voluntaria, desde una posición victimista y autocomplaciente, debería hacer que los huesos de Nora Zeale Hurston, Bessie Head, Mariama Bâ y tantas otras luchadoras por la dignidad de las mujeres negras se revolvieran en sus tumbas.] López Rodríguez, "(Des)Madres e hijas," 9.

101. [literariamente huérfana, hija apócrifa del exilio, y que su novela ha nacido por tanto (des)madrada: desvinculada de la tradición literaria de las mujeres negras, de la cultura origen de la escritora, de la oratura africana no menos que de la narrativa escrita del continente y la diáspora, e indiferente a la trágica historia de (Guinea Ecuatorial).] López Rodríguez, "(Des)Madres e hijas," 10.

102. Boampong, "Reconfigurations of the Female Protagonist in Hispanophone African Literature," 107.

103. Homi Bhabha, *The Location of Culture* (London: Routledge, 2004), 1–2.

104. Bhabha, *The Location of Culture*, 37.

105. Edward W. Soja, *Thirdspace: Journeys to Los Angeles and Other Real-and-Imagined Places* (Malden: Blackwell Publishers, 1996), 126.

106. Boampong, "Reconfigurations of the Female Protagonist in Hispanophone African Literature," 106.

107. Bhabha, *The Location of Culture*, 2.

108. [la pureza de vuestros sexos al margen de los hombres.] Mekuy, *Las tres vírgenes de Santo Tomás*, 19.

109. [un fraile que vivió en el siglo XIII y que consideraba a las mujeres seres biológicamente inferiores a los hombres.] Mekuy, *Las tres vírgenes de Santo Tomás*, 16.

110. [La semilla masculina contiene el poder de reproducción, y la madre sólo proporciona un vientre que da alimento a esa semilla.] Mekuy, *Las tres vírgenes de Santo Tomás*, 21.

111. [Como individuo, la mujer es un ser endeble y defectuoso.] Mekuy, *Las tres vírgenes de Santo Tomás*, 95.

112. Judith Butler, *Gender Trouble* (1990. Reprint, New York: Routledge, 2008), 42.

113. [En ese momento vi el cielo abierto. No el lugar seráfico del que hablaba mi madre, sino la posibilidad de ser libre, de, en nombre de no sé qué revelación o del amor repentino de Teresa, escapar definitivamente. Y lo que era más, convertirme en esa buscadora del placer que me arrastraba y sentía que era la única fuente de vida y que iba a convertirme en una virgen tocada y deseada.] Mekuy, *Las tres vírgenes de Santo Tomás*, 108–19.

114. [—Sólo te pido una cosa: puedes ofrecer tu cuerpo a la lujuria, emular a todas las mujeres del mundo que se han prostituido . . . pero . . . seguirás siendo virgen. Serás deseada, acariciada, lamida, sojuzgada, pero nadie penetrará en ti, ni aun

cuando estés en medio de una orgía de hombres que te quieran poseer y a los que les darás todo menos una cosa: el húmedo tesoro de tu virginidad.

Asentí con un movimiento de cabeza y pensé que le debía eso por haberme ayudado a librarme de vivir, de nuevo y para siempre, prisionera. Pensé además que, de esa forma, cumplía mis más íntimos deseos y que nadie me dominaría, pues sólo yo decidiría lo que podía ser terreno libre para todos.] Mekuy, *Las tres vírgenes de Santo Tomás*, 110.

115. Allan, *Silenced Resistance*, 70.

116. Allan, *Silenced Resistance*, 70.

117. [Era consciente—y más adelante lo sería aún más—de que cuando los hombres me miraban, deseaban poseerme y, sin embargo, era este mismo deseo lo que me daba poder sobre ellos, lo que me daba capacidad de dominarlos, de ser su dueña.] Mekuy, *Las tres vírgenes de Santo Tomás*, 125.

118. [gran hechicera blanca] Mekuy, *Las tres vírgenes de Santo Tomás*, 205.

119. Mekuy, *Las tres vírgenes de Santo Tomás*, 32.

120. Allan, *Silenced Resistance*, 70.

121. [mezclo la cultura africana y la europea a través de una mujer blanca que es la que vive la vida de una africana, porque está metida en el animismo, en las prácticas de la magia negra, la brujería y todo eso. ¿Y por qué lo hice así? Porque al vivir en Europa, teniendo una mujer blanca como protagonista de una novela donde ella sí que actúa con los ritos africanos, es mucho más fácil que la gente entendiera. Si fuera todo una familia negra, la gente diría "bueno, claro típico de cosas de África" y vuelve a ser algo exótico y algo diferente. Pero cuando es una mujer blanca, era muy fácil que la gente se pusiera en la piel de esa mujer porque ya ven en ella algo que otra podría haber hecho. Y luego el que el padre, siendo negro, fuera el que viviera con las prácticas religiosas, era para hacer la crítica.] Rizo, "Entrevista a Guillermina Mekuy," 1135.

122. María Nsué Angüe's *Ekomo* is the first book published in Spanish by an Equatorial Guinean woman (Madrid: Universidad Nacional a Distancia, 1985). In her article "(Des)Madres e hijas: De *Ekomo* a *El llanto de la perra*," Marta Sofía López Rodríguez examines some of the ways in which Mekuy's writing is connected to that of Nsué Angüe, and in how it departs from it.

123. Allan, *Silenced Resistance*, 75.

124. Enrique S. Okenve-Martínez, "Equatorial Guinea 1927–1979: A New African Tradition" (PhD diss., School of Oriental and African Studies, University of London, 2007), 127.

125. Allan, *Silenced Resistance*, 74.

126. Allan, *Silenced Resistance*, 75.

127. Allan, *Silenced Resistance*, 75.

128. James C. Scott, "Everyday Forms of Resistance," *The Copenhagen Journal of Asian Studies*, vol. 4 (1989): 34.

129. [Me gustaba jugar y provocar deseo, y sabía que la fuerza de la provocación y los actos no finalizados me darían más poder sobre los hombres que el sexo consumado. Sabía que la imaginación era el arma más poderosa.] Mekuy, *Las tres vírgenes de Santo Tomás*, 123.

130. Allan, *Silenced Resistance*, 75.

131. [la que algunos considerarían sucia e inmoral, y vi con claridad que, aunque podía ser una pequeña viciosa para la sociedad, para mí era mejor que tantos que vivían en la hipocresía y, en vez de comprar cuerpos, compraban almas. Mejor que aquellos cuyo poder esclavizaba a los que nada tenían y que vivían al margen de cualquier conciencia moral en lo más importante: permitir la libertad y el desarrollo de los que viven en la pobreza y la ignorancia. Lo nuestro eran simplemente juegos inocentes en medio de una sociedad que convertía a los débiles en víctimas y a los poderosos en verdugos, que hacía de la vida no un divertimiento, sino un mercado en el que siempre solían perder los mismos.] Mekuy, *Las tres vírgenes de Santo Tomás*, 155.

132. [juegos inocentes] Mekuy, *Las tres vírgenes de Santo Tomás*, 155.

133. [está involuntariamente reforzando un denigrante estereotipo acerca de la insaciable sensualidad de la mujer negra que la mayoría de las autoras africanas han combatido y denunciado con ferocidad en sus textos.] López Rodríguez, "(Des)Madres e hijas," 7.

134. [*Naked Woman, Black Woman*]

135. Boampong, "Reconfigurations of the Female Protagonist in Hispanophone African Literature," 105.

136. Boampong, "Reconfigurations of the Female Protagonist in Hispanophone African Literature," 106.

137. Allan, *Silenced Resistance*, 89.

138. Allan, *Silenced Resistance*, 90.

139. López Rodríguez, "(Des)Madres e hijas," 7.

140. [La sensualidad sigue siendo algo que a la mujer en sí le corta a la hora de escribir. Pero cuando tú lees los libros escritos por hombres, lo que más emplean de todo eso, pero nadie les cuestiona. Porque son hombres . . . emplean todo tipo de lenguaje, pero como son hombres se les puede perdonar eso. Pero cuando una mujer toca algún aspecto, ya se les cuestiona un poco.] Rizo, "Entrevista a Guillermina Mekuy," 1135.

141. Abbeele, *Travel as Metaphor*, xxv. For examples in Spanish letters, see Eduardo Saavedra y Moraga's or Joaquín Costa y Martínez's descriptions of Morocco in Flores Morales's *África a través del pensamiento español* (89, 170).

142. Said, *Orientalism*, 179, 210, 213, 294.

143. [*Geographies of the Exotic*]

144. [el tratamiento de la temática femenina por parte de la corriente orientalista española enfatiza su vulnerabilidad [la de África] para justificar y alentar la penetración colonial.] Rosa Cerarols Ramírez, *Geografías de lo exótico: El imaginario de Marruecos en la literatura de viajes [1859–1936]* (Barcelona: Edicions Bellaterra, 2015), 226.

145. Gloria Nistal Rosique writes that "Mekuy's writing is fluid, natural, easy to read, with a good handling of childish and adolescent registers in memory, frequent repetitions and a colloquial tone. Both novels follow the pattern of the subgenre known traditionally as melodrama, in which one appreciates a peculiar modernization of the era of the television serials." [La escritura de Mekuy es fluida, natural, fácil de leer, con un buen manejo del lenguaje y de los registros infantiles y adolescentes

en el recuerdo, frecuentes repeticiones y tono coloquial. Ambas novelas (*El llanto de la perra* y *Las tres vírgenes de Santo Tomás*) responden al esquema del subgénero tradicionalmente conocido como melodrama en el que se aprecia una modernización propia de la época de los seriales televisivos.] (Original and translation in Marvin Lewis, *Equatorial Guinean Literature in its National and Transnational Contexts* [Columbia, Missouri: University of Missouri Press, 2017], 90)

146. Said, *Orientalism*, 6.

147. Concha Roldán, "diálogo interreligioso: hablamos con . . . Montserrat Abumalham," *Todos Uno*, accessed May 16, 2020, www.todosuno.org/dimontserrat.htm.

148. [*Do You Remember Shahrazad?*]

149. [*From the Ceiba and the Quetzal*] Montserrat Abumalham Mas, *De la ceiba y el quetzal*, Murcia: Gollarín, 2016.

150. See bibliography for a sampling of some of Abumalham's most recent and most relevant articles.

151. [bien concebido, dispuesto (y) graduado] Martínez Montávez, "Prólogo," 9–10.

152. Pedro Martínez Montávez, "Prólogo," Prologue to *¿Te acuerdas de Shahrazad?* by Montserrat Abumalham Mas (Madrid: Sial Ediciones, 2001), 7, 10.

153. [*Variable Cloud*] Carmen Martín Gaite, *Nubosidad variable* (Madrid: Anagrama, 1992).

154. [*Letter That's Ten Year's Late*] Olga Guirao, *Carta con diez años de retraso* (Madrid: Espasa-Calpe, 2002).

155. Also relevant is Rueda's work *Cartas sin lacrar: La novela epistolar y la España ilustrada, 1789–1840* [*Unsealed Letters: The Epistolary Novel and Enlightened Spain, 1789–1840*] (Madrid: Iberoamericana Vervuert, 2001) which examines the tradition of literary epistolarity during the Spanish enlightenment.

156. [*The Devil of Yudis*] See Ellison, "*Un reino tan lejano*: Yudis, Shahrazad, and the Imaginary Space in the Contemporary Hispano-Moroccan Novel" (*Research in African Literatures* 48, no. 3 [2017]: 98–115) for a comparative analysis of Daoudi and Abumalham's works.

157. [*The Woman*] Mohamed Bouissef Rekab, *La señora* (Madrid: Sial Ediciones, 2006).

158. [*After Tangier*] Larbi el-Harti, *Después de Tánger* (Madrid: Sial Ediciones, 2003).

159. Monterrat Abumalham's father is Nayib Abumalham, credited as the first person to translate Cervantes's *Quijote* into Arabic. He emigrated to Morocco in 1937 and worked for High Commissary in the administration of the Moroccan Protectorate, received a doctorate from the University of Granada, and served as a professor at the Universidad Complutense de Madrid (Zakaria Charia, "Una breve biografía de Nayib Abumalham, el primer traductor del *Quijote* al árabe," articulo.org, May 18, 2011, www.articulo.org/articulo/43050/una_breve_biografia_de_nayib_abumalham_el_primer_traductor_del_quijote_al_arabe.html).

160. This group of authors has been examined and documented in the anthology *Calle del Agua: Antología contemporánea de Literatura Hispanomagrebí*, edited by Manuel Gahete, et al. and also in Ana Rueda and Sandra Martín's *El*

retorno/El reencuentro: La inmigración en la literatura hispano-marroquí (Madrid: Iberoamericana Vervuert, 2010).

161. Shahrazad is the story-teller of *The Arabian Nights*, folk tales originating in the Middle East and South Asia during the Islamic Golden Age (circa 750 CE to 1250 CE). In the stories, she marries the king Shahrayar who executes each wife at dawn following the wedding night and marries a new virgin. Shahrazad is able to stall her own execution by entertaining the king with a continuous story that creates suspense. He ultimately spares her life. See Mernissi's *Scheherazade Goes West: Different Cultures, Different Harems* or Robert Irwin's introduction to *The Arabian Nights* (Penguin Classics, 2010).

162. Mernissi, *Scheherazade Goes West*, 5–7.

163. Mernissi, *Scheherazade Goes West*, 56.

164. The general anglicized spelling is "Scheherazade" and the hispanicized is "Shehrezada," but for consistency purposes and fidelity to the author's specific orthographic choice, here I will use the spelling found in the text: "Shahrazad."

165. Mernissi, *Scheherazade Goes West*, 61–62.

166. See chapter 3 for an analysis of Daoudi's *El diablo de Yudis*.

167. [la sensualidad de *Las mil y una noches*] David Castillo, "De la belleza como un estado de ánimo," prologue to *Después de Tánger* by Larbi el-Harti (Madrid: Sial Ediciones, 2003), 8.

168. I refer here to the limited canon examined within this book, namely of contemporary Spanish and African authors, writing in Spanish about Africa.

169. *¿Te acuerdas de Shahrazad?* was published as a part of the Casa de África collection by Sial Ediciones. This serves to show that even if Abumalham's novel is not representative of the Maghreb or Africa in and of itself, for the Spanish reading public and specifically the Sial Ediciones publishing house, it belongs to a collection of works thematically dealing with Africa.

170. [un hombre que no era rey, pero vivía en un reino tan lejano como las últimas brumas del alma humana.] Abumalham, *¿Te acuerdas de Shahrazad?*, 13.

171. Abumalham, *¿Te acuerdas de Shahrazad?*, 13.

172. [No era una carta larga ni corta. Era una carta ni concisa ni prolija. No era respetuosa ni atrevida. Tampoco era extravagante ni vulgar. No supo qué pensar de aquella carta que no era ni anónima ni de firma conocida. Al final del texto sólo aparecía un nombre: Shahrazad.] Abumalham, *¿Te acuerdas de Shahrazad?*, 14.

173. Abumalham, *¿Te acuerdas de Shahrazad?*, 14.

174. Abumalham, *¿Te acuerdas de Shahrazad?*, 14.

175. [Sin fecha] Abumalham, *¿Te acuerdas de Shahrazad?*, 78.

176. ["The power of the private letter"] Ana Rueda, "El poder de la carta privada: *La incógnita* y *La estafeta romántica*," *Bulletin of Hispanic Studies* 77, no. 3 (2000): 375–391.

177. [la producción epistolar problematiza las dicotomías entre ficción y realidad, espacio privado y público, falsedad y verdad, pasado y presente, personaje y autor.] Rueda, "El poder de la carta privada," 376.

178. [la distancia epistolar] Rueda, "El poder de la carta privada," 378.

179. [los más profundos pliegues del corazón humano.] Abumalham, *¿Te acuerdas de Shahrazad?*, 13.
180. [las últimas brumas del alma humana.] Abumalham, *¿Te acuerdas de Shahrazad?*, 13.
181. [Tu reino está demasiado lejos.] Abumalham, *¿Te acuerdas de Shahrazad?*, 15.
182. [ni serio ni riendo a carcajadas.] Abumalham, *¿Te acuerdas de Shahrazad?*, 19.
183. [Cada cual ponga la excusa que mejor le parezca; era tímido y no se atrevía a decirle nada . . . o mil y una posibilidades más.] Abumalham, *¿Te acuerdas de Shahrazad?*, 13.
184. [Siempre existen diferencias entre la realidad y la ficción.] Abumalham, *¿Te acuerdas de Shahrazad?*, 15.
185. Abumalham, *¿Te acuerdas de Shahrazad?*, 16.
186. [tan negra como (la noche)] Abumalham, *¿Te acuerdas de Shahrazad?*, 18.
187. [los poetas orientales] Abumalham, *¿Te acuerdas de Shahrazad?*, 21.
188. [tan lejano como las últimas brumas del alma humana] Abumalham, *¿Te acuerdas de Shahrazad?*, 13.
189. Mernissi, *Scheherazade Goes West*, 52–53.
190. Said, *Orientalism*, 203.
191. Said, *Orientalism*, 49.
192. Abumalham, *¿Te acuerdas de Shahrazad?*, 14.
193. [Amanece y debo callar. Si mi señor lo estima oportuno, mañana continuaré.] Abumalham, *¿Te acuerdas de Shahrazad?*, 18.
194. [No obstante, he vivido y he muerto varias veces. Pero, sobre todo, he vivido. Mi vida ha sido plena y lo ha sido más gracias a ti. Yo inicié estas cartas pensando darte la vida, ¡vanidad mía! y la vida me la has dado tú. Mientras aliente, mi soplo de vida será siempre tuyo, porque mía es la palabra, única razón de vida, y porque tuyo es el silencio y, sin silencio, no existe la palabra.

Ya no importa si vuelven otros amaneceres, ya Shahrazad no tiene que pelear por conservar la vida, la ha ganado. Shahrazad está viva, aunque muera.] Abumalham, *¿Te acuerdas de Shahrazad?*, 78.
195. [Pero deberás ser paciente y constante. No debes saltar sobre las líneas. Debes leer cada una de las letras, porque no hay letra ociosa.] Abumalham, *¿Te acuerdas de Shahrazad?*, 15.
196. [¿mi nombre soy yo, yo soy un nombre? Si me llamara árbol, ¿sería un árbol o seguiría siendo una mujer? Si soy Shahrazad, ¿soy una mujer, una voz, una palabra, un sueño, una imaginación de tu mente? ¿Soy yo la que te escribe o eres tú mismo que finge escribir una carta y luego leerla como proveniente de lejos, obligándome con tu ficción a ser, sin que yo sea?

¿Es esto literatura?] Abumalham, *¿Te acuerdas de Shahrazad?*, 33.
197. Mohanty, *Feminism Without Borders*, 31.
198. [Quizá algun día, tenga el valor necesario para . . . reconocer a la persona que fui o que vivió dentro de mí. / . . . Tal vez tú seas siempre alguien distinto de quien eres ante ti y estés acostumbrado a convivir con un otro yo diferente que actúa autónomamente.] Abumalham, *¿Te acuerdas de Shahrazad?*, 33.

199. [Los niños de Occidente sueñan con que los Magos de Oriente les colmen de bienes. ¿Qué sueñan, entre tanto, los niños de Oriente? . . . ¿dónde está el Oriente, si en cada tierra, que vive ignorando a las demás tierras, hay un Este y un Oeste?] Abumalham, *¿Te acuerdas de Shahrazad?*, 42.

200. [¿Soy yo la que te escribe o eres tú mismo que finge escribir una carta y luego leerla?] Abumalham, *¿Te acuerdas de Shahrazad?*, 33.

201. [¿Hombre o fantasma de mi imaginación? . . . / Es posible que seas mi invención y por ello te amo como me amo yo misma.] Abumalham, *¿Te acuerdas de Shahrazad?*, 62.

202. [fantasma]

203. [la gracia creadora de la palabra] Abumalham, *¿Te acuerdas de Shahrazad?*, 53.

204. Mohanty, *Feminism Without Borders*, 79.

Chapter 3

Travel and the Other

In the two hundred years since Domingo Badía y Leblich donned his alter-ego of Alí Bey and traveled through North Africa attempting to pass as Muslim, many Spanish writers have traveled through and written about travels in the continent. From Alí Bey on up to contemporary travel writing on Africa as in Javier Reverte's *Caminos perdidos de África* (2004),[1] *Vagabundo en África* (2005),[2] and *El sueño de África* (2007),[3] there is a rich collection of travel writing with Africa as the topic in Spanish letters.[4] And yet it would be remiss to limit a consideration of travel in the Spanish novel to only explicit travel narratives. Therefore, my examination of texts will not adhere to a strict definition of travel writing, but will instead seek to consider the dynamics of travel within a variety of fictional texts.[5] Travel writing cannot be confined to the personal memoir or the explicit travel narrative; Jan Borm suggests that mimetic faithfulness is a mistaken attribute of travel writing and it is much more rewarding to include all genres or expressions because travel writing should represent "multiple crossings from one form of writing into another and, given the case, from one genre to another."[6]

An inclusive understanding of travel literature permits consideration of José Cadalso's *Cartas marruecas* (1789)[7] or Ramón Sender's *Imán* (1930), and it is such an understanding that will most effectively illuminate the dynamics of representation of the Other within the texts here. As various critics have noted, and as Georges Van den Abbeele has so clearly theorized, travel is more than just a verb—an action—it is also, quite often, a metaphor. The "theme of the voyage"[8] serves not only as a space upon which narrative action occurs, but also as a realm of possibility, an opportunity for loss or gain—"a zone of potential loss or profit."[9] Within this zone, the capacity for—or exertion of—physical movement displays nuanced representations of privilege, power, and culture. The representation of the traveler is laden with significance and metaphor. Abbeele notes that "Western ideas about travel and the concomitant corpus of voyage literature have generally—if not characteristically—transmitted, inculcated, and reinforced patriarchal values and ideology from one male generation to the next,"[10] and I would add that, parallel to the preservation of the patriarchal paradigm, Western ideas about travel have often perpetuated Orientalist stereotyping of the Other. It is this metaphor of travel that will serve as the analytical lens for this chapter as I examine three novels: Javier Reverte's *El médico de Ifni* (2005),[11] Alberto Vázquez-Figueroa's *Los ojos del Tuareg* (2000),[12] and Ahmed Daoudi's *El diablo de Yudis* (1994).[13] A consideration of these themes in these three works will articulate my thesis, that contemporary Spanish authors are moving beyond traditional Orientalist discourses and writing new ways of representing the encounter with the African Other.

This chapter specifically examines three recurrent themes in contemporary Spanish novels that deal with Africa. These themes are archetypes of travel: tourism, nomadism, and immigration—the first representing a traditionally more Western phenomenon while the second is stereotypically Other, and the last is an often-polemic issue diametrically opposed to the luxury of tourism. The intersections between these voyagings[14] often define Spanish conceptualizations of Africa. This chapter will rely on the work of Georges Van den Abbeele and his contention that Western travel writings often do little more than reinforce and preserve hegemonic paradigms of cultural value. This study specifically examines to what extent the contemporary Spanish novel continues to transmit this Occidental hegemony or ventures in an expansion of this paradigm. Abbeele theorizes that the place considered as home—the *oikos*—can potentially shift and change through time, travel, and experience, thereby offering the opportunity to examine whether the *oikos* of Spain as a starting, ending, and favored point for the Spanish author and traveler, has indeed shifted or evolved in the narratives of Africa, or whether it remains emphatically indifferent to the movement and passage of time. Travel will also be understood as making possible what I will call the *encounter* with the Other, and the dynamics of these encounters will be analyzed to illuminate representations of the Other and whether or not they perpetuate Orientalist stereotypes.

Orientalism and exoticism of the Other have a long tradition in Spanish letters. Antonio Carrasco González's extensive study of the Hispano-African colonial novel traces this history across Africa. Alterity and the filter of the "European character"[15] form an integral part of the colonial narrations: "this manner of narrating about distant countries without belonging to their natural community and with a feeling or mentality, greater or lesser, of alterity, is colonial literature."[16] Carrasco González traces this tendency back to the fifteenth century and the exotic representation of the Arabic past on the Iberian Peninsula.[17] In his study, he asserts that the exoticism was often more evident than actual literary quality.[18] These observations emphasize the importance of a critical analysis on the current Hispano-African literary production. I find that the authors under consideration here do not follow the exotic fascination of their colonial, literary predecessors. As mentioned before, Said affirms that "Orientalism depends for its strategy on [a] flexible *positional* superiority, which puts the Westerner in a whole series of possible relationships with the Orient without ever losing him the upper hand,"[19] and while a certain "European character" may persist in the narration, neither Reverte, Vázquez-Figueroa, nor Daoudi suggest any inherent superiority of the West over its African Other. Their break with a sustained tradition of representation marks the diminishing power of the Orientalist discourse that has dominated Hispano-African literature for centuries.

Due to Africa's geographical separation from Spain, travel becomes an almost inherent aspect of any work about Africa from a Spanish viewpoint— to an extent that a Spanish novel about Africa that lacked this component, whether it be physical or figurative travel, would indicate a glaringly unique example. The early travels were clearly of colonizing intent: information gathering (spying or anthropological) expeditions, war, and evangelical missions. Carrasco González outlines the predominance of colonial and war literature throughout the nineteenth century; previously largely ignored, "The War of Africa [1859–1860] aroused, without a doubt, interest in Morocco in the Spanish novel."[20] The beginning of the twentieth century offered a brief respite from the war novel, focusing instead on "some stories of exotic taste, Orientalist in the classical terminology of Said."[21] Expansion, war, and colonization again predominate the Hispano-African narrative throughout the wars of the early twentieth century,[22] and the period of the Moroccan Protectorate and Guinean colony. It is not until the late twentieth century, however, that the balance between colonizing/war travel and pleasure travel shifts to more (presumably benign) tourist trips.[23] Javier Reverte provides an example of the tourist in *El médico de Ifni* (2005). In this novel, privileged, Westernized tourism and contact with the African Other drastically change what Abbeele conceptualizes as *oikos* and redefines assumptions of Same and Other. Questions of financial and cultural mobility and privilege intersect with a reconceptualization of the African Other, inviting us to question whether this reconceptualization is subversive to Orientalist discourse or whether it continues the legacy of patronizing representations.

Any examination of the theme of travel in these novels cannot exclude the North African reality of the nomad—the permanent traveler—as evidenced in the Saharawi, Bedouin, Berber, Tuareg, and other ethnic groups. The nomadic lifestyle is a repeated motif in novels by Javier Reverte, Ramón Mayrata, and Alberto Vázquez-Figueroa as a symbol of the distinct Otherness of the African reality. The presentation of the nomad vacillates between one of idealization (even idolization) and enigma to vilification and revulsion. As Spanish novelists attempt to understand and represent these indigenous

African tribes through their own understandings of travel, I will trace how certain Orientalist stereotypes play out, and how others are surpassed. The nomad, like the traveler, frequently represents a highly respected free spirit, physically powerful yet often politically marginalized. Abbeele's theorization of the *oikos* and travel, combined with James C. Scott's articulation of local knowledge—*mētis*—versus technical knowledge—*techne*—in *Seeing Like a State,* serve to analyze Vázquez-Figueroa's narrative as one that emphasizes Western hubris while offering a re-evaluation of the West's interaction with and portrayal of the nomadic cultural Other.[24]

Contemporary Spanish authors such as Reverte and Vázquez-Figueroa often compare their European protagonists to the nomads of North Africa. Such comparisons can very easily fall into the Orientalist pitfall of essentializing or patronizing, but occasionally open the door into new representations of this Other. And so it is with Alberto Vázquez-Figueroa's *Los ojos del Tuareg* (2000). It is a delicate balance any time a Western voice attempts to speak for its Other, and the manner in which these novels attempt to do so must be examined closely in order to understand how contemporary Spanish authors conceptualize their relationship to Africa, be it the geographically proximate North Africa, the historically connected former colonies, or the zones of adventure traced by explorers and thrill seekers.

The third archetype of travel that will contribute to my analysis is that of the immigrant. Immigration is a deeply polemical political topic at the moment, one which at times dominates national discourses in both Europe and the Americas. The immigrant is marginalized on a number of levels—politically, legally, financially, among others—and yet represents an essential component of the modern, globalized, neoliberal economy. Political and popular discourses against immigration often seek to represent the immigrant as a threatening, inhuman Other, carrying out an invasion of the Western *oikos*.[25] As Leo Chavez notes in *The Latino Threat*, these caricatures serve to erase the humanity from these cultural Others, thereby justifying inhumane actions against them.[26] My analysis of the immigrant focuses on the novel *El diablo de Yudis* by the Moroccan author Ahmed Daoudi, and it considers the act of narration and immigration by a Maghrebi author. This novel goes beyond the unidimensional, popular image of the immigrant, and will serve to contribute an understanding of the narration of immigration within this study. Rueda and Martín's *El retorno/el reencuentro: La inmigración en la literatura hispano-marroquí*,[27] Juliane Tauchnitz, and Khalid Amine will provide a theoretical framework for analyzing the narration of the migrant's experience. The migrant's experience shares much with Abbeele's theory of travel, but is specifically marked by "inequality and dependence on those more powerful, thereby s/he must face the clashes between the two cultures and identities, that of the original and the adopted."[28] It is this marginalized position that makes the immigrant an appropriate contrast to the consideration of the privileged tourist.

I have divided this section into a trichotomy—that of the tourist, the nomad, and the immigrant—for a very specific reason. I considered expanding the categories to include the soldier or the missionary, among others, and yet I find that the tourist, nomad, and immigrant can serve as powerful archetypes for the study at hand. The tourist represents a dominant and imposing force with (post)colonial tones; it is a penetrating force in foreign lands. On the other hand, the nomad is the indigenous, migrant force that inhabits and roams, often with a very intimate relationship with the geographical space through which s/he moves. The immigrant falls somewhere in between, with little social or financial capital, and little to no personal knowledge of the terrain s/he traverses; the immigrant actively travels for the potential gain of which Abbeele writes. For these reasons, I find that the umbrella terms of "tourist," "nomad," and "immigrant" serve to encapsulate various other dynamics at play in literary representation. This brief clarification attempts to avoid the pitfalls of both essentializing and also of being over-zealous in reach within this work, and it serves to establish the parameters of analysis that will be most useful in examining the literary encounters between the West and Africa. I hope to show that Reverte, Vázquez-Figueroa, and Daoudi are writing in ways that prove the essentializing demarcations of "Same" and "Other" limiting in scope.

These three novels not only offer considerations of distinct archetypes of travel, but also represent distinct literary genres. *El médico de Ifni* can be described as a crime novel, while *Los ojos del Tuareg* is an adventure novel, and *El diablo de Yudis* is both a fantasy and an adaptation of traditional Moroccan oral-storytelling genres. As examples of literary genres that can often be formulaic in structure and content, with clear lines of protagonist versus antagonist, Reverte, Vázquez-Figueroa, and Daoudi are careful not to draw these distinctions along solely cultural lines. Reverte develops his characters and "criminals" to problematize motives and reverse preconceptions of Same and Other. Vázquez-Figueroa employs the adventure novel genre to criticize the West's corrupt neo-capitalism that disregards other cultural lifestyles and values and reconsiders the West's understanding of the "terrorist" label. Daoudi's narrator creates an interactive narrative that invites the reader to react and respond. The value of these three novels extends beyond their literary genre; that is, regardless of the chosen genre of expression, Reverte, Vázquez-Figueroa, and Daoudi reconsider any presumed Western "*positional superiority*," offering more nuanced narratives.[29] At the very least, these three generically different works suggest that the influence of Orientalist discourse is waning throughout contemporary literary production.

When Abbeele in *Travel as Metaphor* discusses the essential product of travel, he describes it as a loss or gain of value. If we bring Said's *Orientalism* into our consideration, this initially economic term acquires cultural, racial, and personal nuances. *Travel—voyaging*[30]—can serve as a way to establish superiority, support cultural value, and concede or deny value to Others, or to acquire value[31] and recognition. A more equitable approach would avoid assumptions of cultural superiority and "reductive polarizations"[32] in characterizing the Other, because Orientalism is based on an unequal consideration of cultures—"the apparent ontological inequality of Occident and Orient."[33] A less imbalanced approach should include a consideration of the transculturation that cultural contact brings with it. As Bronislaw Malinowski and Fernando Ortiz coined the term "transculturation" to avoid the pitfalls of "acculturation," it is apparent that they recognized the dialectical contributions of two cultures in contact, as opposed to a one-sided, hegemonic influence.[34] Mary Louise Pratt's theorization of transculturation in her book *Imperial Eyes: Travel Writing and Transculturation* (1992) will also serve as a guide as I consider whether these three novelists approach Africa as Orientalists, or whether they are open to the transcultural possibilities.

Transculturation, transcultural valoration, can only occur in a zone of intercultural contact. Same and Other must come face to face and participate in an exchange. I define here this moment of the *encounter* as an unmediated, physically proximate, interpersonal exchange between two or more individuals. This specific term is borrowed from Louis Althusser, as outlined in his essay "The Underground Current of the Materialism of the Encounter,"[35] described through the imagery of atoms, and building on Epicurus's thesis. The *encounter* begins with isolated entities that are brought into contact through chance (the *swerve* or *clinamen*) and their physical concurrence precipitates a new reality from two formerly distinct atoms. Mary Louise Pratt describes the spaces for the potential encounter as

> "contact zones," social spaces where disparate cultures meet, clash, and grapple with each other, often in highly asymmetrical relations of domination and subordination—like colonialism, slavery, or their aftermaths as they are lived out across the globe today.[36]

In more interpersonal terms, it is an understood prerequisite in the humanistic philosophy of Emmanuel Levinas, specifically in his book *Humanism of the Other* (1972), and also in *The Other* (2008) by Ryszard Kapuściński, which builds on Levinas's writings. Travel brings the traveler into close physical proximity with his Other, and it is this encounter between distinct cultural, racial, and personal entities that is at the heart of my analysis of the representation of the Other. Travel makes possible this encounter and the literary representations which result from it can tell us much about the status of Orientalist discourse in the contemporary Spanish novel. The encounter is a moment of interaction—interpersonal, intercultural, and interactive—within the voyage that will illuminate the dynamics of representation at play within these texts.

A consideration of the tourist, the nomad, and the immigrant will offer the opportunity to examine the contemporary realities of the traveler, as portrayed in the novel. Javier Reverte, Alberto Vázquez-Figueroa, and Ahmed Daoudi represent three contemporary Spanish authors that offer new considerations of Spain's African Other. Their contributions represent a variety of viewpoints and genres, suggesting that Orientalism's omnipresence in Spanish letters is waning. With the theoretical guides of Said, Levinas, Kapuściński, and others, this chapter hopes to serve as a critical voyage through these novels, touring the sites, and the ruins, of Orientalist discourse.

THE TOURIST IN JAVIER REVERTE'S *EL MÉDICO DE IFNI*

Javier Reverte's long career includes many years as a journalist, a dozen travel books, as well as at least nine novels, among other writings. His travel books include a *Trilogía de Centroamérica*;[37] three books published between 1986 and 1992 covering his travels in Nicaragua, Guatemala, and Honduras; and his *Trilogía de África*,[38] which was written between 1998 and 2002 and includes the titles: *El sueño de África: En busca de los mitos blancos del continente negro*,[39] *Vagabundo en África*,[40] and *Los caminos perdidos de África*.[41] More recently, he published a collection of poems titled *Poemas africanos*[42] and a book published in the fall of 2011, *La canción de Mbama*.[43] Sadly, he passed away in October 2020 as I was working on revisions to this book.[44]

His 2005 novel, *El médico de Ifni,* takes up the issue of Western Sahara (formerly the Spanish Sahara), and the messy final years of Spanish occupation (1960–1976) and subsequent withdrawal from the region (1976), a move precipitated by the death of Franco, the Moroccan Green March (November 6, 1975), and effective takeover of Spanish Sahara.[45] The drama unfolds primarily in the present day as the protagonist Clara Canabal seeks clues to uncover the story of the father she never knew, a former Spanish soldier in Africa who became a renegade and defected to the Saharawi Polisario fight for independence. The narration is in a third person omniscient voice, with sections that include the poetry,[46] letters, and journal of Clara's father, Gerardo Canabal. The storyline progresses primarily along a simple chronological development, aside from the temporal jumps of the journals and letters, and except for the first scene which begins *in media res* with an uncontextualized narration of a murder scene. The reader is not returned to this moment until the final pages of the novel, when context is introduced. The reader discovers that the murdered couple of the initial pages is the presumed murderer of Clara's father—his former best friend, and in many ways his rival or amoral double.

Clara had thought her father dead for the majority of her life; at the very least, she believed that he had abandoned her and her mother and therefore wanted nothing to do with him. When a representative of the Saharawi Polisario informs her of his death in the Saharawi refugee camps in Aousserd, Algeria, she begins to learn more about the man who was her father, and she discovers that she has a Saharawi half brother and family. In her search to uncover the past, Clara travels to Ifni and meets her half brother's aunt; she also travels to the refugee camps in Algeria, meeting her half brother and his family and learning the mysteries of her father's life and death.

Even though the novel centers on uncovering the truth about Gerardo Canabal's renegade life, Clara is the focal point of the narration as she seeks to understand his apparent abandonment of her and his nation. It is, in essence, an examination of why her father chose to embrace the African Other and to reject his own culture and country. As Clara retraces her father's route, her travel—as her father's before her—leads her to reject her own Same and embrace her cultural, African Other. Same and Other remain as distinct demarcations, and yet Reverte shows that they can be overcome through personal, intercultural encounters. *El médico de Ifni* recognizes the stereotypical divisions between the European and the African, and simultaneously emphasizes the fact that they are social constructs that can be challenged and exchanged. While this is not necessarily a new trope, since it can be found in works such as Cervantes's "La gitanilla" (1613) or in the *novelas moriscas* of the sixteenth century,[47] Reverte's narrative does depart from the tradition of Orientalism that dominated Western discourse about the African Other throughout the frenetic centuries of European colonial expansion, specifically during the nineteenth and twentieth centuries.

The clearest markers of Otherness are evident in the travel undertaken by the respective cultural representatives. Clara, as the main, Western protagonist, travels frequently and for pleasure; she is able to engage in tourism on a whim. Her relative wealth can afford her a certain caprice when it comes to mobility. She and her partner, Beatriz, regularly vacation on the Greek island Kastellorizo, and Clara's own trajectory takes her from Morocco to Greece two weeks later. She also contemplates a last-minute trip to New York in the near future. Clara's frequent travel is made possible through her personal affluence, and even as the trips to Morocco and the Saharawi refugee camps become less touristically motivated, she is capable of making these trips because of her status as an economically privileged European. It is clear that Clara views travel as "exciting and interesting, as liberating, and as what 'opens up new horizons.'"[48] In her travels, Clara is in search of answers and adventures that will liberate her from her ambiguous personal history; in "open[ing] new horizons," she hopes to uncover her family history. In fact, Beatriz attempts to challenge Clara's romantic obsession with travel during their vacation to Kastellorizo, when she complains that Clara did not call her once during her last trip:

> "I forgot about my previous life, everything that is normal."
> "That's what's so bad: that I belong to what you call your normal life."
> "Is there something bad about normal life?"
> "That it's detestable."
> "Why?"
> "It's monotonous, boring. And you are for me, precisely, the opposite of fucking normalcy, the other face of all that overwhelms me, of what bores me and what I despise."
> . . .
> "Don't overthink things. . . . Out there" and she pointed . . . "is the desert."
> "And over here" Beatriz brought her hand to her chest "normalcy, right? That's a bitch, don't you think?"[49]

In this exchange, Beatriz attempts to convince Clara that her *oikos*, or home, is to be found in their comfortable, domestic relationship, not in the obsessive movement that Clara wishes to undertake. And yet her argument is not convincing, as Clara operates under what Abbeele calls "The dearest notions of the West nearly all appeal[ling] to the motif of the voyage: progress, the quest for knowledge, freedom as freedom to move, self-awareness as an Odyssean enterprise, salvation as a destination to be attained by following a prescribed pathway."[50] By reminiscing about the early days of Clara and Beatriz's partnership, the text suggests that Clara's ability to undertake these trips is a result of her profitable business, an art gallery she co-owns with Beatriz.[51] Clara's social and cultural privileges enable her to engage in this self-revelatory act of travel, a voyaging which she hopes will bring her knowledge, help her to feel free, and offer her a deeper self-awareness.

This privilege of travel that is afforded to the Westerner is contrasted with the travel of Clara's father (also a Westerner), and most importantly, with the forced travel of the Saharawi exiles. Gerardo's travel is distinct from his daughter's in that his is not a travel for pleasure or personal gain; it is the travel of the soldier. He first went to the then-Spanish Sahara as a soldier, a military doctor, and found his way to the Algerian refugee camps as a deserter and renegade. His status as a doctor hints at his complicated identity within established paradigms; he is not the archetypical soldier sent to engage in violence, but rather one who heals. This nuance establishes Gerardo's uniqueness within the conformity of the military. His individuality is later asserted in the cultural sphere as he becomes a renegade. Gerardo's rejection of his nation and army, and his acceptance of life as a political exile with the Saharawi, also suggest his explicit rejection of financial stability and/or lucrative wealth that could have been his, a wealth and opportunities that were offered to him by his friend-turned-enemy Alberto Balaguer. In this sense, he willingly turns his back on the underlying conditions that make possible Clara's freedom of movement: cultural/political dominance as an identified Westerner and financial wealth. He is forced into his renegade status by the decision to collaborate with the Saharawi cause and the refusal to cooperate completely with his longtime friend and nemesis Alberto Balaguer. In fact, Gerardo is caught in between the machinations of Balaguer and the Saharawi Polisario, as his old friend Salek reveals to Clara and her half brother Omar. Gerardo died believing that his greatest moment of treachery was of his own making, but Salek confides in Clara and Omar that Gerardo was an unwitting and innocent pawn in a larger political game;[52] he was, effectively, unknowingly used by both parties for their own ends. Gerardo, in this sense, is little more than a puppet manipulated by those around him. The underlying message is that his motivations for travel may have been superficially driven by ideals of right and wrong, justice, or the search for adventure, but he was, at times, no more than a naïve pawn compelled by a movement greater than him.

Gerardo's traveling is also less linear than a traditional voyage; it is a more muddled process. This supports Abbeele's assertion that "The 'place' of the voyage cannot be a stable one,"[53] and also calls into question the idea of a "fixed point of reference" an *oikos* for the voyage.[54] Omar describes his father as "a man without a place, someone who didn't belong anywhere,"[55] and Gerardo himself contemplates a return to Spain in his journals but concludes that "I have stopped belonging to Spain. I don't think that I am a part of any place on the earth . . . the desert is the only possible fatherland for me."[56] Gerardo is a tortured pariah. He cannot return to Spain; he is never able to embrace the Saharawi Other completely, to become transculturated, and the novel's title ascribes to him a belonging that he cannot achieve either, due to Morocco's control of Ifni. These compounding points emphasize his physical loss of the *oikos,* and yet his repeated use of Spain as a fixed point of reference indicates that it is still a psychic referent. For Gerardo, Spain is a point of departure, and a point to which return is impossible. In fact, as Abbeele notes: "The concept of a home is needed . . . only *after* the home has already been left behind."[57] The dynamics of Gerardo's travel are distinct from those of his daughter Clara, and yet they both operate with Spain as an *oikos*, a point of reference that is psychically important for them both.

The other travelers of the novel are the Saharawi, the nomadic soldiers and exiles, dispersed throughout North Africa, and, within the novel, primarily found in Ifni and the refugee camps in Algeria. Their travel is a forced exile, driven out of their homeland, their *oikos*, by the occupying Moroccan forces. However, as nomads, they still inhabit a familiar geography, that of the desert, and therefore, while they are exiled from the epicenter of their *oikos*, they still travel within a generalized area of that space. It is not a luxurious lifestyle or a capricious travel that they experience. In fact, Fatma, Omar's mother and Gerardo's first love, tells Gerardo (relayed through his journals), that the Saharawi are accustomed to the hard life of the desert.[58] As Clara contemplates the refugee camps from her departing airplane window, she also considers that the Saharawi must be "cursed by the world, expelled from any hospitable space on the Earth that they could call fatherland."[59] In this sense, travel for the Saharawi in *El médico de Ifni* is more of what Ryszard Kapuściński envisions in expressing, "When I say travel, naturally I do not mean tourist trips. In a reporter's understanding, a journey is a challenge and an effort, involving hard work and dedication; it is a difficult task, an ambitious project to accomplish."[60] Obviously the Saharawi are not engaged in the same travel as Kapuściński in his role as reporter, but their voyaging is more similar to his in its difficult nature, as opposed to the frivolous, diversionary travel of the tourist. This distinction in travel dynamics contributes to the Otherness of the Saharawi, an Otherness that also distinguishes them from the Moroccans who are not traditionally nomadic. In fact, Suelma reflects on this unique identity (the complete Otherness of her nomadic identity) when she explains to Clara that it

> is the only manner in which I can explain my feelings to myself. Nomads are accustomed to submerging themselves in the desert, to following the rain and to never having a stable place to live because it is never the same place where water is found. For this reason they call us 'children of the clouds' and our country is not the land, but the water. We are made to roam, because the desert is an inhospitable place.... And no one will ever take the desert away from us because only we understand it. Those who occupy it today, the desert will expel: because they do not understand it nor have they learned to love it.[61]

Therefore, in Reverte's representation, Saharawi nomadic identity is auto-conceptualized as a unique identity, a completely Other identity. Even though it is expressed through a Saharawi character in the novel, as an actor in a Westerner's plot line, these words are more representative of how the West views the Saharawi Other than how they conceptualize themselves. It is, perhaps, a romanticized view, but it is not derogatory. It neither functions on tropes of paternalistic representation nor offers a valorization of the lifestyle for better or for worse. It emphasizes the Saharawi's understanding of the unique desert landscape, a localized knowledge that James Scott calls *mētis*.⁶² The concept of *mētis* in regard to the Saharawi offers a localized privilege to the desert nomads. It establishes and recognizes the otherness of the Saharawi, based on their travel catalysts, and this geographic-specific aspect of Saharawi identity emphasizes the importance of the desert as a perceived *oikos*.

Omar, son of Gerardo and Fatma and Clara's half brother, forges his identity through his nomadic travel. In contrast with Clara and Gerardo, he feels a very deep tie to the geographical space of his *oikos*, stating that he "would be nothing without the desert."⁶³ While Gerardo is exiled from his home and Clara is continuously uneasy with her natal culture, Omar has a physical tie with and a localized knowledge of his psychic home; he inhabits its space and moves within its confines. However, complicating his intense self-identification as a "son of the clouds," is the fact that he is ethnically interstitial, the son of a Spanish father and Saharawi mother, racially neither Same nor Other. His racial hybridity and identification with a physical *oikos*—when contrasted with the racial homogeneity of Gerardo and Clara and their detachment from their geographical *oikos*—indicates that conceptualizations of belonging and lines of Same/Other are social or psychic constructs. When Suelma says that the desert will expel its current occupiers because they do not understand or appreciate it,⁶⁴ lines of racial difference are blurred as she perhaps unintentionally suggests that *difference* can be overcome by learning to understand and to love. That is to say, the tourist, the renegade soldier, and the nomad may travel for distinct purposes, but *El médico de Ifni* does not leave it as an irreconcilable difference. There still exists the hope of meaningful exchange between Same and Other, made possible by travel. So it can be understood that the differences established in the nature of travel serve to establish Same/Other distinctions that, upon further analysis, the encounter can undermine.

In addition, Reverte's racially mixed protagonists offer a racial hybridity that undermines essentialized demarcations of Same and Other. The miscegenation of the novel explicitly destabilizes the totem of any homogenous Western identity and authority. Therefore, not only are psychic constructs of Same and Other rendered arbitrary, but so is physical (i.e., ethnic) difference shown to be a reconcilable one.

Reverte accomplishes this subversion by subtly shifting lines of Otherness from phenotypical difference to more ideological distinctions. Clara's search to uncover her past and familial history is a search for her identity. Throughout her life, she has felt an emotional distance from her closest family members and acquaintances. This emotional distance is made clear to her as she undertakes physical travel. When she thinks about her first failed marriage and her failing relationship with Beatriz, she describes the failings in terms of distance.⁶⁵ Clara's relationship with her biological mother is strained.

The mother as a psychic provider of home—*oikos*—is unstable; Clara resents her mother for betraying her father, even when Clara knows very little about their relationship. She always viewed her mother as cold and emotionally distant, and these differences are contrasted with her warm reception by the sister of her father's first wife, Suelma, in Ifni, with whom she shares an instant personal bond and later a physically intimate bond, and with her half brother Omar in Aousserd as he welcomes her into his home. Clara feels an almost immediate affection for both Suelma and Omar, a familial connection that she never felt with her biological mother. Their cultural differences are not obstacles to the formation of relationships. Conversely, Clara does not feel any significant ties of loyalty or identification with her cultural, racial, or even biological Sames. By problematizing Clara's relationship with these Sames, Reverte effectively destabilizes justifications of Same/Other as nothing more than artificial constructs.

This reduction in the importance of phenotypical Otherness versus ideological otherness is further supported in Clara's relationship with Beatriz; that is, in the realm of interpersonal relationships, superficial differences—be they gender, race, or others—are supplanted in importance by character traits, be they congeniality, shared concerns, or other emotional bonds. In discounting the prominence of physical difference, Reverte's novel emphasizes a shared humanity that avoids a hegemonic Orientalist discourse of the Other; one that denies the "ontological and epistemological distinction made between 'the Orient' and . . . 'the Occident.'"[66] The intercultural demarcations of "the Orient" and "the Occident" are reduced to irrelevancy, empathy and interpersonal congruence trump cultural difference.

Clara's traveling, analyzed above as a luxury afforded to her as a Westerner, still provides the opportunity for her to question established precepts of Same and Other. It takes her into direct contact with a distinctly different culture, and ultimately leads her to reject her own cultural heritage and to prefer the newly discovered one. Her travels bring her face to face with her Other, an Other that is also tied to the Same through her father's relationship with Fatma and the son Omar born from it. These face-to-face encounters actualize a recognition of shared bonds that transcend cultural Otherness. In *Humanism of the Other*, Levinas describes this encounter in saying

> I find myself facing the Other. He is neither a cultural signification nor a simple given. He is, primordially, *sense* because he lends it to expression itself, because only through him can a phenomenon such as signification introduce itself, of itself, into being.[67]

The intimacy of the *sensory* experience of the Other—Clara's physical approximation to Suelma and Omar (one which does lead to a literal *sensual* experience with Suelma)—preempts and overrides the cultural narratives that a traveler metaphorically carries in her journeys. The immediacy of the sensorial has the power to disrupt inherited preconceptions. The encounter is therefore a necessary step towards a reconceptualization of Same and Other.

Clara's first trip to Morocco and Ifni, to investigate the existence of her father's first son and her own possible extended family, brings her into contact with Suelma, the twin sister of her father's Saharawi lover. Her encounter with Suelma is initially mediated by a group of Moroccan men who help her to locate Suelma and act as translators for the exchange. There is an instant intimacy between the two,[68] even though relatively little practical information is relayed. As the Moroccan men conclude the conversation and leave, Suelma addresses Clara directly in Spanish, and invites her to stay for dinner.[69] Unmediated, Clara and Suelma are able to have a meaningful encounter. Suelma reveals to Clara part of the family history that Clara desperately sought. Their few days together ends in a sensual evening together, and the dynamics of this encounter are worth noting. As their eyes connect, Suelma asks a simple "'Would you like to . . . ?,'" prompting Clara to nod "with a small movement of her chin. And offered her open mouth to Suelma's."[70] Suelma's agency initiates the physical exchange; she is the pursuer in this scene, a scene which both alludes to the erotic Oriental female as a powerful motif in Orientalist discourse[71] and yet also subverts the motif in making a female Other the initiator and dominant force within the exchange, overturning the Orientalist hierarchy of West over Other and countering Said's assertion that "There are Westerners, and there are Orientals. The former dominate; the latter must be dominated."[72] This relationship is initiated by Suelma, but predicated on an extended offer—"¿Quieres?"—to which Clara affirmatively responds. In this intimate exchange, this act of "facing the Other"[73] leads to a moment that transcends the hierarchy of Same over Other and male over female; Clara and Suelma's sensual encounter is an intercultural exchange where the Oriental is the agent of instigation within a sphere deprived of both Western and (the often concomitant) masculine privilege. The encounter leads to a reduction of this Other to "*sense*,"[74] a moment that reduces the Other to Same through common sensorial capacity. Thus, what is at play in the romantic moment between Clara and Suelma is a dynamic that does not privilege Same over Other, but moderates these distinctions through a biological commonality, deemphasizing cultural or phenotypical distinctions.

The ease with which Clara is able to interact with Suelma is contrasted with the tension of her relationship with Beatriz or her mother back in Spain. Suelma's intimacy causes Clara to reconsider her own conceptualization of her *oikos*, and her relationship to her Same and Other. Clara's awareness of the Others she comes across in her travels evolves through her intimate encounter with Suelma and her newfound family. Whereas her trips to

Kastellorizo exclude the Greek Other almost completely, her trips to Ifni and Aousserd highlight her growing interest in knowing her cultural Other. As she learns about and meets her extended, formerly unknown family, she begins to fantasize about moving to El Aaiún with Omar, Muluma, and also Suelma "To begin there a new life without hate or rancor . . . and [to] recover the remains of her father, to bury them next to those of Fatma in the lost oasis. / What would she do in Madrid?"[75] She dreams of establishing an *oikos* in Western Sahara with her newly discovered family, an *oikos* bolstered by the proximity of her father's grave, reuniting the family that might have been possible in a hypothetical "homeland"—made even more hypothetical by the fact that Clara never personally visits the Western Sahara territory within the text.

Like Clara's encounter with Suelma, her meeting with her half brother Omar in the refugee camps in Aousserd also hints at dynamics that disrupt Orientalist discourse and a reconceptualization of the *oikos*. Clara appears to take Omar literally when he welcomes her into his *jaima*[76] saying "Welcome to your home, sister."[77] In fact, this encounter with Omar in many ways is nuanced as an approximation to her father. Clara does, in fact, come to know the father she never met through Omar, and her half brother assumes a metaphorical position as a father figure to Clara through his knowledge of Gerardo. Omar's role as a father figure is supported in several admissions from Clara. Omar provides a sense of protection, "Clara felt a new sensation: that someone was protecting her";[78] she is envious of the affection Omar shows towards his own daughter, "Clara noticed how a forgotten infantile yearning reemerged. . . . For an instant she envied her niece,"[79] and she feels submissive in his presence, "Clara nodded with a small movement of her chin. She felt a strange sensation in the presence of Omar: her rebellious instincts calmed in front of him, as if the presence of her brother awoke in her a certain submission."[80] In both the seductive "¿Quieres?" of Suelma and the moment of submission to Omar, Clara responds with a subtle movement of her chin.[81] She is rendered voiceless in front of her supposed Other. She respects their authority in ways that surprise her, because she never felt such respect in the presence of her Same. The West's hegemony is undermined by these personable and familiar Orientals. As Clara learns about her estranged father, finds paternal authority in her half brother and (complicated) maternal warmth in Suelma, she reevaluates her own *oikos*. As Clara interacts with her cultural Others, she reorients her loyalties and reconceptualizes her ideas of Same and Other. The encounter serves as a powerful moment of transcultural exchange that takes Clara beyond being a mere tourist, operating in an economic sphere of relation to the Other, to an interpersonal exchange that recognizes the humanity of the Other.

Clara's personal submission is perhaps better understood as an awakening of empathy. A basic definition of *tourism* emphasizes the "practice of traveling for pleasure,"[82] a pleasure that is intended to benefit primarily the tourist. Eugenia Afinoguénova and Jaume Martí-Olivella, drawing on the work of Dean MacCannell, offer a more theorized definition, summarized as "travel against the space/time divide opened by modernity: a quest for an escape from the separation of work from leisure and the compartmentalization of land, a search for an experience that would allow one to touch the 'authentic' in order to 'reconstruct a cultural heritage or a social identity,' now removed in time (to history) or in space (to natural, 'primitive' or exotic destinations)."[83] The pursuit of pleasure posits the tourist in a range of primarily economic transactions with the Others encountered through travel, and MacCannell's definition emphasizes the project of tourism as a search for difference. By traveling "against the space/time divide," *tourism* effectively functions on an Orientalist base of exotic and primitive difference. Yet, as Clara validates the personhood and authority of Omar and Suelma through her submissive response, she responds to the affective power of the encounter. Her empathetic attachment to Omar and Suelma overturns the tourist dynamic of her previous (Other-less) trip to Kastellorizo, as she engages in the interpersonal exchange of humans and not merely the economic relationship of the tourist. Omar and Suelma are valued as family and companions, not exotic relics of a lifestyle incompatible with Western modernity.

Clara's encounter with Suelma and Omar also leads her to question her relationship with her own Same, with the Spanish and the West.[84] As she learns more about her father, through his own journals that Omar lends to her, Clara comes to understand the military renegade that she never knew. What she learns solidifies her newfound identification with the Saharawi cause, and her repulsion at the actions of her own relatives in Spain. She bears intense anger towards her mother for never revealing the truth about her father to her; she despises her father's brother Juan for his cowardice, and she plans to assassinate Alberto Balaguer, the man who was her father's best friend and later arch-enemy and rival and her mother's lover. Clara's newfound allegiances highlight how Reverte subtly emphasizes the importance of ideological differences over more superficial phenotypic otherness. Clara realizes that she holds little in common with her fellow countrymen, and more in common ideologically with the extended family she has just met. Reverte considers how phenotypic, cultural difference is often the most obvious when Suelma relates to Clara the story of her father and Fatma, Suelma's sister:

> They belonged to two different worlds. On one side, that of the Spanish, people who considered themselves superior, even though that was not the case with your father . . . despite the fact that he tried to marry Fatma, our father was opposed to it: he would not consent to a wedding with someone through whose veins Saharawi blood did not run.[85]

Evident in this admission from Suelma is both the colonial discourse of cultural superiority on the part of the Spaniards, and a concern for racial purity on the part of the Saharawi; both of these concerns implode in the relationship that covertly continues between Gerardo and Fatma. Gerardo is not concerned with the pervasive ideas of cultural hegemony that he, as a colonialist soldier in 1970s Spanish Sahara, is ostensibly sent to enforce, and Fatma is unconcerned about the mixing of blood as is proven with the birth of Omar. Their encounter is intimate and personal, unmediated by hegemonic ideas of cultural or racial superiority. Even though intercultural relationships abound in the Spanish colonial history, and at times form the basis of conquest, this is a relationship that leads Gerardo to reject and be rejected by the colonial paradigm due to the subversive political activities of the Saharawi. It is an encounter which leads Gerardo to question his own ties with his cultural Same and assume the role of a military renegade, supporting the Saharawi cause for independence.

Clara's loyalties shift so dramatically that she ends up assassinating Alberto Balaguer, the man she suspects was responsible for her father's death. She commits this crime under the assumption that he is the one ultimately responsible, however it is never confirmed that Gerardo's death was murder; it remains a distinct possibility that he died of purely natural causes. The essential analysis of this final, violent act that Clara commits is that she follows her father's renegade path in rejecting her cultural Same to a point where she commits treason against her own nation. Alberto Balaguer is an unscrupulous politician, closely affiliated with both parties, depending on which is in power. His political stances are ideological only in the sense that they shift and align with the controlling ideology. In this understanding, Reverte sidesteps accusations against specific political philosophies by criticizing the abuse of power in general. Balaguer represents all that is devious and manipulative about the Spanish political system, and her crime against him is both a personal act of revenge for the death of her father, but also a political response to the Spanish betrayal of the Saharawi people, personified in the political history of Balaguer. Balaguer's assassination is Clara's decisive rejection of the Spanish political paradigm; it is a treasonous crime that highlights her personal and political sympathies.

Her crime is first prefaced in the novel's initial pages, opening with Alberto Balaguer's assassination and returning to the scene in the final pages. This parenthetical narrative device emphasizes the plot's development towards a known climax. Considering *El médico de Ifni* as an example of the crime novel, these first few pages function to establish the crime initially and then explain the motives and execution behind the act. However, as I mentioned in the introduction, the literary genre does not limit the narrative's reach, but rather opens the text to additional insights. Within the current analysis, the crime (the murder of Alberto Balaguer) represents not only Clara's vengeance for the death of her father, but also the culminating moment of her rejection of the Same for the African Other. The initial pages gain this nuance retroactively as the novel develops and Clara's motives are made clear. Both narratively and theoretically, this is an engaging device; plot development justifies both Clara's desire for vengeance and her realigned loyalties. That is not to say that the novel justifies murder, but Reverte effectively destabilizes the West's moral high-ground through the under-handed political dealings of Alberto Balaguer and Spain's abandonment of the Saharawi territory and people. The reader is forced to reevaluate the "crime" of the first few pages with all of the background information provided through the plot development.

The murder of Alberto Balaguer reinforces the idea that knowing the Other, encountering the Other face-to-face, has the power to cause reverse polarization in preconceptions of Same and Other, effectively rendering the cultural Same into a strange and revolting Other. Ultimately, Clara's betrayal of her cultural Same, in the assassination of Alberto Balaguer, causes her to simultaneously alienate her partner (and enlisted co-assassin), Beatriz. Clara effectively uses Beatriz's skills as a markswoman to commit the crime, even though she has emotionally distanced herself from Beatriz. In the final pages, Clara contemplates her physical distancing from Beatriz and a return to Suelma in Morocco, thoughts which stir in her a sense of adventure.[86] Momentarily, she hears a noise on the opposite sidewalk, then she sees the movement of a shadow, and "she then immediately felt a terrifying thunder exploding inside her head."[87] Despite the veiled narration, the reader can reasonably assume that Beatriz has learned of Clara's planned departure and exacted her own revenge, shooting her lover on the doorstep of her apartment. The reader is led to assume Beatriz's guilt in much the same way that Clara accused Balaguer of her father's death.

This climactic conclusion is effective on a number of levels. The first being its dramatic and shocking twist of the plot in the final lines. Secondly, within a text that has diminished the importance of phenotypical difference and emphasized the importance of ideological otherness, it is, perhaps, metaphorical that Clara meet her end with a "terrifying thunder exploding inside her head."[88] The psychic site of identification for Clara is pierced by a bullet, destroyed. In choosing the bullet placement for this final shot, the choice of the head over the heart lends an important element to the narration. As the metaphysical locus of reason, as opposed to the heart as a locus of emotion, her betrayal of Beatriz and her cultural Same, elicits a violent response that is a direct shot to metaphorical reason. That is, Clara fully accepts the Other and rejects the Same, recognizing the superficiality of Western distinctions of Same and Other and the instability of perceived Western cultural superiority.

This cultural "betrayal" is met with Beatriz's vengeance as she directs her fatal shot at Clara's site of ideological formation—the brain.

The third level of interpretation stems from the ambiguity of the narration. The reader can reasonably assume that Beatriz has exacted her revenge on Clara by shooting her, and yet this is not explicitly conveyed. Similarly, the reader is led to understand that Alberto Balaguer is responsible for Gerardo's death, even though explicit linkage to the crime is never made. These two crimes subtly imply that life and death decisions are often made on incomplete evidence; passion is the culprit of both crimes and encounters, and it is a fickle impetus. Throughout the novel, interpersonal communication is strained between Clara and her cultural Sames; in such a setting stereotypes and hegemonic discourses are able to flourish in a space lacking authentic communication. Interpersonal communication offers the potential to break down walls of difference as evidenced in Clara's interactions with Suelma and Omar. The implication is that interpersonal/intercultural communication overcomes the stereotypes and discourses that inhabit a place of communicative and narrative ambiguity.

Reverte's *El médico de Ifni* offers a reconsideration of Same and Other—a consideration where the Same becomes Other and Other, Same. As Neal Ascherson notes in the introduction to Kapuściński's *The Other*, "the recognition of selfhood . . . can only be brought about by contact with and recognition of the Other."[89] Clara's travels bring her into contact and exchange with her Others, forcing her to reflect on her own conceptualizations of familiarity and the unknown. Reverte examines and emphasizes what Kapuściński calls the "problem . . . [of] this relationship existing within each of us, between the person as individual and personality and the person as bearer of culture and race,"[90] ultimately choosing to approach and know the Other as individual and personal. Clara's voyaging "displace[s] the home," and her crime effectively "prevent[s] any return to it," an activity that "undermin[es] the institution of that economy."[91] The metaphor of travel as economy is posited on a return to the *oikos*, a fixed point of reference, and yet, Clara's conceptualization of this *oikos* is interrupted by her interaction with Suelma and Omar, and her preconceived route is shifted as her ideas about the Other are changed. This unsettling of the *oikos* can be theorized to also represent the preconceptions of the Other with which one begins the journey, and so, the re-positioning of the *oikos* for Clara suggests an undermining of these previous stereotypes and discourses of the Other.

What her physical travel does support is the "Western metaphysics to privilege presence over absence . . . the near over the far"[92] and her voyage, as she physically approximates to the Other, causes her to shift cultural dynamics of privilege in a parallel movement. This shift of privilege also causes an ideological exchange of valoration for Clara (as her *oikos* is relocated), such that when she physically returns to Spain it does not revert; she values the far over the near. This new stance reflects her shifting loyalties and expresses the fact that "the identity of the home is breached by the very movement that constitutes it."[93] Clara does find a familial bond in Africa, which offers empathetic support to her reconceptualization of Same and Other, but aside from this, her shift is drastic and perhaps somewhat excessive. The best response to incredulity at Clara's repositioning of her loyalties is found in the humanism of Levinas. The face-to-face encounter with another human being is a powerful moment of self-reflection. Reverte narrates the power of this encounter to radically reimagine discourses of Same and Other, subverting hierarchies of privilege that Orientalist discourse has long promulgated.

The African Other of *El médico de Ifni* is not a subjugated, second-class human, nor a noble savage, s/he is a warm and personable human being. Additionally, ties of blood and history provide indelible links between Spain and its African Other. What superficially appears Other, shares much in common with the Occidental subject. Reverte's novel effectively destabilizes euro-centric narratives of exceptionalism and authority, and for this Reverte represents an author writing his African Other in new and engaging ways that deviate from the Western Orientalist tradition. In short, the tourist loses her privileged authority when she comes into unmediated contact with her Other.

THE NOMAD IN ALBERTO VÁZQUEZ-FIGUEROA'S *LOS OJOS DEL TUAREG*

Little critical attention has been paid to the work of Alberto Vázquez-Figueroa, despite the fact that he has published over forty novels since 1975, nine of which have been adapted to film, and he was awarded the Premio de Novela Histórica Alfonso X El Sabio in 2010 for his novel *Garoé* (2010).[94] His bookjackets and personal website biography credit him as "one of the most widely read contemporary Spanish authors in the world";[95] his global book sales top 25 million copies, and his work has been translated into more than 30 languages.[96] His prolific publications spanning more than a quarter of a century deserve a closer critical look, one which has been sadly missing.

His work is important for this project specifically as he consistently returns to the theme of Africa for inspiration. A quick review of his published novels shows that several of them take place in or focus directly on Africa, among them: *Ébano* (1975),[97] *Tuareg* (1980), *África llora* (1996),[98] and *Los ojos del Tuareg* (2000).[99] His abundant literary production, his focus on the African continent, and his status as a popular, contemporary Spanish author make him an ideal author for this study, and his portrayal of the African Other offers a valuable example for this analysis.

Vázquez-Figueroa's first autobiographical biographical novel *Arena y viento* (1953)[100]—which deals with his family's flight from the Canary Islands to the Spanish Sahara during the Spanish Civil War—and his later novel *Ébano* (1975) show that he has been considering the themes of Africa and the African Other throughout his career. These dates also indicate that the breadth of his literary production straddles the monumental publication of Edward Said's *Orientalism* in 1978. For this reason, it is pertinent that Vázquez-Figueroa's recent works be examined for their current treatment of the Other within the contemporary Spanish literary canon. He falls squarely within the scope of this analysis as an author who is actively portraying the African Other in his current literary production, and his portrayal offers a nomadic Other that serves as a lens through which to critique the West.

For this analysis, I focus on Vázquez-Figueroa's 2000 novel *Los ojos del Tuareg*, which is a loose sequel to his 1980 *Tuareg*.[101] It follows the family of Gacel Sayah, son of the protagonist of *Tuareg* (also named Gacel Sayah), as they flee the dramatic events of the first novel which led to the patriarch Gacel's death, and search for a new life deep in the Saharan desert.[102] They are both fleeing as political exiles and also fulfilling the lifestyle of dedicated Tuareg nomads.[103] The first chapter opens on the immediate flight of the family, now led by the eldest son, as they search for a remote oasis that will sustain them. They find an isolated oasis and begin to dig a well. The second son, Ajamuk, is killed by a cave-in during the process, and yet, against the odds, the family succeeds in digging a barely functioning well on which they survive. In the space of a few paragraphs, years pass. They live in the oasis cut off from the rest of the world for those years, isolated from almost all contact with other families or society at large, until one day an airplane flies overhead, circles the oasis, and leaves.

A few days or possibly weeks later they spot dust trails on the horizon. A rally car approaches and asks for water, which they provide. In conversing with the European rally car drivers, Gacel and his family learn that the airplane from earlier had been mapping the rally car race route and had incorrectly labeled their meager oasis as a different, more plentiful water source.[104] This mistake is proven when a second rally car shows up and the driver demands water to clean his car. The Tuareg family refuses his wasteful request, and in a fit of rage the driver dumps motor oil into their well and leaves abruptly.

The plot hinges on this unforgivable act. Gacel and his family offer reasonable hospitality to the driver, one Marc Milosevic, and his malicious actions betray the honored Tuareg rules of hospitality, as well as permanently contaminating the only water source for a family and their livestock. Gacel proceeds to take the next few rally car "visitors" hostage, and demands, not money or ransom of some sort, but rather the return of the criminal, promising to cut his hand off as effective retribution in accordance with tribal laws. Gacel's family flees to a remote mountainous area with its prisoners as the rally organizers attempt to deal with the situation. Gacel refuses any financial remuneration, and the organizers are unwilling to hand over a European to a small band of Tuaregs for such a gruesome punishment. The desperate solution that the trans-Saharan rally organizers implement is to hire a team of vicious mercenaries and air drop them into the desert to quickly and quietly take out Gacel and his family, and possibly (but not necessarily) to rescue the hostages.

In this showdown, Gacel and his brother Suleiman outsmart and overpower the mercenaries. Gacel has a change of heart in his plans to dismember the man who poisoned his well, and he sets the hostages free. Two points of note punctuate the conclusion, the first is that helicopter pilot Nené Dupré, who also functions as the appointed mediator by the rally organizers, gives Gacel (against Gacel's wishes) the one million francs at his disposition to offer as a ransom.[105] The second is that one of the hostage's fathers has ties to the Mafia underworld and arranges to have Marc Milosevic brought clandestinely to Gacel for vengeance. Gacel has mercy on the man, leaving him nothing more than a scar on his hand, but the mafioso captors decide to leave Milosevic stranded in the desert to die. The novel ends with Milosevic stumbling across a discarded aluminum can that he believes was his own trash from a few weeks prior, and then discovering his car tracks and following them. His fate is unknown as the book closes, open to interpretation or perhaps a continuation of the story in a future book. This brief plot summary serves to introduce a novel that contains a trove of encounters between Same and Other, encounters which I analyze in the pages that follow.

This fast-paced adventure novel, written by a white, European author and unfolding in the Saharan desert, offers a consideration of the encounter between the West and its African Other. Western sport, in particular the rally race car driver, literally collides with the nomad protagonist. Generalizations of the Occidental Same and its Other are generalized in the motives and modes of travel through the barren expanse. Vázquez-Figueroa does fall into Orientalized descriptions of the nomad and the African terrain; the former is occasionally presented as a noble savage and the latter often "[wears] away the European discreteness and rationality of time, space, and personal identity. In the Orient one suddenly [confronts] unimaginable antiquity, inhuman beauty, [and] boundless distance."[106] And yet, this novel offers surprising considerations that also undermine traditional Orientalist rhetoric, explicitly subverting Orientalist rhetoric that considers geographical knowledge as "the material underpinning for knowledge about the Orient."[107] In short, *Los ojos del Tuareg* does represent a break from a history of representation of the Other that is unequal and essentializing; Vázquez-Figueroa's Other is human—different and mysterious, yes, but very human nonetheless. Alberto Vázquez-Figueroa, in his overall project with this novel, goes beyond simple Orientalist representations of the African Other and offers a nuanced consideration of the encounter between disparate cultures.

It is, perhaps, best to begin with a consideration of the title itself. As a sequel to his 1980 *Tuareg*, *Los ojos del Tuareg* begins with a humanization. The title no longer refers simply to the ethnic heritage of the protagonist, but emphasizes a common human characteristic, the eyes. The reader is offered a *visage*, and Levinas's theorization of the face offers a useful interpretation: "The nudity of the face is a stripping with no cultural ornament—an absolution—a detachment of its form in the heart of production of form."[108] These titular eyes are modified by the adjectival phrase of culture, and yet humanity is emphasized in the title. The reader confronts another human, not simply an ethnically charged noun that encompasses an entire people group. The image that it creates is also one of presence; the face—the eyes—are made present in the title and so it alludes to an encounter with the Other: *Los ojos del Tuareg* contains a subtle intimacy in its phrasing that is lacking in the concise *Tuareg*. Levinas's articulation of the encounter with the Other, which was useful in the previous section of this chapter, can serve as a starting point for my analysis here: "I find myself facing the Other. He is neither a cultural signification nor a simple given. He is, primordially, *sense* because he lends it to expression itself, because only through him can a phenomenon such as signification introduce itself, of itself, into being."[109] An encounter with the Other, a recognition of the humanity of the Other, can produce far greater considerations than a mere cultural evaluation that reinforces "belligerent collective identity";[110] it can offer the opportunity for ontological reflection "understanding and intellectual exchange."[111] Just as textbook Orientalism "has less to do with the Orient than it does with 'our' world,"[112] so does a less hegemonized encounter with the Other offer a critical lens through which to see the Same. In this sense, the Other routinely serves as a refracting lens, but the valorization of this Other within the textual context, the evaluation of the discourse at play, is key to avoiding Orientalist platitudes and portrayals.

In Vázquez-Figueroa's depiction of Same and Other, the lines are clearly drawn. The European—the Same—is wealthy, capriciously traveling across the Saharan expanse in a foolhardy race, while the nomad explicitly rejects the actions and values of these Westerners. Gacel and his family repeatedly state that they have no use for money, for Western-sanctioned "justice," and that they cannot comprehend the motivation that would compel men to risk their lives in a sporting event such as the rally. These distinctions are clear, and yet comparisons are made that link the two sides. Westerners undertake frivolous risks for the sake of little more than adventure,[113] while the nomad undertakes similar risky ventures, without the luxury of options. Desert travel is inherently risky—"only a Tuareg would be so crazy as to embark upon the adventure of attempting to find water in a such a remote part of the desert,"[114] but there remain few other options as Gacel notes that they have nowhere else to go, and only the desert has supported them.[115] The two cultural spheres are ideologically distinct, and yet compared equally in their willful confrontation with the hostile desert. In writing the Tuareg, Vázquez-Figueroa establishes a parallel Other, different in almost every way, but justified and valued. While the two cultures set out across the desert, the Westerner is motivated by whim and adventure, and the Tuareg does so out of necessity.

The metaphor of travel underpins the novel. The nomad is, by definition, one who wanders as a lifestyle, and Vázquez-Figueroa contrasts this traditional desert lifestyle with the trans-Sahara rally, a sporting event that is undertaken voluntarily. These contrasting motives represent the largest distinction between the West and its Other, and Vázquez-Figueroa aptly uses the Tuareg protagonists to examine and criticize the vapid Western consumerist worldview and culture. Since the Westerners embark on their race voluntarily and seeking adventure, it will be more concise to distinguish them here as tourists since they travel for pleasure, and in this dichotomy of the tourist and the nomad can be found the dynamics at play in the encounter between cultures.

It is also important to highlight the distinction between tourist and nomad here because this Westernized travel-for-pleasure/thrill-seeking carries with it a blatant disrespect for the indigenous cultures of the land they traverse and an exploitation of scarce desert resources. This thrill-seeking tourist represents Said's Orientalist *par excellence.* The brazen arrogance of Alex Fawcett, the public relations manager for the rally, is posited on his own perceived authority over the indigenous, African Other. Further, his and the rally's focus on the media representation of the race to the Western world reflects the exteriority of the concerns and motivations behind the organization and participants.[116] These are deeply critical representations of the West, and specifically the evils of neo-Capitalism, and therefore Vázquez-Figueroa's narrative, primarily sympathetic with the Tuareg, undermines the Western moral authority through this characterization.[117] "The West," exemplified in the arrogance of Alex Fawcett, holds no narrative privilege.[118]

For Alex Fawcett and the corporate sponsors of the rally, the bottom line is a financial one. Fittingly, as we previously saw, Georges Van den Abbeele, theorizes travel—the voyage—as a "zone of potential loss or profit."[119] There is an economy at play in all voyaging, be it nomadic or touristic. The profits can be cultural or financial, among other possibilities, and the losses can be fatal or monetary. It is these "profits" that motivate travel, and also reveal distinctive catalysts that lead individuals to voyage. In *Los ojos del Tuareg*, the desert race for the Westerner is a zone of adventure and personal profit. The rally car drivers are able to undertake the race because they have vast personal wealth or significant corporate sponsorship. Additionally, the winners can relish in the glory of having "conquered" the vast Saharan expanse with their technology and skill. Vázquez-Figueroa reduces this space, the desert, to a zone of loss that only local knowledge—the knowledge a Tuareg inherits and acquires—can navigate. James C. Scott in *Seeing Like a State* elaborates on the importance of "local knowledge" for navigating specific environs. Scott draws from the Greek in calling it "*mētis*," literally wisdom, skill, or craft. Scott's *mētis* is "vernacular and local, keyed to the common features of the local ecosystem,"[120] just like the Tuareg's ability to survive for generations in the desert. In Vázquez-Figueroa's depiction of "an authentic Tuareg,"[121] *mētis* is an indispensable quality: "When a Tuareg died of thirst he was accepting that he had not learned the lessons of generations of ancestors that for centuries had proudly maintained a foothold in the most desolate landscapes of the planet."[122] This is perhaps the romanticized vision of a Western author, but it emphasizes the indigenous and *local* source of knowledge that the Tuareg wields, contrasted with the imported, technology-supported cars of the European ralliers. Western corporations—Western media outlets, car and weapons manufacturers, among others—finance this spectacle, pitting the capital of the Occident against the brutality of the desert, with the indigenous residents as the collateral victims and, in this case, unexpected rivals.

Within Abbeele's framework of travel, the *oikos*[123] operates as a spatialized relation which "defines or delimits the movement of travel."[124] Since "travel" necessarily involves movement towards or away from locations, the *oikos* functions as a reference point for understanding the profit or loss such travel provides. This concept is complicated in the case of the nomad. Since a nomadic lifestyle is one of constant movement, the Western conceptualization of home/*oikos* must be adapted. I suggest that for the purpose of this analysis the *oikos* be linked to Scott's *mētis*. *Mētis* is spatially located because "much of his [the indigenous subject] knowledge would be irrelevant if he were suddenly transposed to a different [location]."[125] For example, in the initial pages Gacel and his family dig a well "in the middle of nowhere,"[126] confident that their inherited knowledge of the desert would guide them to water. The nomad travels, yes, but within a locality that is familiar in a broad sense. The Western tourist, upon leaving home on his voyage, must rely on the Greek concept of *techne*[127] to navigate the unfamiliar. Thus, it can be understood that Vázquez-Figueroa, while writing two types of travelers, distinguishes them in their reliance on *mētis* versus *techne*: "Where mētis is contextual and particular, techne is universal."[128] The Westerner sets out across the Sahara armed with science and technology (*techne*), and his worldview is one that supports his confidence in his ability to conquer unknown geography with superior geographical knowledge provided by technology. This is a distinctly Orientalist mindset as Said notes that "Geography was essentially the material underpinning for knowledge about the Orient."[129] Through the novel, Vázquez-Figueroa undermines this mindset, and chips away at Orientalist confidence and prowess, rendering it helpless in the face of the Tuareg's *mētis*.

This previous complication of the term *oikos* in relation to the nomad does not detract from the analysis at hand, it is simply a clarification of the limits of the theory as it pertains to a non-Western subject. The nomadic, self-exiled family of *Los ojos del Tuareg* physically moves within the narrative and is fully conscious of the risks of travel and life in the desert. In the beginning, when they flee society into the desert and search for water, they undertake an itinerary full of risks and dangers, in fact losing the middle son in the process. Abbeele does posit that "the very activity of traveling may also displace the home . . . thus undermining the institution of that economy and allowing for an infinite or unbounded travel"[130] which would appear to solve the problem of an unfixed *oikos*, and yet, the Tuaregs of this novel never leave a geographical space to which they do not feel indigenously tied, that is, their movement is contained within a familiar zone. Even if the specific locations are unfamiliar, their *mētis* is still relevant. This is not the case for the ralliers; they have transported themselves beyond a range where tradition and experience can guide them and must therefore rely on their *techne*—both their technology and their book knowledge—and in this scenario they are fitting portrayals of the arrogant Orientalist or colonizer, setting out to conquer, confident that their knowledge is geographically transferable and universal.

In fact, Milosevic's poisoning of the family well represents the extremes of Orientalist arrogance contrasted with the tempered existence of the nomadic Other. Prior to dumping the motor oil into the well, he attempts to wash the dust from his car, an action which horrifies the Tuaregs in its blatant waste of precious resources. His subsequent rash action threatens the nomad's very survival. Milosevic essentially acts under the "universal," Western conception that water is plentiful, an example of a non-transferable mindset that, when transposed to the desert setting, threatens survival. This opposition of "knowledges" is the central conflict of the novel.

The Tuareg's relationship with the desert, his familiarity with the terrain, undergirds the novel. Vázquez-Figueroa portrays this relationship as intrinsic in the Tuareg being. In their search for water, Gacel compares the Tuareg existence to that of a desert palm: "the day that an *Imohag*[131] is not capable of doing what a palm can, our race will be condemned to disappearing from the face of the earth. And that moment has not arrived yet. . . . This is something that your father taught me and that you will have to teach to your children."[132] This representation is not one of the simplistic and naïve "noble savage"; there is little naiveté in Gacel and his family. Instead, it serves to emphasize the Westerner's failure to understand its African Other, an Other which is both this nomadic family and the desert. This tie to the land supports the interpretation that the Tuaregs, even though they travel as a mode of life, remain consistently within a defined space that can be understood to be their *oikos*. This *oikos* is inherently dangerous, and they are subject to the same potential for loss or profit that other travelers are, and yet their familiarity with the terrain makes for successful navigation of the same. Lacking this territorial familiarity, the traveling ralliers must rely on their *techne*, which ultimately fails in the crucial moments of crisis within the novel. In this sense, Vázquez-Figueroa's novel "has less to do with the Orient than it does with 'our' world."[133] Therefore, Gacel Sayah's fight is not against individuals, but rather against a worldview that assumes control over a foreign territory on the basis of superior technology and capital (neither of which hold any effective power in the desert). Vázquez-Figueroa uses the Tuaregs to examine and criticize the corrupt and vapid Western consumerist worldview and culture.

In this sense, Vázquez-Figueroa exploits the archetype of the nomad as an esperpentic lens through which to return the gaze upon the West. I would hesitate to suggest that Vázquez-Figueroa penetrates the ethos of the Tuaregs in his portrayal of them; his use is perhaps more appropriately symbolic. *Los ojos del Tuareg* is a somewhat simplistic novel, in that it is more interested in working a thesis than creating a moving literary piece. That said, intentionally or not, the narrative suggests a cultural awareness on the part of the author to write against Orientalist discourse. His use of the Tuaregs still achieves a narrative that is counter to traditional Orientalism.

Therefore, in this confrontation between the Tuaregs and the West, Gacel Sayah and his family are forced to engage with the rally car drivers and, by extension, the rally organizers. The nomads effectively face off against the powerful corporate sponsorship of the race that is in close partnership with global media to promote sales. This global media and financial structure has little to no concern for the inhabitants of forgotten corners of the desert. The nomads are marginalized and ignored because they have no effective purchasing power, and yet conversely, the backdrop of the desert—suggesting adventure and the prowess of Western technology when corporate logos are foregrounded in the global media—is a profitable motif for international advertising.

Within this indifference to the inhabitants of the desert, the person of the Other is consciously manipulated by the West, specifically through the character of Alex Fawcett. Fawcett has at his disposal access to and certain power over media outlets around the world. He is the one who is ultimately responsible for the media coverage of the race, a race that is supported by advertising money and which depends on adherence to a certain Westernized script. After learning of the hostages and meeting with Gacel, Alex Fawcett is counseled by his associate, Yves Clos:

> who the fuck cares that some so-and-so that they've never heard of wins a section of a car race that occurs in a corner of Africa of which they also have never heard of before? . . . no one. But your department is in charge of creating this 'useless necessity,' ensuring that our images are emitted when a ton of bored people are seated in front of the television, because these will be the people who buy the products that our clients advertise.[134]

This conversation betrays the dynamics that undergird the race: (1) it is dependent upon Western capital, and (2) it is a televised spectacle that has little to do with Africa and everything to do with the spectacle of televised adventure. Vázquez-Figueroa highlights the West's ultimate disinterest in Africa. The interest is on the Westerner's exploits occurring at previously scheduled, broadcast moments that conform to audiences' and advertisers' preconceived expectations. The novel focuses on the way that perceptions are molded by the media and controlled by capital. The Other is who big money finds it most beneficial to be. This truth is made even more explicit as Nené Dupré discusses with Hans Scholt—an Austrian reporter who seeks to write a piece that undermines the race's official narrative—the ultimate importance of positive publicity over all else:

> "If the hostages die they will be satisfied with taking some photographs and giving them to the press as irrefutable proof that some 'heartless bandits' assaulted, robbed, and murdered some innocent athletes who had done no harm to anyone."
> "But that is not the truth."
> "It will be 'their truth' and I don't think that they will leave alive anyone who can offer a different version."[135]

Vázquez-Figueroa highlights this battle over the power to represent: who has the power to represent the Other?

This question on representation is considered from various angles. The Austrian reporter, Hans Scholt, writes an exposé of the race that presents Alex Fawcett in unflattering terms, and yet Fawcett is so well connected that Scholt is fired from his position on Fawcett's request. Fawcett tells Scholt that he was able to accomplish this by "reminding his director that without our collaboration no reporter in the world would be able to cover this information."[136] Vázquez-Figueroa also flirts with the consideration that the catch-all term of "terrorist" is a construction of the Western world that benefits the West by never offering a voice to the Other. Gacel's request of Milosevic's hand horrifies the Western sensibility. In a reunion of Tuareg leaders (which does not include Gacel Sayah or his family) with a representative of the rally, they consider the possibilities of organizing and fighting against the injustice perpetrated on their land and people:

> "[We should order] all of the Imohag . . . to impede at whatever price the passage of your cars, your vehicles, and your trucks."
> "This sounds like terrorism."
> "No! Not at all! Do not try to confuse the terms. The terrorist is a despicable creature that attacks by betrayal hiding in anonymity. Ours is a declaration of war, one in which the enemy does not hide. The enemy is the Tuareg Nation in force."
> "Are you prepared to kill?"
> "In any war there are deaths."[137]

This popular resistance is effective in disrupting the race, and yet, Fawcett maintains the power of representation to the world press and is able to portray the *Imohag* as little more than roving bandits and stereotypical "terrorists." That is, the West's *techne* may not serve to guide them in navigating the desert, but it does connect them with the West and afford them the power of representation to the West. As Fawcett uses his power to manipulate the international discourse, ignoring local realities, the novel questions which is more horrifying: a Tuareg seeking the hand of a man who attempted to kill him and his family by contaminating their water supply, or the acts that are carried out in the name of Western capitalism which cause untold damage and cruelty?

This explicit question comes as Hans Scholt reveals his investigations to Nené Dupré, showing him photos of children missing limbs from land mines fabricated by the very companies that sponsor the race.[138] Sponsorship and capital motivate every Western action; however, money is shown to be a false motivation in life and death situations such as the final showdown in the desert. Gacel Sayah never has any interest in what money can afford him; Alex Fawcett has millions at his disposal and yet cannot accomplish his goals easily. Bruno Serafian, a mercenary sent to attack Gacel, realizes that he would return "all [of the money] that they have paid us in order to not find myself in this place."[139] Ultimately, the Westerners are at the mercy of capital and Western society. Comparatively, the nomadic Tuareg is at the mercy of the desert. The juxtaposition of these two colliding worldviews in the diegetic space of the novel offers up the intriguing metaphor that modern, Western society is nothing more than a bleak desert—both *techne* as well as money are superficial resources for navigating it in a meaningful way.

Vázquez-Figueroa strips away the Western might of technology in favor of the interpersonal encounter. He admits the power of the media in controlling representation of the Other: "The spectacle is inhuman, but colorful and brilliant."[140] And yet he finds a more honest approach in the face-to-face exchange of two individuals. Nené Dupré forms a friendship with Gacel Sayah, and the first rally car drivers to stop at the oasis establish a cordial relationship with the Tuareg family also. Even the hostages and the mercenaries learn to respect Gacel Sayah because he treats them humanely. Within the text, interpersonal interaction leads to mutual respect for the Other, whereas personal isolation (and interaction with the forms of media) leads to paranoia and fear, as in the case of Alex Fawcett. There is no cultural high-ground afforded the West. Through the trope of travel, Vázquez-Figueroa shows the limited utility of the West's accumulated knowledge in practical situations. He still admits the power of portrayal that the West's media controls, a power which allows the West to classify persons as "terrorists" or "heroes," and yet he holds that

> It is usually joked that this rally is like a circus, but to tell the truth it is not an innocent circus of clowns and tightrope walkers, but rather an authentic 'Roman circus' in which the emperors have been substituted for television cameras, the roaring lions for roaring vehicles launched at full speed . . . and the 'Christians' for poor natives who from time to time get run over by a car. The spectacle is inhuman.[141]

Los ojos del Tuareg offers this subversive alternative to the popular media, and therefore represents a significant deviation from historic Orientalist discourse.

This subversion, however, is not the only merit to the novel. I have examined how Vázquez-Figueroa establishes a parallel Other, distinct from the Westerner, with its own system of values and beliefs. These two worlds collide, resulting in conflict; a conflict which unravels through exchange, through the encounter.[142] While Vázquez-Figueroa does occasionally poeticize his portrayal of the nomadic Tuareg, he stops short of romanticizing this Other into either a noble savage or a symbolic martyr. He does not even go as far as Levinas in "proclaiming praise for and the superiority of the Other,"[143] but he does emphasize the value of the personal encounter between individuals for furthering understanding of the Other. As Gacel Sayah holds several ralliers hostage, they come to respect one another. Even the mercenaries that are sent to exterminate the nomads find mercy from and respect for their adversaries. Nené Dupré forms a close friendship with Gacel, and Gacel ultimately shows mercy on Milosevic, who insulted and imperiled his family in the first place. That is, through interpersonal interaction a common humanity is realized and valued. Gacel ultimately places this recognition of shared humanity above the upholding of traditional laws—the Tuareg laws which demand the hand of Milosevic—and when Milosevic is delivered to

Gacel for his punishment, he lets him go leaving only a small scar on his hand as a reminder.[144] This physical mark on flesh, therefore, forces Milosevic to recognize the Other through a recognition of his own skin.

Gacel Sayah's evolution from hardline fundamentalist to merciful humanist is a dialectical process that evolves as he dialogues with his hostages, Nené Dupré, and Hans Scholt. The ultimate recognition of shared humanity arises from the face-to-face encounter unmediated by the media. As Kapuściński paraphrases Levinas in saying: "Stop. . . . There beside you is another person. Meet him. This sort of encounter is the greatest event, the most vital experience of all. Look at the Other's face as he offers it to you. Through this face he shows you yourself."[145] This is why the title *Los ojos del Tuareg* is apt to emphasize the personal encounter that transcends stereotyping and cultural narratives of the Other. It reaches beyond the spectacle, showing those representations to be unreliable, and considers the implications that dialogue can bring.

While Vázquez-Figueroa's presentation of the Tuareg Other may not be entirely realistic, it engages with the question of reality behind the spectacle that the media offers and considers the human that is called Other. In focusing on the struggles of the individual Gacel Sayah and his family, the novel avoids grand stereotypes of what it means to be "African," a "nomad," "Muslim," or other categories that are so common, and it is able to focus on a family's fight for recognition in a world that wants to fit them into a clearly marked category and exploit them. While the other Tuareg tribes do stand in solidarity with Gacel against the international ralliers, there is no physical contact between Gacel's family and them and this support is more symbolic than reinforcing. The dramatic conflict plays itself out between Gacel and the international ralliers and their mercenaries. Gacel and his brother single-handedly decimate a team of highly trained and equipped hired guns; it is an individual fight against the corporate power of Western capital. Even though Gacel's demand for vengeance horrifies the Western sensibility, Vázquez-Figueroa shows that Western capitalism and the media are the true horrors unleashed upon the world that cause untold damage and cruelty.

In adhering to the generic conventions of an adventure novel, every clue throughout the plot development builds toward the moment when Gacel Sayah will chop off the hand of Marc Milosevic and receive his vengeance. When Gacel chooses not to follow through, he undermines the expectations placed on him throughout the narrative due to his cultural heritage as a Tuareg. As he rejects the readers' expectations, so does Vázquez-Figueroa reject the mantle of Orientalist discourse that would resolve such a story in easy cultural platitudes. What the reader is left with at the end is not a flat representation of an emblematic Other; Gacel Sayah is an individual with the ability to deviate from hegemonic narratives of representation that would trap him in models of tradition or acculturation. I hesitate to term his stance at the end of the novel "transculturation" because there is no hybridized culture that develops, and yet, through his encounter with the European Other, Gacel Sayah recognizes a shared humanity that transcends his own traditional views and is also ignored by the corporate West with whom he is at war. It is a neutral third ground that recognizes humanity first above culture, tradition, and difference. This is the most subversive element of Vázquez-Figueroa's novel, and the one which explicitly deviates from the traps of Orientalism. Vázquez-Figueroa offers a place beyond the binaries of Occident and Orient that emphasizes the encounter of human-before-human, and while the binaries exist in the background, the encounter provides an opportunity to step beyond the limits of group identity into the moment of interpersonal contact.

In concluding this analysis of *Los ojos del Tuareg*, it serves to return to Said and the consideration of travel. Said briefly discusses travel in *Orientalism*. He offers two situations: (1) "One is when a human being confronts at close quarters something relatively unknown and threatening and previously distant," or conversely (2) "A second situation [relies on] the appearance of success."[146] Both options juxtapose textual information versus reality by highlighting that "Many travelers find themselves saying of an experience in a new country that it wasn't what they expected it to be, meaning that it wasn't what a book said it would be," and leading to the idea that "the book (or text) acquires a greater authority, and use, even than the actuality it describes."[147] Vázquez-Figueroa undermines both of these Orientalist approaches to travel writing, albeit through a text. In the first case, he offers an encounter with an Other ("relatively unknown and threatening and previously distant"[148]) and builds on the readers' expectations throughout the novel—that Gacel will demand the hand of Marc Milosevic in revenge—ultimately to deny the readers' expectations in the final pages, showing that not only is the narrative different from "what [the reader] expected it to be" but also that the book itself is admitting that it wasn't what it "said it would be." It destabilizes readers' expectations, simultaneously destabilizing the Orientalist tropes on which it occasionally relies.

As noted above, Said also offers a second scenario:

> If one reads a book claiming that lions are fierce and then encounters a fierce lion ... the chances are that one will be encouraged to read more books by that same author, and believe them.[149]

Said discusses that this appearance of success can lead to the expectation of the fierceness of lions, thereby increasing their perceived fierceness. According to Said, then, the text serves to strengthen preconceived notions of the Other (in his example of a lion), exaggerating essentialist observations.

Vázquez-Figueroa's conclusion avoids this textual attitude by admitting in the final pages that cultural expectations are unreliable. By denying the readers' expectations, Vázquez-Figueroa relinquishes his authority on the Other by offering the consideration that the rules of representing the Other are not hard and steadfast. These characters are not just flat, cultural stereotypes, but individuals with the power to support or depart from hegemonic norms as they see fit.

In *Los ojos del Tuareg,* Vázquez-Figueroa effectively destabilizes his own authority over representation, employing the adventure novel genre and yet also departing from a conventionally anticipated climax. His emphasis on the personal encounter between the European and the African avoids grand narratives of Otherness and finds a common point of relation and understanding between the two. The theme of travel—the rally drivers versus the nomads—serves to underpin this interaction, highlighting the cultural differences that thrust competing cultures into contact. As a result, the mechanized Westerner with his *techne* collides with the indigenous African and his *mētis*. These contrasts establish the difference that the personal encounter overcomes. The novel offers the consideration that, despite the Otherness of the Other, a face-to-face encounter can reconcile these differences in light of shared humanity.

THE MIGRANT AND NARRATION IN AHMED DAOUDI'S *EL DIABLO DE YUDIS*

Ahmed Daoudi, was born in 1965 in Fez, Morocco. He received a degree in Spanish philology in Morocco and then moved to Madrid, Spain, to pursue a doctorate degree, which he completed in 1992. While in Spain, he published *El Diablo de Yudis*[150] in 1994; this is his first and only published work.[151] Published by Ediciones Vosa in Madrid, this text is considered to be the first novel by a Moroccan author to be published originally in Spanish by a Spanish press.[152] It was well received at the time but had a limited distribution.[153] Upon his return to Morocco, Daoudi was briefly affiliated with the Spanish Department at the University Hassan II in Casablanca,[154] but, in the early 2000s, he disappeared completely, to the great concern of those that know him.[155] Close friends and acquaintances have not heard from him in many years; his publishers have been unable to contact him, and the *Nueva asociación de escritores marroquíes en lengua española*[156] has expressed continued concern over his disappearance.

The novel has been examined from various perspectives by a number of academics. Ana Rueda considers its focus on trans-Mediterranean migration;[157] Adolfo Campoy-Cubillo focuses on the performance of identity and postcoloniality in *Memories of the Maghreb* (2012), and Brian Bobbitt's 2016 dissertation examines the imagery and semantics of burial in the novel.[158] Juliane Tauchnitz further analyzes the construction of identity in the novel through migratory movements in "Identity Questions in *El diablo de Yudis* by Ahmed Daoudi" (2018), and I examined the creation of imaginary spaces in the novel in "*Un reino tan lejano*: Yudis, Shahrazad and the Imaginary Space in the Contemporary Hispano-Moroccan Novel" (2017). The novel's complex narrative structure and multiple narrative threads create a text that is open to various interpretations and analyses. This narrative richness and the novel's status as the first novel by a Moroccan author to be published in Spanish by a Spanish press confirms its value as a text that merits continued attention.

The novel develops on multiple narrative planes. It is divided into eight chapters, and throughout each chapter, the narration jumps between the imaginary story of Yudis to the frustrated emigration(s) from Morocco to Spain of the unnamed narrator. The novel is foregrounded with the story about a fictional land called Yudis that is plagued by a demon. An army from the continent of Burwilasch is sent to aid the citizens of Yudis in their fight against this demon. The reader soon discovers that this story is the creation of a storyteller in the plaza of Boujloud in Fez. This storytelling strategy employs the traditional Moroccan form of oral storytelling called *al-halqa*.[159] This unnamed narrator begins to interweave his own personal story with his invented story, and he narrates his difficult life, attempted clandestine emigrations, and subsequent repatriations, all leading to his current life as an impoverished plaza storyteller. Daoudi's novel was inspired by the stories of his fellow Moroccan immigrants in Spain,[160] and its publication coincided with other contemporaneous attempts in Spanish literature (by Spanish authors) to highlight the plight of Maghrebi immigrants in Spain.[161]

The novel is structurally creative, richly narrated, and unique. Since its publication in 1994, there has been a boom of Moroccan authors writing in Spanish, but Daoudi's work still stands as one of the most internationally recognized examples. The novel's treatment of a frustrated emigration story, written by an immigrant Maghrebi author, offers the opportunity to examine the representation of the African migrant from a non-European viewpoint. In his book, *Memories of the Maghreb* (2012), Adolfo Campoy-Cubillo highlights the contemporaneous publication of two other novels to Daoudi's: *Yo, Mohamed*,[162] published in 1995 by Rafael Torres, and *Dormir al raso*,[163] published in 1994 by Pasqual Moreno Torregrosa and Mohamed El Ghreyb. Campoy-Cubillo notes that, of the three novels, Daoudi's is the most "direct expression of Spanish, postcolonial identity."[164] And while there have been a number of other books or short stories by African authors in Spanish that take up the theme of immigration in the years since,[165] *El diablo de Yudis'* distinction as the first novel by a Moroccan author published in Spanish by a Spanish press highlights the importance of its voice and historical position.

This study approaches Daoudi's work by focusing on the work's strategies of narration and the theme of migration. In Daoudi's narrative, these two themes are intricately intertwined. The unnamed narrator is a traditional story-teller in Fez, Morocco that weaves his fantastical story of the devil in Yudis in the traditional Moroccan oral storytelling tradition of *al-halqa*. The narrator's role as a *hlayqi* creates a narrative space that is uniquely non-Western, and yet it is produced in and disseminated in Spanish in its novelistic format. These two essential elements of the text construct a narrative space that employs traditional Moroccan narrative techniques to disrupt Orientalist readings of the text by highlighting the power of narration with its concomitant inherent unreliability. With *El diablo de Yudis,* Daoudi adapts the *halqa* theatrical genre to the novel format and exploits the affective powers of the theatrical genre to engage the reader on the issues of migration, marginalization, and postcoloniality.

In *Memories of the Maghreb*, Adolfo Campoy-Cubillo analyzes the use of the *halqa* narrative format as a strategy for expressing an allegory of recent Moroccan history in order to engage with the complications of postcolonial identity. Campoy-Cubillo's analysis is strong and convincing but focuses on the fantastic plot of the imaginary Yudis, and I would like to expand it to consider the frustrated emigrations and narrative circles that the novel develops. I argue that Daoudi not only includes an example of the *halqa* in his novel, but also develops a *halqa* in the novel format. Moroccan theater scholar Khalid Amine describes the *halqa* in the following:

> *Al-halqa* is a public gathering in the form of a circle around a performer or a number of performers (*hlayqi/hylaqia*) in a public space, be it a marketplace, a medina gate, or a newly devised town square. It is a space of popular culture that is open to all people from different walks of life. Al-halqa hovers between high culture and low mass culture, sacred and profane, literacy and orality. Its repertoire combines fantastic, mythical, and historical narratives from *A Thousand and One Nights* and *Sirat bani hilal*, as well as stories from the holy Quran and the Sunna of the prophet Mohammed.[166]

In later work, Amine expands his description of the *halqa* to note its contestatory and inclusive characteristics:

> The space [of the performance] is a neutral area for presentation with spectators totally surrounding the action, and an action that continually sought to involve those spectators. This liminal performance arrangement, most commonly called the *halqa* (circle), has become widely employed in the modern Arabic theatre

and provides a distinct alternative to the traditional European proscenium stage. *Al-halqa* has a managed environment that is strictly opposed to the traditional European closed theatrical space. Its audience is called upon "to drift" spontaneously into an arc surrounding the performances from all sides. The space required by the *hlayqi* (the maker of the spectacle) is not a specific space, and the performance may take place at any time. No fourth wall with hypnotic fields is erected between stage and auditorium, for such binary opposition does not exist in *al-halqa*.[167]

Campoy-Cubillo notes that the *halqa* oratory strategy was employed as "a vehicle of expression of anticolonialist aspirations"[168] and that it was an "especially effective tool to question the authority of the hegemonic colonial discourse."[169] It is a deceptively subversive storytelling strategy that, in practice, depends on body language and audience participation for its full power. Daoudi's adaptation of the *halqa* storytelling framework adds significant cultural nuances to his narration, and the multiple narrative layers of the novel draw readers into the story while repeatedly reminding them of their status as audience, effectively employing the Brechtian *Verfremdungseffekt*.

Amine and Campoy-Cubillo both apply the term *Verfremdungseffekt* to the *halqa* theatrical tradition[170] as a strategy that highlights the "distanciation" of the audience.[171] However, the term can be applied specifically to Daoudi's narrative choices in the novel format as well.[172] Daoudi adapts the *halqa* genre and exploits its key elements of circular structure,[173] audience distanciation/alienation,[174] and inclusivity[175] to create a novel that disrupts the Western/Orientalist gaze.

Estrangement and alienation imbue many elements of the novel. The narrator of the novel, the *hlayqi*, is unnamed. Juliane Tauchnitz notes that "he is the only character whose name is never disclosed. Hence, he is even deprived of an own identity."[176] Tauchnitz's analysis of this is that he is one more of the unnamed "clandestine immigrants, . . . those who fail in societies such as the Spanish or Moroccan ones."[177] Brecht might suggest that this lack of a name converts the narrator into "an empty sheet of paper that can be written on";[178] it alienates the reader of the text as "everyday things are removed from the realm of the self-evident."[179] By denying the narrator a name, the reader/audience is prevented from full empathy (*Einfühlung*) with a named protagonist. The narrator's lack of a name serves the dual function of positioning the narrator as a migrant archetype—one more of the "clandestine immigrants"—while also developing a theatrical/narrative distancing effect for the reader.

The narrator's migrant aspirations are repeatedly frustrated. His legal status in Morocco is tenuous; his family lives in a poor, illegally developed neighborhood, and he and his wife become increasingly dissatisfied with their attenuated legal and economic status. He makes two attempts to cross the

Mediterranean to arrive in Spain so that he can make his way on to France and eventually England to be able to return to his wife and family "to buy a house or a parcel of land; I would return in a big car; I would return as if I had been born again, but this time with more luck."[180] Both of his attempts are clandestine; the first is by *patera* in a dangerous crossing of the Strait at night; they are intercepted by the *Guardia Civil* upon reaching the coast of Spain and he is immediately repatriated. The second attempt is by ferry with a fake visa. With this attempt, he makes it past customs in Algeciras and boards a bus to go and find work in Murcia but is caught by the police at a bus stop and again repatriated. For the narrator, each aspiration of success, both in Morocco and in his migration journeys, is frustrated. He is impotent to improve his life, and he is continually forced to live on the margins of society.

The narrator's repeatedly frustrated aspirations reflect a core element of the *halqa*, "suspense, a device as old as *A Thousand and One Nights*."[181] At each turn, the narrator hopes for a positive turn of events and finds disappointment instead. Suspense and hope imbue each stage of his life, but the reader, along with the protagonist, is denied a positive resolution. The recounting of the narrator's life follows the same narrative structures as the *halqa* tale that he spins in Boujloud plaza, and the story of Yudis becomes a *mise en abyme*—another hallmark of the *halqa*[182]—for the narrator's life as the search for the devil in Yudis is inconclusive and ends in absurdity.

While the narrator is performing the *halqa* within the novel, the narrative planes create a meta-*halqa*. This re-creates the circular structuring of the *halqa*'s performance; the audience in the plaza forms in a circle around the narrator to hear the story of Yudis, and the reading audience forms another, extra-diegetic circle witnessing the novel's performance of a *halqa*.[183] This is one subtle way in which Daoudi breaks the fourth wall, by creating narrative circles that expand and metaphorically include the reader in the performance of *halqa* about his migration experience.

In addition, the narrator also *"makes it clear that he knows he is being looked at"*[184] in both subtle and direct ways through repeated comments that highlight the artificiality and impotence of narration. The narrator develops this sense of futility in narration through two anecdotes from his hard life in Morocco; truthful narration is shown to be ineffective and powerless. In the first, the narrator's friend and brother-in-law, Tawawan, works with the union at the factory where they are both employed in order to organize a strike for better hours and consistent pay. The factory's security frames him for drug possession and for stealing from the factory. Tawawan is arrested and at the trial

> the owner's witnesses were the guard, the manager, and an employee that saw him when he was caught leaving the building: it was all indisputable. Tawawan's

declarations didn't count for anything, even though his lawyer, given to him at no cost by the union, tried to demonstrate that it was all a set up. The court was only convinced by the proof . . . we knew that it was a set up, but no one paid attention to us. It's impossible, impossible, sometimes it's impossible to demonstrate the truth.[185]

The anecdote highlights the marginalized position of Tawawan and the narrator in society, where truth is a matter of political power and privileged perspective, neither of which they have. The truthful words of Tawawan and his supporters are unable to convince others of their veracity.

This short anecdote is immediately followed by a similar story of the neighborhood resident Bailabú who is repeatedly robbed by "the thief Sardaf."[186] When the police refuse to help, Bailabú decides to catch the thief in the act and raises the alarm, drawing neighbors that promise to serve as witnesses when they observe Sardaf stealing from Bailabú. In the drawn-out time until the trial, Sardaf intimidates the witnesses such that none appear at the trial and there is insufficient evidence to convict the thief. Realizing that he cannot trust the testimonies of his neighbors, Bailabú then sets out to photograph Sardaf in the act, but when Sardaf sees the camera flash catching him in the act, he proceeds to steal Bailabú's camera. Bailabú is again left unable to prove the crimes:

It was all unbelievable to the justice because there was no proof. Only Bailabú was able to demonstrate the truth, but his truth was not demonstrable because he lacked the proof that was required. On the contrary, the lie was able to be converted, through proofs, into the truth, just like what happened with Tawawan.[187]

These exchanges call to mind Lyotard's articulation of the *differend* where "reality is not what is 'given' to this or that 'subject,' it is a state of the referent,"[188] directly applicable to Daoudi's skepticism of the effectiveness of narration as the protagonists find that they are "endowed with language [but] . . . placed in a situation such that none of them is now able to tell about it . . . their testimony bears only upon a minute part of this situation."[189] These stories highlight the marginalized position of the narrator and his neighbors, while displaying the relative impotence of their words and testimony to bring about change or justice, or to convince those with the power to help of their credibility.

As Daoudi's narrator highlights the subjectivity of narration, he also reflects on his own act of narrating. In the plaza in Fez, he describes the strategy of effective narration:

The experience had taught me sufficiently well how to draw a crowd from among the plaza's loiterers. I know that to start the narration you have to attract attention and highlight the plight of the protagonists.[190]

He notes the importance of suspense as essential for capturing the attention of an audience, in a metanarrative reflection, and then builds suspense as the police enter the plaza and begin to break up the crowds around the public entertainers, threatening his story. This metanarrative reflection is *"the actor look[ing] at himself . . . from time to time he looks at the spectator as if to say: Isn't it just like that?"*[191] This compounds the *Verfremdungseffekt*; Brecht writes that

> To look at himself is for the performer an artful and artistic act of self-estrangement. Any empathy on the spectator's part is thereby prevented from becoming total, that is, from being a complete self-surrender. An admirable distance from the events portrayed is achieved. This is not to say that the spectator experiences no empathy whatsoever. He feels his way into the actor as into an observer. In this manner an observing, watching attitude is cultivated.[192]

The narration winks at the reader; it is an "instant of intrusion into the everyday: it is what constantly demands to be explained and re-explained—in other words, it is an estrangement which asks to be further estranged."[193] It is the *hlayqi* winking knowingly at his audience, acknowledging awareness but awareness of an act that is simultaneously impotent to express truth.

As the police search the plaza to break up illegal merchants and undesirable storytellers, the metanarrative reflection considers the value of the story and its audience. The narrator's friend Airut, a snake charmer in the plaza, remarks to him that

> "You're the only lucky one."
> "Why's that?"
> "They can't confiscate your stories."
> "Get out of here! And what about my money?"[194]

Airut compares the narrator's stories to a commodity sold in the medina's market. He suggests that the intangible nature of stories protects the narrator from having his product taken from him by the police, but the narrator contests that his ability to generate income is equally disrupted as the authorities exert policing power over the marginalized vendors and storytellers in the public plaza.

Here, the narrator also highlights the limited audience for his stories:

The foreign tourists that so often visited us would walk by Airut to watch his dancing serpents, or by Buschif to inspect the flame that didn't burn. But they never benefit me at all, because they don't understand what I'm saying, or, maybe, they don't even understand what I'm doing. My clientele is always the same class of people and my earnings are disastrously limited.[195]

The audience that can understand his stories is linguistically limited; his public storytelling can only be accessed through a shared linguistic knowledge with his audience, and, as such, it is not accessible visually (such as Airut's snake-charming) or tangibly (such as the artisans or vendors). The power of story-telling, of narration, is limited, unappreciated, and unvalued.

This observation of the narrator further functions to alienate the reader of the text. The novel is narrated in the first-person, directed at the reading audience, and expressed in Spanish, but here the narrator suggests that the "tourist" audience is unable to understand his tales or even what it is that he does. Through this distancing/alienation/estrangement trick, Daoudi forces the reader of the text to question their ability to understand or empathize with the narrator's tales. This distancing strategy reflects Brecht's *Verfremdungseffekt*, but, more importantly, it participates in the *halqa* tradition of "constantly distanc[ing] the audience from the theatrical action."[196]

This estrangement strategy is multiplied by the fact that the novel was written and published in Spanish. Campoy-Cubillo asserts that the narrator is engaging in a harsh critique of Spanish colonialism:

The postcolonial subject is doomed to live with a corrupted image of his/her traditional identity. But the postcolonial subject is not the only one that is unable to purge the devil of colonization, as the narrator of Daoudi's novel, published in Spanish for the descendants of the Spanish colonizers, in a gesture that is reminiscent of the interactive nature of the halqa, addresses the reader directly to remind him/her of his/her role in the postcolonial drama.[197]

But there is more, Ngũgĩ wa Thiong'o, in his essay "Decolonising the Mind," argues that literary production by postcolonial subjects in a colonial language should be described as "colonial alienation."[198] And, in following the circular format of the *halqa*,[199] this postcolonial literary production creates a

deliberate disassociation of the language of conceptualization, of thinking, of formal education, of mental development, from the language of daily interaction in the home and in the community. It is like separating the mind from the body so that they are occupying two unrelated linguistic spheres in the same person.[200]

As Daoudi alienates his novel's audience, so also does he participate in a self-alienating practice that draws attention to himself as narrator, performer, and alienated "postcolonial subject."[201] It effectively highlights the Otherness of the narrator and the readers, following in the tradition and the potential of the

> halqa's capacity to implicate "Others," it negotiates the differing relationships among its participants. And in the process, it reformulates cultural values and self-knowledge as it engages its audience in a constant game of role-playing. The performance imbues the human actions of the narratives with a heightened potential to shape, reflect, and mirror cultural identity.[202]

Narratively, Daoudi adapts the oral *halqa* format for the novel, maintaining core elements of structure, alienation, and theatricality. These elements engage the Spanish-reading audience with a critique and an invitation to participate in the sense of alienation that the postcolonial subject lives. As Amine notes, the *halqa* storytelling tradition holds great potential to engage with its audience and to "re-formulate" and "shape" values and identity. This is a powerful possibility as Daoudi employs the novel format to direct a *halqa* tale towards a Spanish audience.

While many of Daoudi's narrative strategies are subtle, the final two pages of the novel make this engagement with the reader direct and unmistakable. These final two pages are two separate, very short chapters (chapters 7 and 8). Chapter 6 concludes the tale of the devil in Yudis with a somewhat ambiguous finale, and chapter 7 opens in the second person plural directed at the audience, "With the applause, my story comes to an end, but I need other, more real, shows of appreciation, that of your generosity."[203] In the entire novel, these final two pages are the only place where the narrator directly addresses the plural crowd in the second person. The request for a few dirhams from the audience is a standard component of *al-halqa* performances and Amine notes that "they bear a matrix of exteriority; meanwhile, they are legitimate parts of the whole body of al-halqa."[204] As the narrator makes this request of his audience, the police raid the plaza to disperse the various unlicensed vendors. The one-paragraph of chapter 7 ends with the narrator's words to the police officers as the text suggests that he is arrested: "They're not talking. Where are you taking me? Hey, hey! I haven't done anything; I was only telling a story about the devil here in the plaza."[205] Chapter 8 is one line only, a cryptic "Shut up. You're the devil,"[206] and with that line the novel ends.

This is an ambiguous ending, open to multiple interpretations. Daoudi plays with the narrative and this ambiguity to unsettle the reader's complacency. If there were no chapter break, the reader might easily assume that this final line followed the narrator's detention by the police and was something that one of the officers said to him as they apprehended him, but its separation—its distancing—into a separate chapter disrupts the narrative flow and casts doubt onto both the question of speaker and the intended diegetic audience of the utterance. In addition, the noted silence of the officers—"They're not talking."[207]—creates uncertainty that it is an officer's response to his protestations. So, within an ambiguous narrative context, the reader encounters two solitary uses of the second person in these final pages, on page 126 an appeal for "your generosity. One, two, or three dirhams,"[208] and on page 127 "Shut up. You're the devil."[209] This has the effect of rupturing the fourth wall as the text suggests that the final insult could, in fact, be directed to the reader. Campoy-Cubillo interprets this final chapter as "address[ing] the [Spanish] reader directly to remind him/her of his/her role in the postcolonial drama,"[210] and his analysis of the novel is strong and compelling. What I would like to add to his argument is a contextualization of Daoudi's narrative strategy here within the *halqa* tradition in order to exploit the theatrical genre's "heightened potential to shape, reflect, and mirror cultural identity."[211]

As the narration of the final two chapters turns to face the reader with the use of the second person, Amine notes that these "comments and accompanying transitory devices" directed at the audience have tremendous power:

> Mostly, these comments are sources of humor, yet, they are also demythologizing mechanisms. They bear a matrix of exteriority; meanwhile they are legitimate parts of the whole body of al-halqa. And this is how al-halqa can be seen as a performance that is both representing and represented. Its narrative utterances elevate it to an explicit space of textual practice that is discursively contextualized. And this fact constitutes the traversing of al-halqa from a geographical space (ringlike circle) to a cultural space, from narrative to narratives, from text to con-texts.[212]

This final line, therefore, confirms the novel's status as a novelistic *halqa*, and it draws on the potential of the theatrical genre to demythologize, "shape, reflect, and mirror cultural identity."[213]

The insult directed at the reader ruptures the fourth wall, enhancing the Brechtian *Verfremdungseffekt*, "turning off or shutting down . . . *Einfühlung*, . . . empathy or even sympathy."[214] This alienation/estrangement forces the reader to accept or reject the narrator's words, requiring a reaction from "the conscious realm, not . . . [from] the spectator's subconscious."[215] It is an accusation, as Campoy-Cubillo notes, but in the *halqa* tradition, it is also an invitation to interact. Amine speaks on the *halqa's* "capacity to implicate 'Others,' it negotiates the differing relationships among its participants. And in the process, it reformulates cultural values and self-knowledge as it engages its audience in a constant game of role-playing."[216] In producing this novel in Spanish, Daoudi is speaking to a specific audience that is normally linguistically excluded from the *halqa* (as he notes on page 68 of the novel).

It is an accusation, but it is also an invitation to engage with the text "in the conscious realm"[217] and it is an "intrusion into the everyday: it is what constantly demands to be explained and re-explained—in other words, it is an estrangement which asks to be further estranged."[218]

Daoudi employs the *halqa* and the Brechtian *Verfremdungseffekt*, therefore, as a way to write beyond an Orientalist framework. As "Orientalism is premised upon exteriority,"[219] Daoudi invites the reader into a dynamic narrative paradigm that suggests more possibilities. It invites and then disrupts the Western gaze through the use of the *Verfremdungseffekt* and introduces the reader to the alienation and estrangement that its migrant/postcolonial narrator shares.

As the narrator repeatedly highlights the inadequacy of truthful narration to effect change and the ability of the powerful to reify truth, Daoudi undermines Orientalism's assumptions of narrative objectivity. His narrative highlights the alienation of the postcolonial subject, the migrant, the poor and marginalized, as he employs a traditional Moroccan story-telling strategy to engage and upset the passive Western (Spanish) observer. In the 2003 preface to *Orientalism*, Said reflects on Humanism as an alternative to Orientalism as "humanism is centered upon the agency of human individuality and subjective intuition, rather than on received ideas and approved authority."[220] Daoudi's novel is one that is centered on the narrator's individuality and intuition. The *halqa* format plays with the passive reception of ideas and the narration undermines its own authority, creating a text that contests Orientalist strategies of narration.

Daoudi's migrant narrator is alienated and frustrated; his experiences create a "demythologizing mechanism"[221] that contextualizes the cultural archetype of the migrant. The narrator's marginalized and undocumented existence is not a product of clandestine immigration, but rather a reality of his entire life. In *El retorno/El reencuentro*, Rueda notes the themes of persecution, invisibility, marginalization, and exploitation that structure the lives of the narrator and his poor neighbors.[222] These are realities that also structure, but are not exclusive to, undocumented migration. And by combining the narrator's migrant journeys into a complex narrative of his life and his fabricated stories, Daoudi develops a multi-faceted protagonist that cannot be reduced to a simple, pitiable archetype. Juliane Tauchnitz notes that the narrator

> turns out not only to be the stereotypical image of a failing migrant, but he also must be recognized as a singular and complex individual. In other words, one (essential) part of this narrator is, in fact, characterized by this traumatic moment all the illegal fugitives share who cross the Mediterranean Sea hoping to find a better life in Europe—but that moment doesn't describe the entirety of highly diverse and heterogeneous traits that constitute a human being.[223]

And in denying the reader the facile option of pitying the poor, unfortunate migrant, Daoudi exploits the Brechtian *Verfremdungseffekt* to place the migrant and the postcolonial subject "in a new light."[224] Frederic Jameson explains the power of the *Verfremdungseffekt* to contextualize and disrupt:

> the familiar or habitual is reidentified as the 'natural', and its estrangement unveils that appearance, which suggests the changeless and the eternal as well, and shows the object to be instead 'historical', to which may be added, as a political corollary, made or constructed by human beings, and thus able to be changed by them as well, or replaced altogether.[225]

This suggests that Daoudi's novel has a subversive power to challenge existing narratives of migration and marginalization. The narrative techniques employed combined with the emphasis on the subjectivity of truth function to undermine established traditions of narration and reception, directly responding to Orientalism's legacy with an alternative that demonstrates the power of narrative creativity to traverse "from a geographical space . . . to a cultural space, from narrative to narratives, from texts to con-texts."[226]

And lastly, Daoudi's text draws on the power of the *halqa* tradition in order to draw the Spanish reader into a shared state of estrangement, disrupting passive reception, and, in using the *halqa*, it invites the reader into a conscious engagement with the themes of migration, postcoloniality, and the construction of truth. As Daoudi's narrator performs the role of *hlayqi*, sharing the fantastic tale of the devil in Yudis with a circle of onlookers in the plaza of Boujloud in Fez, the structure of the broader diegetic space forms a wider audience circle and creates a second meta-*halqa* that exploits the provocative potential of the theatrical genre to engage "in the conscious realm" with the narrative.[227]

In his 2008 article with Marvin Carlson, "'Al-Halqa' in Arabic Theatre: An Emerging Site of Hybridity," Amine ponders the as yet untapped potential of the *halqa*, writing that

> The enormous potentialities of *al-halqa* still remain unexplored at the practical level. There has been little interdisciplinary experimentation with *al-halqa's* repertoire of pre-expressivity, and its acting techniques, which might open new perspectives on the actor's energy and presence, remain largely unexplored. There has also been to date no effective use of *al-halqa's* political agency and praxis in a way similar to Boal's Theatre of the Oppressed. The *halqa* is still informed by the conventional "art as presentation," as opposed to Grotowski's last phase of research labeled by Brook, "art as vehicle." As presentation, it is still conceived within the age-old confines of the actor/spectator binary; if, however, *al-halqa* were to be elevated to the level of *art* as vehicle, then there would be no actors/spectators, only doers. The circularity of the *halqa* offers

that visionary potential—a performance that would transmit energy and harmonize bodies and minds.[228]

Daoudi's novel exploits the affective power of the *halqa* while experimenting with its vehicle of expression. It does not, perhaps, achieve the aspirational potential that Amine hopes for, but it does suggest that many of the *halqa's* strengths can be translated into the novel format with powerful results. And Daoudi's expansion of the *halqa* tradition offers a framework that undermines the legacy and strategies of Western Orientalist narration.

NOTES

1. [*Lost Trails of Africa*]
2. [*Vagabond in Africa*]
3. [*The Dream of Africa*]
4. See Carrasco González, *Historia de la novela colonial hispanoafricana*, for an extensive consideration of the Spanish colonial novel about Africa.
5. Jan Borm, in her article "Defining Travel: On the Travel Book, Travel Writing and Terminology" offers this insight: "The point to determine, therefore, is whether *travel writing* is really a genre at all. I shall argue here that it is not a genre, but a collective term for a variety of texts both predominantly fictional and non-fictional whose main theme is travel" (In *Perspectives on Travel Writing*, eds. Glenn Hooper and Tim Youngs [Burlington, Vermont: Ashgate, 2004], 13).
6. Borm, "Defining Travel," 21, 26.
7. [*Moroccan Letters*] José de Cadalso, *Cartas marruecas / Noches lúgubres* (1789. Reprint, Madrid: Cátedra, 2004).
8. Abbeele, *Travel as Metaphor*, xiii.
9. Abbeele, *Travel as Metaphor*, xvi.
10. Abbeele, *Travel as Metaphor*, xxvi.
11. [*The Doctor from Ifni*]
12. [*The Eyes of the Tuareg*]
13. [*The Devil in Yudis*]
14. See Abbeele: "*VOYAGE* . . . transport of a person from the place where one is to another place that is far enough away" (*Travel as Metaphor*, epigraph).
15. [carácter europeo] Carrasco González, *Historia de la novela colonial hispanoafricana*, 9.
16. [esa manera de narrar sobre países alejados sin pertenecer al pueblo natural de ellos y con un sentimiento o mentalidad, mayor o menor, de alteridad, es literatura colonial.] Carrasco González, *Historia de la novela colonial hispanoafricana*, 9.
17. Carrasco González, *Historia de la novela colonial hispanoafricana*, 11.
18. "In general, there is more quaintness, of tourist chronicles, of easy astonishment for the bourgeois traveler that arrives in a savage world in the colonial novel, than there is of quality and work on the content and in the complexity of the story."

[Generalizando, hay en la novela colonialista más de pintoresquismo, de crónica turística, de asombro fácil en el viajero burgués que llega al mundo salvaje, que de calidad y trabajo en el contenido y en la complejidad del relato.] Carrasco González, *Historia de la novela colonial hispanoafricana*, 28.

19. Said, *Orientalism*, 7.

20. [La guerra de África [1859–60] avivó, sin duda, el interés por Marruecos en la novela española.] Carrasco González, *Historia de la novela colonial hispanoafricana*, 36.

21. [unos relatos de gusto exótico, orientalistas en la terminología clásica de Said.] Carrasco González, *Historia de la novela colonial hispanoafricana*, 61.

22. The most famous examples being Ramón J. Sender, José Díaz Fernández, and Arturo Barea, but including many others.

23. See Reverte's travel and historical novel *El sueño de África: En busca de los mitos blancos del continente negro* [*The Dream of Africa: In Search of the White Myths of the Black Continent*] which details European exploration and visitation of Africa from David Livingstone in the mid-nineteenth century up to the author's own travels.

24. This consideration of nomadism is also tangentially considered in chapter 1 in my analysis of Ramón Mayrata's *El imperio desierto*.

25. See Leo Chavez, *The Latino Threat: Constructing Immigrants, Citizens, and the Nation* (Stanford, California: Stanford University Press, 2008), 6.

26. Chavez, *The Latino Threat*, 6.

27. [*The Return/The Reencounter: Immigration en Hispano-Moroccan Literature*]

28. [desigualdad y dependencia del más poderoso, por lo que deberá enfrentarse a los choques entre las dos culturas e identidades, la del origen y la adoptiva.] Rueda, *El retorno/el reencuentro*, 50.

29. Said, *Orientalism*, 7.

30. Abbeele's assertion that travel (voyaging) "necessarily implies a crossing of boundaries or a change of places. A voyage that stays in the same place is not a voyage. Indeed, the very notion of travel presupposes a movement away from some place, a displacement of whatever it is one understands by 'place'" (*Travel as Metaphor*, xiv) suggests both physical displacement and also the potential for ideological "movement." This "topos" of the voyage can (and perhaps should) serve to question "the status of literary discourse itself." (*Travel as Metaphor*, xiv)

31. A value that could be economic as in the hopes of the immigrant, or a value of sustenance as in the case of the nomadic lifestyle.

32. Said, *Orientalism*, xxiii.

33. Said, *Orientalism*, 150.

34. See Santí, "Fernando Ortiz," for a useful study of Malinowski and Ortiz's development and theorization of the term, especially pp. 204–210.

35. Louis Althusser, "The Underground Current of the Materialism of the Encounter," in *Philosophy of the Encounter: Later Writings, 1978–1987*, ed. François Matheron and Oliver Corpet (New York: Verso, 2006), 163–207.

36. Pratt, *Imperial Eyes*, 4.

37. [*Trilogy of Central America*] Made up of *Los dioses bajo la lluvia* [*The Gods Under the Rain*] (1986. Reprint, Madrid: Plaza & Janés Editores, 1986), *El aroma del Copal* [*The Scent of the Copal Tree*] (Madrid: Editorial Debate, 1989), and *El hombre de la guerra* [*The Man of the War*] (Madrid: Editorial Bitácora, 1994).

38. [*Trilogy of Africa*]

39. [*The Dream of Africa: In search of the White Myths of the Black Continent*]

40. [*Vagabond in Africa*]

41. [*The Lost Trails of Africa*]

42. [*African Poems*]

43. [*Mbama's Song*]

44. On Reverte's death, writing for *El país*, Jacinto Antón wrote "He was our man in Africa, the one who took many of us for the first time to the black continent, hand in hand with the great classics, and we will never be able to appreciate him enough." [Fue nuestro hombre en África, el que nos llevó a muchos por primera vez al continente negro de la mano de los grandes clásicos, y nunca se lo agradeceremos bastante.] Jacinto Antón, "Muere Javier Reverte, escritor de viajes, a los 76 años," *El país*, October 31, 2020, https://elpais.com/cultura/2020-10-31/muere-javier-reverte-escritor-de-viajes-a-los-76-anos.html.

45. See Hodges, *Western Sahara: The Roots of a Desert War*, for a complete history of the Western Sahara region. In brief, Spain controlled the now contested territory in various manifestations from 1884 to 1976. In the early 1970s, amid a popular Saharawi push for independence, Spain was in the process of granting autonomy to the region. Both Morocco and Mauritania also claimed governing rights over the territory, and King Hassan II organized the unarmed march of Moroccan civilians into Spanish Sahara on November 6, 1975. Franco died shortly thereafter on November 20, 1975, and the following political crisis in Spain led to the literal abandonment of Western Sahara in Moroccan hands. The Saharawi independence organization (the Polisario) was forced to flee to refugee camps in Algeria, but continues fighting for international recognition to this day. Western Sahara remains one of the few remaining non-self-governing territories in the world. For a more recent examination of the Saharawi political struggle for recognition, see Jacob A. Mundy, "Performing the Nation, Pre-Figuring the State: The Western Saharan Refugees, Thirty Years Later," *Journal of Modern African Studies* 45, no. 2 (2007): 275–297.

46. Many of the poems found in *El médico de Ifni* are compiled in *Poemas africanos*.

47. The "novelas moriscas" are a literary genre from sixteenth-century Spain (though experiencing a revival in the Romantic Movement of the nineteenth century). They typically employed Muslim protagonists and idealized the portrayal of the relationship and interaction between Moors and Christians. See Ryan Prendergast's *Reading, Writing, and Errant Subjects in Inquisitorial Spain* (New York: Routledge, 2016).

48. Abbeele, *Travel as Metaphor*, xv.

49. [Clara:] —Olvidé mi vida anterior, todo lo que es normal.
[Beatriz:] —Eso es lo malo: que yo pertenezca a eso que llamas tu vida normal.
—¿Hay algo de malo en la vida normal?

—Que es detestable.
—¿Por qué?
—Es monótona, aburrida. Y tú eres para mí, precisamente, el lado contrario de la puta normalidad, la otra cara de todo lo que me abruma, de lo que me aburre y de lo que detesto.
. . .
[Clara:] —No les des tantas vueltas a las cosas . . . Más allá—y señaló . . . — está el desierto.
—Y más acá—Beatriz se llevó la mano al pecho—la normalidad, ¿no? Eso es una putada, ¿no crees?] Reverte, *El médico de Ifni*, 94.

50. Abbeele, *Travel as Metaphor*, xv.
51. Reverte, *El médico de Ifni*, 122.
52. Reverte, *El médico de Ifni*, 206.
53. Abbeele, *Travel as Metaphor*, xv.
54. Abbeele, *Travel as Metaphor*, xvii.
55. [un hombre sin un lugar, alguien que no pertenecía a ningún sitio] Reverte, *El médico de Ifni*, 155.
56. [he dejado de pertenecer a España. Creo que no formo parte de ningún sitio de la Tierra . . . el desierto es la única posible patria para mí.] Reverte, *El médico de Ifni*, 185.
57. Abbeele, *Travel as Metaphor*, xviii.
58. Reverte, *El médico de Ifni*, 168.
59. [malditos por el mundo, expulsados de cualquier espacio amable de la Tierra al que pudieran llamar patria.] Reverte, *El médico de Ifni*, 220.
60. Kapuściński, *The Other*, 16.
61. [es la única manera con que puedo explicarme mis sentimientos. Los nómadas están acostumbrados a hundirse en el desierto, a seguir la lluvia y no tener un lugar estable donde vivir porque nunca es el mismo lugar donde se encuentra agua. Por eso nos llaman "los hijos de las nubes" y nuestra patria no es la tierra, sino el agua. Estamos hechos para vagar, porque el desierto es un duro lugar. . . . Y nadie nos quitará nunca más el desierto porque sólo nosotros lo comprendemos. A los que hoy lo ocupan, el mismo desierto los expulsará: porque ellos no lo comprenden ni han aprendido a amarlo.] Reverte, *El médico de Ifni*, 68–69.
62. In *Seeing Like a State*, Scott defines the term "*mētis*" as skill relevant to a specific situation, offering the example of "When a large freighter or passenger liner approaches a major port, the captain typically turns the control of his vessel over to a local pilot, who brings it into the harbor and to its berth. . . . This sensible procedure . . . reflects the fact that navigation on the open sea (a more 'abstract' space) is the more general skill, while piloting a ship through traffic in a particular port is a highly contextual skill. . . . Much of this knowledge would be irrelevant if he were suddenly transposed to a different port." Scott, *Seeing Like a State*, 316–317.
63. [no sería nada sin el desierto.] Reverte, *El médico de Ifni*, 155.
64. Reverte, *El médico de Ifni*, 69.
65. Reverte, *El médico de Ifni*, 118.
66. Said, *Orientalism*, 2.

67. Levinas, *Humanism of the Other*, 30.
68. Reverte, *El médico de Ifni*, 62.
69. Reverte, *El médico de Ifni*, 64.
70. [—¿Quieres? — . . . con un movimiento de la barbilla. Y ofreció su boca entreabierta a la de Suelma.] Reverte, *El médico de Ifni*, 87.
71. See Said and Mernissi. Said examines the image of the erotic Oriental female in *Orientalism*, noting that "Woven throughout all of Flaubert's Oriental experiences, exciting or disappointing, is an almost uniform association between the Orient and sex" (188). Mernissi, in *Scheherazade Goes West*, discusses the powerful images of Muslim artists in depicting highly erotic, voluptuous, and active female figures, contrasting their representation with the passive nudes of Matisse, Ingres, and Picasso (14–15).
72. Said, *Orientalism*, 36.
73. Levinas, *Humanism of the Other*, 30
74. Levinas, *Humanism of the Other*, 30.
75. [Empezar allí una vida nueva sin odios y sin rencores . . . y recoger los restos de su padre, para enterrarlos al lado de los de Fatma en el oasis perdido. / ¿Qué haría en Madrid?] Reverte, *El médico de Ifni,* 220.
76. The *jaima* is a tent that is used by many of the nomadic peoples of North Africa.
77. [Bienvenida a tu casa, hermana.] Reverte, *El médico de Ifni*, 150.
78. [Clara tuvo una sensación nueva: que alguien la protegía.] Reverte, *El médico de Ifni*, 145.
79. [Clara percibió cómo renacía un olvidado anhelo infantil. . . . Envidió por un instante a su sobrina] Reverte, *El médico de Ifni*, 151.
80. [Clara asintió con un movimiento leve de la barbilla. Percibía una extraña sensación en presencia de Omar: su instinto de rebelión se dormía ante él, como si la presencia de su hermano despertara en ella cierta sumisión.] Reverte, *El médico de Ifni*, 153.
81. Reverte, *El médico de Ifni*, 87, 153.
82. "Tourism," *The American Heritage Dictionary* (Houghton Mifflin, 1992).
83. Eugenia Afinoguénova and Jaume Martí-Olivella, "Introduction: A Nation under Tourists' Eyes: Tourism and Identity Discourses in Spain," in *Spain is (Still) Different*, eds. Eugenia Afinoguénova and Jaume Martí-Olivella (Plymouth, UK: Lexington Books, 2008), xi–xii. Afinoguénova and Martí-Olivella's summarization represents a more concise articulation of the theoretical definition of "tourism" that Dean MacCannell further (and originally) elaborates in *The Tourist: A New Theory of the Leisure Class* (1976. Reprint, Berkeley: University of California Press, 1999), 9–16.
84. In this sense, the novel explores the complex historical relations between Spain and the Arab world through a suggestion of the ethnic ties that form a basis for modern Spanish identity. This complicated history is examined in Martin-Márquez, see specifically chapter 1 (*Disorientations*, 12–63).
85. [pertenecían a dos mundos distintos. Por un lado, el de los españoles, gente que se consideraba superior, aunque ése no era el caso de tu padre . . . a pesar de que él

trató de casarse con Fatma, nuestro padre se opuso: no consintió una boda con alguien por cuyas venas no corría sangre saharaui.] Reverte, *El médico de Ifni*, 70–71.

86. Reverte, *El médico de Ifni*, 251.

87. [sintió enseguida que un pavoroso trueno estallaba dentro de su cabeza.] Reverte, *El médico de Ifni*, 251.

88. Reverte, *El médico de Ifni*, 251.

89. Neal Ascherson, introduction to *The Other*, by Ryszard Kapuściński (New York: Verso, 2008), 8.

90. Kapuściński, *The Other*, 14.

91. Abbeele, *Travel as Metaphor*, xx.

92. Abbeele, *Travel as Metaphor*, xx.

93. Abbeele, *Travel as Metaphor*, xxiii.

94. Alberto Vázquez-Figueroa, *Garoé* (Madrid: Mr Novela Histórica, 2010).

95. [uno de los autores españoles contemporáneos más leídos en el mundo]

96. Vázquez-Figueroa has both an official Spanish and English website.

97. [*Ebony*] Alberto Vázquez-Figueroa, *Ébano: La ruta de los esclavos* (1975. Reprint, Barcelona: Plaza & Janés Editores, 1983).

98. [*Africa Cries*]

99. [*The Eyes of the Tuareg*]

100. [*Sand and Wind*]

101. *Tuareg* (1980. Barcelona: DeBols!llo, 2004) was made into a movie in 1984; directed by Enzo G. Castellari and starring Mark Harmon, Luis Prendes, and Ritza Brown. Original title: *Tuareg: Il guerriero del deserto*, English title: *Tuareg: The Desert Warrior*.

102. In *Tuareg*, Gacel Sayah the senior finds himself at odds with the government when he offers traditional Tuareg hospitality to political renegades that stumble upon his encampment. His showdown with the government authorities eventually leads to his death. *Los ojos del Tuareg* begins shortly after his death.

103. The family's status as "self-exiled" is significant in that it marks them as even more marginalized. This added marginalization does force the nomadic lifestyle upon them, and yet the narrative emphasizes their participation in the long tradition of Tuareg nomadism rather than their politically motivated flight.

104. While no explicit ties are made between the text and the race or specific organizers, this is a rally that has taken place under the auspices of various groups and names since the 1970s. The most famous race is the Dakar Rally ("Dakar," Amaury Sport Organisation, accessed May 20, 2020, dakar.com). The year *Los ojos del Tuareg* was first published (2000) marks the first and only time that the race extended from Dakar to Cairo (previously it traced a north to south route such as Paris to Dakar), a route which is reflected in the novel. Also, in 2008, the race was canceled due to "fears of terrorist attacks" and has since been relocated to South America (Paul Hamilos, "Dakar Rally Cancelled at Last Minute over Terrorist Threat," *The Guardian*, January 4, 2008, www.theguardian.com/world/2008/jan/05/france.sport).

105. Gacel adamantly refuses the "bribe," but Nené drops the bag containing the cash from his helicopter as he flies away. Vázquez-Figueroa, *Los ojos del Tuareg*, 312.

106. Said, *Orientalism*, 167.

107. Said, *Orientalism*, 216.
108. Levinas, *Humanism of the Other*, 32.
109. Levinas, *Humanism of the Other*, 30.
110. Said, *Orientalism*, xxii.
111. Said, *Orientalism*, xxii.
112. Said, *Orientalism*, 12.
113. Vázquez-Figueroa, *Los ojos del Tuareg*, 75.
114. [únicamente un targui sería tan loco como para lanzarse a la aventura de intentar encontrar agua en tan remoto lugar del desierto] Vázquez-Figueroa, *Los ojos del Tuareg*, 22.
115. Vázquez-Figueroa, *Los ojos del Tuareg*, 15.
116. See Said, *Orientalism*, 19–21, where he discusses Western *authority* and *exteriority* as fundamental elements of Orientalism.
117. But not necessarily "The Westerner," as I examine below, Vázquez-Figueroa offers a more nuanced presentation of the individual.
118. See MacCannell, *The Tourist*, 9–10, for a consideration of the negative stereotype of the tourist. Many similarities can be found to Vázquez-Figueroa's depreciative portrayal of this arrogant, completely exterior Western stereotype.
119. Abbeele, *Travel as Metaphor*, xvi.
120. Scott, *Seeing Like a State*, 312.
121. [un auténtico tuareg]
122. [Cuando un tuareg moría de sed estaba aceptando que no había aprendido las enseñanzas de generaciones de antepasados que durante siglos se mantuvieron orgullosamente en pie en el más desolado de los paisajes del planeta.] Vázquez-Figueroa, *Los ojos del Tuareg*, 18.
123. As examined previously, "the Greek for 'home' from which is derived 'economy.'" (Abbeele, *Travel as Metaphor*, xviii).
124. Abbeele, *Travel as Metaphor*, xviii.
125. Scott, *Seeing Like a State*, 317.
126. [en mitad de la nada] Vázquez-Figueroa, *Los ojos del Tuareg*, 23.
127. Scott defines *techne* as follows: "techne represented knowledge of an order completely different from mētis. Technical knowledge, or techne, could be expressed precisely and comprehensively in the form of hard-and-fast rules (*not* rules of thumb), principles and propositions" (319).
128. Scott, *Seeing Like a State*, 320.
129. Said, *Orientalism*, 216.
130. Abbeele, *Travel as Metaphor*, xx.
131. *Imohag* and *Inmouchar* are other terms for "Tuareg"—"as the Tuaregs were in the habit of calling themselves." [como solían llamarse a sí mismos los tuaregs.] Vázquez-Figuera, *Los ojos del Tuareg,* 9.
132. [el día que un imohag no sea capaz de hacer lo que es capaz de hacer una palmera, nuestra raza estará condenada a desaparecer de la faz de la tierra. Y aún no ha llegado ese momento. . . . Eso es algo que tu padre me enseñó y que tú tendrás que enseñar a tus hijos.] Vázquez-Figueroa, *Los ojos del Tuareg*, 16.
133. Said, *Orientalism*, 12.

134. [¿a quién coño le importa que un fulano del que nunca ha oído hablar gane una etapa automovilística que acaba en un rincón de África del que tampoco ha oído hablar? . . . a nadie. Pero tu departamento es el encargado de crear esa «inútil necesidad» procurando que nuestras imágenes se emitan cuando un montón de gente aburrida se encuentra sentada frente al televisor, porque ésos serán los que compren los productos que nuestros clientes anuncian.] Vázquez-Figueroa, *Los ojos del Tuareg*, 149.

135. [Nené Dupré:] —Si los rehenes mueren se limitarán a hacer unas cuantas fotografías y entregárselas a la prensa como prueba irrefutable de que 'unos desalmados bandidos' asaltaron, robaron y asesinaron a unos inocentes deportistas que ningún daño les habían hecho.
[Hans Scholt:] —Pero ésa no es la verdad.
—Será 'su verdad' y no creo que dejen con vida a quien pueda ofrecer una versión diferente.] Vázquez-Figueroa, *Los ojos del Tuareg*, 201.

136. [recordándole a su director que sin nuestra colaboración ningún periodista del mundo podrá cubrir esta información.] Vázquez-Figueroa, *Los ojos del Tuareg*, 189.

137. [—Debemos ordenar] a todos los imohag . . . que impidan a cualquier precio el paso de vuestros coches, vuestras motos y vuestros camiones.
—Eso suena a terrorismo.
—¡No! ¡En absoluto! No intentes confundir los términos. El terrorista es un ser deleznable que ataca a traición escudándose en el anonimato. Lo nuestro es una declaración de guerra, y en la que el enemigo no se oculta. El enemigo es la nación tuareg en peso.
—¿Estáis dispuestos a matar?
—En toda guerra hay muertos.] Vázquez-Figueroa, *Los ojos del Tuareg*, 144.

138. Vázquez-Figueroa, *Los ojos del Tuareg*, 169.

139. [todo [el dinero] que nos han pagado con tal de no encontrarme aquí arriba.] Vázquez-Figueroa, *Los ojos del Tuareg*, 305.

140. [El espectáculo es inhumano, pero colorido y brillante.] Vázquez-Figueroa, *Los ojos del Tuareg*, 170.

141. [Se suele bromear asegurando que este rally es como un circo, pero a decir verdad no es un inocente circo de payasos y funambulistas, sino un auténtico 'circo romano' en el que los emperadores han sido sustituidos por cámaras de la televisión, los rugientes leones por rugientes vehículos lanzados a toda velocidad . . . y los 'cristianos' por pobres nativos a los que de tanto en tanto aplasta un coche. El espectáculo es inhumano.] Vázquez-Figueroa, *Los ojos del Tuareg*, 170.

142. See Kapuściński, *The Other*, 20–25, where he discusses conflict and exchange as the two primary modes of historical interaction between cultures.

143. Kapuściński, *The Other*, 35.

144. Vázquez-Figueroa, *Los ojos del Tuareg*, 323.

145. Kapuściński, *The Other*, 34.

146. Said, *Orientalism*, 93.

147. Said, *Orientalism*, 93.

148. Said, *Orientalism*, 93.

149. Said, *Orientalism*, 93.

150. [*The Devil in Yudis*]
151. Rueda, *El retorno/el reencuentro*, 6.
152. Cristián Ricci, *Literatura periférica en castellano y catalán: El caso marroquí* (Madrid: Ediciones del Orto, 2010), 10.
153. Ana Rueda and Constantin C. Icleanu published an annotated version of the novel with StockCERO in 2020.
154. Rueda, *El retorno/el reencuentro*, 63.
155. Mohamed Bouissef Rekab, "Literatura marroquí de expresión española," *El español en el mundo: Anuario del Instituto Cervantes*, Instituto Cervantes (2005): 5.
156. [*New Association of Moroccan Writers in Spanish*] *Nueva asociación de escritores marroquíes en lengua española*, Facebook Group, accessed May 15, 2020, www.facebook.com/NUEVAAEMLE.
157. Rueda, *El retorno/el reencuentro*.
158. Bobbitt, Brian J., "Refusing to Be Buried Alive: Burial and African Immigration in Afro-Hispanic Literature" (PhD diss., University of Texas at Austin, 2016).
159. Cristián Ricci, *¡Hay moros en la costa!: Literatura marroquí fronteriza en castellano y catalán* (Madrid: Iberoamericana Vervuert, 2014), 170.
160. Rueda, *El retorno/el reencuentro*, 63.
161. Campoy-Cubillo, *Memories of the Maghreb*, 129.
162. [*I, Mohamed*] Rafael Torres, *Yo Mohamed* (Madrid: Temas de Hoy, 1995).
163. [*Sleeping Out in the Open*] Pasqual Moreno Torregrosa and Mohamed El Ghreyb, *Dormir al raso* (Madrid: Ediciones Vosa, 1994).
164. Campoy-Cubillo, *Memories of the Maghreb*, 129.
165. Most notably is probably Equatoguinean author Donato Ndongo's novel *El Metro* (Barcelona: El Cobre, 2007), but the themes of immigration is frequent in shorter fiction such as Mohamed Lemrini El-Ouahhabi's 2004 story "Viaje al pasado" (in *La puerta de los vientos: Narradores marroquíes contemporáneos*, eds. Marta Cerezales, Miguel Ángel Moreta, and Lorenzo Silva [Barcelona: Destino, 2004], 217–223) or Mohamed Chakor's fantastic take on trans-Mediterranean immigration in "Las dos orillas, el mar y la muerte" (in *Entre las dos orillas: Literatura marroquí en lengua española*, ed. Carmelo Pérez Beltrán [Granada: Universidad de Granada y Fundación Euroárabe de Altos Estudios, 2007], 47–48).
166. Khalid Amine, "Crossing Borders: Al-halqa Performance in Morocco from the Open Space to the Theatre Building," *TDR* 45, no. 2 (2001): 55.
167. Khalid Amine and Marvin Carlson, "'Al-Halqa' in Arabic Theatre: An Emerging Site of Hybridity," *Theatre Journal* 60, no. 1 (2008): 72.
168. Campoy-Cubillo, *Memories of the Maghreb*, 130.
169. Campoy-Cubillo, *Memories of the Maghreb*, 131.
170. Amine, "Crossing Borders," 58 and Campoy-Cubillo, *Memories of the Maghreb*, 131.
171. Amine, "Crossing Borders," 58.
172. Bertolt Brecht outlined his ideas on *Verfremdungseffekt* in the article "On Chinese Acting" (*The Tulane Drama Review* 6, no. 1 [1961]: 130–136); it is sometimes translated from the German as alienation effect, estrangement effect, distancing effect, or, as Frederic Jameson proposed in *Brecht and Method* (New York: Verso,

1998), simply the V-effect. It is a theatrical strategy meant to alienate the audience so that "the spectator is prevented from feeling his way into the characters. Acceptance or rejection of the characters' words is thus placed in the conscious realm, not, as hitherto, in the spectator's subconscious." Brecht, "On Chinese Acting," 130.

173. Amine, "Al-Halqa in Arabic Theatre," 73, 85.

174. Amine, "Crossing Borders," 58.

175. Amine, "Crossing Borders," 57 and Al-Halqa in Arabic Theatre," 85.

176. Juliane Tauchnitz, "Identity Questions in *El diablo de Yudis* by Ahmed Daoudi," in *The World in Movement: Performative Identities and Diasporas*, eds. Alfonso de Toro and Juliane Tauchnitz (Leiden: Brill, 2018), 221.

177. Tauchnitz, "Identity Questions," 221.

178. Brecht, "On Chinese Acting," 131.

179. Brecht, "On Chinese Acting," 131.

180. [para comprar una casa o una parcela; volvería en un coche grande; volvería como si hubiera nacido de nuevo, pero con más suerte.] Daoudi, *El diablo de Yudis*, 94.

181. Amine, "Crossing Borders," 58.

182. Amine, "Crossing Borders," 58.

183. In his 2001 article, "Crossing Borders: Al-halqa Performance in Morocco from the Open Space to the Theatre Building," Amine examines the practical and symbolic use of the circle in the *halqa* tradition. He notes that it reflects common hierarchical and urban organizational traditions in Morocco, and "thus, the circle is deeply rooted in the morphology of Moroccan architecture as well as the social imaginary of Moroccan people" (56).

184. Brecht, "On Chinese Acting," 130.

185. [Los testigos del empresario eran el vigilante, el director, y un empleado que le vio cuando fue descubierto a la salida: todo era indiscutible. Las declaraciones de Tawawan no valían de nada, a pesar de que el abogado, ofrecido gratuitamente por el sindicato, intentó demostrar que era un montaje. Al tribunal solo le convencían las pruebas . . . sabíamos que era un montaje, pero nadie nos hizo caso. Imposible, imposible, a veces es imposible demostrar la verdad.] Daoudi, *El diablo de Yudis*, 61.

186. [el ladrón Sardaf] Daoudi, *El diablo de Yudis*, 61.

187. [Todo era increíble para la justicia porque no había pruebas. Sólo Bailabú procuraba demostrar la verdad, pero su verdad era indemostrable por carecer de las pruebas que se exigían. Por el contrario, a la mentira era posible convertirla, mediante pruebas, en verdad, tal como ocurrió con Tawawan.] Daoudi, *El diablo de Yudis*, 63.

188. Jean-François Lyotard, *The Differend: Phrases in Dispute*, trans. Georges Van den Abbeele (Minneapolis: University of Minnesota Press, 1988), 4.

189. Lyotard, *The Differend,* 3.

190. [La experiencia me había enseñado lo suficiente como para lograr reunir a una parte de los merodeantes de la plaza. Sé que iniciar la narración siempre supone llamar la atención, (y) recalcar la preocupación (por los protagonistas).] Daoudi, *El diablo de Yudis*, 69.

191. Brecht, "On Chinese Acting," 131.

192. Brecht, "On Chinese Acting," 131.

193. Jameson, *Brecht and Method*, 84.
194. [—Eres el único que tienes suerte.
—¿Por qué?
—Tus historias no se pueden confiscar.
—¡Anda ya!, ¿y el dinero?] Daoudi, *El diablo de Yudis*, 69.
195. [Los turistas extranjeros que tantas veces nos visitan se dirigen al corro de Airut para contemplar las serpientes que bailan, o al de Buschif para escudriñar el fuego que no quema. Pero a mí no me benefician nada, porque no entienden lo que cuento o, quizá, ni siquiera entienden lo que hago. Mi clientela es siempre de la misma clase y mis recaudos son fatalmente limitados.] Daoudi, *El diablo de Yudis*, 68.
196. Campoy-Cubillo, *Memories of the Maghreb*, 132.
197. Campoy-Cubillo, *Memories of the Maghreb*, 136.
198. Thiong'o, "Decolonising the Mind," 103.
199. Amine, "Al-Halqa in Arabic Theatre," 73.
200. Thiong'o, "Decolonising the Mind," 103.
201. Campoy-Cubillo, *Memories of the Maghreb*, 136.
202. Amine, "Crossing Borders," 57.
203. [Con los aplausos, se termina mi cuento, pero yo necesito otros más reales, los de vuestra generosidad.] Daoudi, *El diablo de Yudis*, 126.
204. Amine, "Crossing Borders," 60.
205. [Éstos no hablan, ¿a dónde me llevan? ¡Oye, oye!, yo no he hecho nada; solo estaban contando en la plaza la historia del diablo.] Daoudi, *El diablo de Yudis*, 126.
206. [—Cállate, tú eres el diablo.] Daoudi, *El diablo de Yudis*, 127.
207. [Éstos no hablan.] Daoudi, *El diablo de Yudis*, 126.
208. [vuestra generosidad. Uno, dos o tres dirhams.] Daoudi, *El diablo de Yudis*, 126.
209. [Cállate, tú eres el diablo.] Daoudi, *El diablo de Yudis*, 127.
210. Campoy-Cubillo, *Memories of the Maghreb*, 136.
211. Amine, "Crossing Borders," 57.
212. Amine, "Crossing Borders," 60.
213. Amine, "Crossing Borders," 57.
214. Jameson, *Brecht and Method*, 39.
215. Brecht, "On Chinese Acting," 130.
216. Amine, "Crossing Borders," 57.
217. Brecht, "On Chinese Acting," 130.
218. Jameson, *Brecht and Method*, 84.
219. Said, *Orientalism*, 20.
220. Said, *Orientalism*, xxix.
221. Amine, "Crossing Borders," 60.
222. Rueda, *El retorno/El reencuentro*, 67–69.
223. Tauchnitz, "Identity Questions," 223.
224. Jameson, *Brecht and Method*, 40.
225. Jameson, *Brecht and Method*, 40.
226. Amine, "Crossing Borders," 60.
227. Brecht, "On Chinese Acting," 130.
228. Amine and Carlson, "'Al-Halqa' in Arabic Theatre," 85.

Conclusion

This study does not pretend to be an exhaustive and definitive analysis of current trends among contemporary Spanish authors, but it has sought to analyze a selection of works that point to a diminishing presence of Orientalist discourse in Spanish literature on Africa. The authors examined here share a focus on Africa and the African Other, but also do not form a unified literary movement. Each of these authors has chosen to write about Africa for very personal reasons, and so therefore it would be both brash and artificial for me to classify these nine authors as a unified and concerted group. However, it is their very difference that signals a broader trend within recent Spanish fiction that I have highlighted here. From authors as dissimilar as Abumalham and Vázquez-Figueroa or Mekuy and López Sarasúa, we can identify certain reactionary elements within their works that respond to the concerns articulated by Said in 1978. The generic and thematic differences between these authors suggest that, just as Orientalism continues to be a pervasive force, so there also exists a counter-current in Spanish letters that reacts to Orientalism's legacy. This work hopes to have identified the trend, and while I do not want to suggest that these authors are unified in their ideological projects, I do hope to have shown that Said's theories on Orientalism are less applicable to recent Spanish fiction than in the past.

I am encouraged by my findings. The majority of the authors examined here seem to be conscious of the pitfalls in writing about their Other. Mayrata, Daoudi, and Abumalham all make specific efforts to avoid authoritative narrations about the Other. Mekuy and Abumalham's narrative voices reflect a growing diversity within Spanish fiction. And Silva and Vázquez-Figueroa's works are strong critiques of any assumed Western superiority. These accomplishments may not be completely novel; Silva's war writing draws on and reflects the projects of Sender and Díaz Fernández from the 1920s, and similar literary examples of Reverte's intercultural interaction may be found as far back as Cervantes's story "La gitanilla" or in the *Novelas moriscas*. However, the combined effect of these works signals a significant movement away from the totalizing and essentializing discourse of Orientalism in contemporary Spanish literature.

This was the ultimate goal of this project, to consider the status of Orientalist discourse in the contemporary Spanish novel. Does Said's monumental work still serve to analyze the contemporary Spanish literary reflections on Africa? Is Orientalism as a mode of representation alive and well? The answer to both of these questions must be "yes," but that does not mean that Orientalism exists with unflagging force. The legacy of Orientalism instead persists in subtle ways. Dueñas's novel shows that it often hides beneath the explicit text, a subtle dynamic exerting its force. In contrast, Mayrata, Abumalham, and Daoudi all confront the authority of the Western author to speak for and represent its Other, implicitly engaging with the haunting force of Orientalism. Thirty years later, Said still offers a valuable theoretical framework with which to understand the dynamics at work in these Spanish reflections on Africa.

Orientalism's power has indeed waned. The works analyzed here reveal that it is no longer the authoritative, authorizing, and explicit voice of the West speaking for its African Other. Instead, it exists as a subtle undertone, a narrative assumption that does not necessarily direct the text but that does influence it. It is a weakened rhetoric. The majority of the authors examined here are moving beyond the strict binary that structures and upholds Orientalism.

Even as they avoid Orientalism, these authors do not avoid Africa. Africa still serves as a fertile inspiration for literary creation. However, it is no longer a totalized vision of Africa that reflects colonial designs; instead, it is a reflection that often admits limitations and nuances. Spain, as part of the West, is not a totemic authority in all interactions with the Other, and Africa is not simply the dark continent awaiting the illumination of Western authority.

To their credit, these authors have also avoided a mere reversal of the Orientalist paradigm. Silva's novel, *El nombre de los nuestros*, does employ the same binary structure of Orientalism, but replaces the categories with economic divisions instead of racial or cultural ones. The narrative ambiguity and humility of Mayrata, Abumalham, and Daoudi avoids totalizing conclusions on either side. And the focus on the interpersonal encounter in the works by Reverte or López Sarasúa undermines any presumed cultural hierarchy. Therefore, the current literary production on Africa is not a simple knee-jerk overturning of Orientalism, but rather a calculated rejection of its limiting structures and characteristics.

The ultimate accomplishment of these authors examined here has been a decentering of the narrative focus. They have written a textual space that is inclusive. The cultural Other has a space within the literary canon (as with Abulmalham, Daoudi, and Mekuy) and within the specific literary works (as with Vázquez-Figueroa or Mayrata). Africa is not merely a cultural contestant,[1] and the West is no longer the hegemonic, authorizing voice that excludes all Others.

If potential readers of this book would appreciate a concise summary of this project, then I offer the following: Africa is still a vibrant inspiration for Spanish authors and Orientalism persists, but these contemporary Spanish authors are writing their African Other in new ways that undermine the historical power of Orientalist discourse. I am heartened by the trend that these works suggest, and I look forward to reading the future works not only by these nine authors, but by the growing number of authors who are writing Spain and Africa in the twenty-first century. The ultimate aspiration of any scholar is that his or her work will spark an insight in a fellow colleague's research; I also hope that this project may open new paths of inquiry for present and future scholars. Spain and Africa's history together is long, and it is far from over.

NOTE

1. Said, *Orientalism*, 1.

Bibliography

Abbeele, Georges Van den. *Travel as Metaphor: From Montaigne to Rousseau.* Minneapolis: University of Minnesota Press, 1992.
Abrighach, Mohamed. "Concha López Sarasúa: novelista de las dos orillas." *Espéculo: Revista electrónica cuatrimestral de estudios literarios*, no. 46 (2010): np. webs.ucm.es/info/especulo/numero46/dorillas.html.
———. *Superando orillas: Lectura intercultural de la narrativa de Concha López Sarasúa.* Rabat: Imprimerie El Maarif Al Jadida, 2009.
Abumalham Mas, Montserrat. *De la ceiba y el quetzal.* Murcia: Gollarín, 2016.
———. "De la ignorancia al conocimiento y la sumisión: de la 'Yahiliyya' al Islam." *Revista de la sociedad española de ciencias de las religiones*, no. 1 (2007): 7–18.
———. "Génesis 1–2, 4 en la Biblia árabe cristiana." *Ilu. Revista de ciencias de las religiones*, no. 7 (2002): 91–100.
———. *El Islam.* Madrid: Ediciones del Orto, 1999.
———. "El juego de los espejos y otros artificios poéticos." *Anaquel de estudios árabes*, no. 11 (2000): 37–46.
———. "Literatura fantástica en lengua árabe." *Revista museo romántico*, no. 3 (2001): 103–108.
———. *¿Te acuerdas de Shahrazad?* Madrid: Sial Ediciones, 2001.
———. "La voz de la revelación y su negación: un ejemplo en el Islam." *Ilu. Revista de ciencias de las religiones*, no. 19 (2007): 239–246.
Afinoguénova, Eugenia, and Jaume Martí-Olivella. "Introduction: A Nation under Tourists' Eyes: Tourism and Identity Discourses in Spain." In *Spain is (Still) Different*, edited by Eugenia Afinoguénova and Jaume Martí-Olivella, xi–xxxviii. Plymouth, UK: Lexington Books, 2008.
Aguilar, Andrea. "La integración no significa que comamos chorizo." *El País*, June 8, 2007, elpais.com/diario/2007/06/09/cultura/1181340005_850215.html.
Alarcón, Pedro Antonio. *Diario de un testigo de la Guerra de África.* Madrid: Imprenta y Librería de Gáspar y Roig, 1859.

Aleixandre, Vicente, ed. *Espejo del amor y de la muerte: antología de poesía española última*. Madrid: Azur, 1971.
Allan, Joanna. *Silenced Resistance: Women, Dictatorships, and Genderwashing in Western Sahara and Equatorial Guinea*. Madison: University of Wisconsin Press, 2019.
Almarcegui, Patricia. "La experiencia como reescritura. *Del Rif al Yebala. Viaje al sueño y la pesadilla* de Lorenzo Silva." In *El viaje en la literatura hispánica: de Juan Valera a Sergio Pitol*, edited by Julio Peñate Rivera and Fancisco Uzcanga Meinecke, 81–88. Madrid: Editorial Verbum, 2008.
Althusser, Louis. "The Underground Current of the Materialism of the Encounter." In *Philosophy of the Encounter: Later Writings, 1978–87*, edited by François Matheron and Oliver Corpet, translated by G. M. Goshgarian, 163–207. New York: Verso, 2006.
Amaury Sport Organisation. "Dakar." Accessed May 20, 2020. dakar.com.
American Anthropological Association. "AAA Statement on 'Race.'" May 17, 1998. Accessed May 20, 2020. www.americananthro.org/ConnectWithAAA/Content.aspx?ItemNumber=2583.
The American Heritage Dictionary. "Tourism." Houghton Mifflin, 1992.
Amine, Khalid. "Crossing Borders: Al-halqa Performance in Morocco from the Open Space to the Theatre Building." *TDR* 45, no. 2 (2001): 55–69.
Amine, Khalid, and Marvin Carlson. "'Al-Halqa' in Arabic Theatre: An Emerging Site of Hybridity." *Theatre Journal* 60, no. 1 (2008): 71–85.
Andrés-Gallego, José, José Luis Comellas, Demetrio Ramos Pérez, and Luis Suárez Fernández. *Historia general de España y América: La Segunda República y la Guerra*. Madrid: Ediciones Rialp, 1986.
Anidjar, Gil. *The Jew, The Arab: A History of the Enemy*. Stanford: Stanford University Press, 2003.
Antón, Jacinto. "Muere Javier Reverte, escritor de viajes, a los 76 años." *El País*, October 31, 2020. https://elpais.com/cultura/2020-10-31/muere-javier-reverte-escritor-de-viajes-a-los-76-anos.html.
The Arabian Nights: Tales of 1,001 Nights. Edited by Robert Irwin, Translated by Malcolm C. Lyons and Ursula Lyons. Penguin Classics, 2010.
Ascherson, Neal. Introduction to *The Other*, 1–10. By Ryszard Kapuściński, New York: Verso, 2008.
Atxaga, Bernardo. *Siete casas en Francia*. Madrid: Alfaguara, 2009.
Bey, Alí. *Viajes de Ali Bey el Abbassi por África y Asia, Tomo Primero*. Valencia: Librería de Mallen y Sobrinos, 1836.
Bhabha, Homi. *The Location of Culture*. London: Routledge, 2004.
Boampong, Joanna. "Reconfigurations of the Female Protagonist in Hispanophone African Literature." In *In and Out of Africa: Exploring Afro-Hispanic, Luso-Brazilian, and Latin-American Connections*, edited by Joanna Boampong, 96–108. Newcastle upon Tyne: Cambridge Scholars Publishing, 2012.
Bobbitt, Brian J. "Refusing to Be Buried Alive: Burial and African Immigration in Afro-Hispanic Literature." PhD diss., University of Texas at Austin, 2016.

Borm, Jan. "Defining Travel: On the Travel Book, Travel Writing and Terminology." In *Perspectives on Travel Writing*. Edited by Glenn Hooper and Tim Youngs, 13–26. Burlington, Vermont: Ashgate, 2004.
Bouissef Rekab, Mohamed. *La señora*. Madrid: Sial Ediciones, 2006.
———. "Literatura marroquí de expresión española." *El español en el mundo: Anuario del Instituto Cervantes*. Instituto Cervantes, 2005. cvc.cervantes.es/lengua/anuario/anuario_05/bouissef/p01.htm.
Bowen, Wayne H. *Spaniards and Nazi Germany: Collaboration in the New Order*. Columbia, Missouri: University of Missouri Press, 2000.
Brecht, Bertolt. "On Chinese Acting." Translated by Eric Bentley. *The Tulane Drama Review* 6, no. 1 (1961): 130–136.
Broeck, Paul Van Den. "Un encuentro con Lorenzo Silva." In *Actas del XIV Congreso de la Asociación Internacional de Hispanistas, III: Literatura española, siglos XVIII–XX*, edited by Isaías Lerner, Robert Nival, and Alonso Alejandro, 623–627. Newark, DE: Juan de la Cuesta Hispanic Monographs, 2004.
Butler, Judith. *Gender Trouble*. 1990. Reprint, New York: Routledge, 2008.
Cadalso, José de. *Cartas marruecas / Noches lúgubres*. 1789. Reprint, Madrid: Cátedra, 2004.
Cairo, Heriberto. "Spanish Enclaves in North Africa." In *Handbook of Global International Policy*, edited by Stuart S. Nagel, 57–78. Boca Raton: CRC Press, 2000.
Calderwood, Eric. *Colonial al-Andalus: Spain and the Making of Modern Moroccan Culture*. Cambridge, Massachusetts: Harvard University Press, 2018.
Campoy-Cubillo, Adolfo. *Memories of the Maghreb: Transnational Identities in Spanish Cultural Production*. New York: Palgrave Macmillan, 2012.
Campoy-Cubillo, Adolfo, and Benita Sampedro Vizcaya. "Entering the Global Hispanophone: An Introduction." *Journal of Spanish Cultural Studies* 20, nos. 1–2 (2019): 1–16.
Carrasco González, Antonio. *Historia de la novela colonial hispanoafricana*. Madrid: SIAL Ediciones, 2009.
———. *El reino olvidado: Cinco siglos de Historia de España en África*. Madrid: La esfera de los libros, 2012.
Carreras Serra, Lluís. *Las normas jurídicas de los periodistas*. Barcelona: UOC, 2008.
Castillo, David. "De la belleza como un estado de ánimo." Prologue to *Después de Tánger*, by Larbi el-Harti, 7–9. Madrid: Sial Ediciones, 2003.
Castillo, Rafael del. *España y Marruecos: Historia de la Guerra de África, escrita desde el campamento*. Cádiz: Imprenta de la Revista Médica, 1859.
Cerarols Ramírez, Rosa. *Geografías de lo exótico: El imaginario de Marruecos en la literatura de viajes [1859-1936]*. Barcelona: Edicions Bellaterra, 2015.
Cercas, Javier. *Soldados de Salamina*. 2001. Reprint, Buenos Aires: Tusquets Editores, 2004.
Cervantes Saavedra, Miguel de. "La gitanilla." In *Novelas ejemplares*, 13–75. 1613. Reprint, Barcelona: Red ediciones, 2012.
Chacón, Dulce. *La voz dormida*. Madrid: Alfaguara, 2002.

Chakor, Mohamed. "Las dos orillas, el mar y la muerte." In *Entre las dos orillas: Literatura marroquí en lengua española*, edited by Carmelo Pérez Beltrán, 47–48. Granada: Universidad de Granada y Fundación Euroárabe de Altos Estudios, 2007.

Chamberlain, Muriel Evelyn. *The Scramble for Africa*. New York: Longman, 1999.

Charia, Zakaria. "Una breve biografía de Nayib Abumalham, el primer traductor del *Quijote* al árabe." *Articulo.org*, May 18, 2011. www.articulo.org/articulo/43050/una_breve_biografia_de_nayib_abumalham_el_primer_traductor_del_quijote_al_arabe.html.

Chavez, Leo. *The Latino Threat: Constructing Immigrants, Citizens, and the Nation*. Stanford, California: Stanford University Press, 2008.

Cixous, Hélène, and Catherine Clément. *The Newly Born Woman*. Translated by Betty Wing. Manchester: Manchester University Press, 1986.

Clarín, Leopoldo Alas. *La Regenta*. 1885. Reprint, Madrid: Castalia, 1981.

Costa, Joaquín. "Los intereses de España en Marruecos." In *África a través del pensamiento español*, edited by Ángel Flores Morales, 141–184. Madrid: Instituto de Estudios Africanos, 1949.

Craig-Odders, Renée. "Sin, Redemption and the New Generation of Detective Fiction in Spain: Lorenzo Silva's Bevilacqua Series." *La novela policial hispánica actual*, special issue of *Ciberletras*, no. 15 (July 2006): 28–42.

Daoudi, Ahmed. *El diablo de Yudis*. Madrid: Ediciones VOSA, 1994.

———. *El diablo de Yudis*. Edited by Ana Rueda and Constantin C. Icleanu. StockCero, 2020.

Deleuze, Gilles, and Félix Guattari. *Kafka: Toward a Minor Literature*. Translated by Dana Polan. Minneapolis: University of Minnesota Press, 1986.

Derrida, Jacques. *Of Grammatology*. 1974. Translated by Gayatri Chakravorty Spivak. Reprint, Baltimore: The Johns Hopkins University Press, 1998.

———. "Plato's Pharmacy." In *Dissemination*, 67–186. 1972. Reprint, New York: Continuum Books, 2004.

———. *Specters of Marx*. New York: Routledge, 1994.

Díaz Fernández, José. *El blocao*. 1928. Reprint, Madrid: Viamonte, 1998.

Diccionario de la lengua española. "Aleya." Real academia española. Accessed February 25, 2020, dle.rae.es/aleya.

———. "Aljamía." Real academia española. Accessed February 25, 2020, dle.rae.es/aljamía.

———. "Esperpento." Real academia española, 2014. Accessed February 25, 2020. dle.rae.es/esperpento.

———. "Harca." Real academia española, 2014. Accessed February 25, 2020. dle.rae.es/harca.

Dueñas, María. *El tiempo entre costuras*. Madrid: Ediciones Temas de Hoy, 2009.

———, screenplay. *El tiempo entre costuras*. Directed by Ignacio Mercero, Iñaki Peñafiel, and Norberto López Amado, performances by Adriana Ugarte, Hannah New, Tristán Ulloa, and Felipe Duarte. Antena 3 Televisión, 2012.

———. "El tiempo entre costuras—María Dueñas." Accessed April 29, 2020. Eltiempoentrecosturas.blogspot.com.

———. *Las Hijas del Capitán*. New York: Harper Collins Español, 2019.

———. *Misión olvido*. Madrid: Atria Books, 2014.
———. *La Templanza*. Madrid: Atria Books, 2015.
———. *The Time in Between: A Novel*. Translated by Daniel Hahn. Madrid: Atria Books, 2011.
Ellison, Mahan L. "*Un reino tan lejano*: Yudis, Shahrazad, and the Imaginary Space in the Contemporary Hispano-Moroccan Novel." *Research in African Literatures* 48, no. 3 (2017): 98–115.
Esquirol, Miguel. "Lorenzo Silva: 'Esta guerra es un fracaso colectivo.'" *Lateral: Revista de Cultura* 11, no. 118, (2004): np. www.circulolateral.com/revista/indice/118.htm.
Estévez Hernández, Pablo. "El censo de 1950 en Guinea Española: La raza como categoría de recuento." *Kamchatka: Revista de análisis cultural* 10 (December 2017): 533–554.
———. "Censos, identidad y colonialismo en el Sáhara español (1950-1974): La imaginación numérica de la nación española." *Papeles de CEIC* 89 (September 2012): 1–34.
Eulalia Martí, Marta. "Pasión por la lectura en su año internacional." *GranadaDigital.com*. April 25, 2012.
Evita Ika, Victoria. *Kanga: La tierra de los sueños*. Madrid: Sial Ediciones, 2016.
———. *Mokámbo: Aromas de libertad*. Majadahonda: Creativa, 2010.
Faszer-McMahon, Debra, and Victoria L. Ketz, eds. *African Immigrants in Contemporary Spanish Texts: Crossing the Strait*. Burlington, Vermont: Ashgate, 2015.
Fernández Parrilla, Gonzalo. "Disoriented Postcolonialities: With Edward Said in (the Labyrinth of) Al-Andalus." *Interventions* 20, no. 2 (2018): 229–242.
Flores Morales, Ángel, ed. *África a través del pensamiento español: De Isabel la Católica a Franco*. Madrid: Instituto de Estudios Africanos, 1949.
Fornieles, Javier, and Inmaculada Urán. "El lugar de Lorenzo Silva en la literatura juvenil." *Tonos digital: Revista electrónica de estudios filológicos* 9 (June 2005): np. www.um.es/tonosdigital/znum9/estudios/lorenzosilva.htm.
Gahete, Manuel, Abdellatif Limami, Ahmed M. Mgara, José Sarria, and Aziz Tazi, eds. *Calle del Agua: Antología contemporánea de literatura hispanomagrebí*. Madrid: Sial Ediciones, 2008.
Ganivet, Ángel, and Miguel de Unamuno. *El porvenir de España*. 1898. Reprint, Madrid: Espasa-Calpe, 2008.
García Figueras, Tomás. *Marruecos: La acción de España en el Norte de África*. Barcelona: Ediciones FE, 1941.
———. *Santa Cruz de Mar Pequeña-Ifni-Sahara (La acción de España en la costa occidental de África)*. 1941. Reprint, Barcelona: Ediciones FE, 1951.
García Jambrina, Luis. "La recuperación de la memoria histórica en tres novelas españolas." *Iberoamericana: América Latina-España-Portugal* 4, no. 15 (2004): 143–154.
Gerling, David Ross. "An Informal Interview with Lorenzo Silva." *World Literature Today* 76, no. 2 (2002): 92–97.

Giménez Caballero, Ernesto. *Notas marruecas de un soldado.* 1923. Reprint, Barcelona: Planeta, 1983.
Gorton, Kristyn. "(Un)fashionable Feminists: The Media and Ally McBeal." In *Third Wave Feminism: A Critical Exploration.* Edited by Stacy Gillis, Gillian Howie, and Rebecca Munford, 212–223. New York: Palgrave Macmillan, 2007.
Gozálvez Pérez, Vicente. "Descolonización y migraciones desde el África española (1956-1975)." *Investigaciones geográficas* 12 (1994): 45–84.
Guirao, Olga. *Carta con diez años de retraso.* Madrid: Espasa-Calpe, 2002.
al-Hakim, Taufiq. *Shahrazad.* 1934. Reprint, Paris: Nouvelles éditions Latines, 1936.
Halstead, Charles R. "A 'Somewhat Machiavellian' Face: Colonel Juan Beigbeder as High Commissioner in Spanish Morocco, 1937-1939." *Historian* 37, no. 1 (1974): 46–66.
Hamilos, Paul. "Dakar Rally Cancelled at Last Minute over Terrorist Threat." *The Guardian*, January 4, 2008. www.theguardian.com/world/2008/jan/05/france.sport.
el-Harti, Larbi. *Después de Tánger.* Madrid: Sial Ediciones, 2003.
Harvey, L. P. *Islamic Spain: 1250–1500.* Chicago: The University of Chicago Press, 1992.
Hodges, Tony. *Western Sahara: The Roots of a Desert War.* Westport, Connecticut: Lawrence Hill & Co, 1983.
Hodgson, Barbara. *Dreaming of East: Western Women and the Exotic Allure of the Orient.* Berkeley: Greystone Books, 2005.
International Court of Justice (ICJ). "Western Sahara: Advisory Opinion of 16 October 1975." Accessed May 20, 2020. www.icj-cij.org/files/case-related/61/6197.pdf.
Jameson, Frederic. *Brecht and Method.* New York: Verso, 1998.
Kapuściński, Ryszard. *The Other.* New York: Verso, 2008.
Lachica Garrido, Margarita. "Poetas árabes del País Valenciano." *Anales de la Universidad de Alicante. Historia Medieval* 9 (1992–1993): 17–37.
Landa, Nicasio. *La campaña de Marruecos. Memorias de un médico militar.* Madrid: Imprenta de Manuel Álvarez, 1860.
Landow, George P. "Edward W. Said's *Orientalism.*" *Political Discourse—Theories of Colonialism and Postcolonialism, Postcolonial Web,* March 18, 2002. Accessed May 20, 2020. www.postcolonialweb.org/poldiscourse/said/orient14.html.
Larequi, Eduardo-Martín. "La guerra de África, desde las trincheras: *El nombre de los nuestros,* de Lorenzo Silva." *La bitácora del tigre,* March 6, 2005. Accessed May 20, 2020. www.labitacoradeltigre.com/2005/03/06/la-guerra-de-africa-desde-las-trincheras-el-nombre-de-los-nuestros-de-lorenzo-silva/.
Leante, Luis. *Mira si yo te querré.* Madrid: Punto de lectura, 2008.
Leguineche, Manuel. *Annual 1921: El desastre de España en el Rif.* Madrid: Extra Alfaguara, 1996.
Levinas, Emmanuel. *Humanism of the Other.* Translated by Nidra Poller. Chicago: University of Illinois Press, 2003.
Lewis, Bernard, Grabar Oleg, and Edward Said. "Orientalism: An Exchange." *New York Review of Books.* June 24, 1982. www.nybooks.com/articles/1982/08/12/orientalism-an-exchange/.

Lewis, Marvin A. *Equatorial Guinean Literature in its National and Transnational Contexts*. Columbia, Missouri: University of Missouri Press, 2017.

———. *An Introduction to the Literature of Equatorial Guinea: Between Colonialism and Dictatorship*. Columbia, Missouri: University of Missouri Press, 2007.

Lewis, Reina. *Gendering Orientalism: Race, Femininity, and Representation*. New York: Routledge, 1996.

López Rodríguez, Marta Sofía. "(Des)Madres e hijas: De *Ekomo* a *El llanto de la perra*." *Afroeuropa* 2, no. 2 (2008): 1–12.

López Sarasúa, Concha. *Celanova 42: La España rural de la posguerra*. Alicante: Editorial Cálamo, 1993.

———. *Cita en París*. Alicante: Editorial Cálamo, 2005.

———. *La daga turca y otros relatos mediterráneos*. Alicante: Editorial Cálamo, 1996.

———. *En el país de Meriem*. Alicante: Editorial Cálamo, 1998.

———. *La llamada del almuédano*. Alicante: Editorial Cálamo, 1990.

———. *Meriem y la ruta fantástica*. Alicante: Editorial Cálamo, 1991.

———. *Los mil y un cuentos de Meriem*. Alicante: Editorial Cálamo, 2003.

———. *¿Por qué tengo que emigrar?* Madrid: Ibersaf, 2009.

———. *¿Qué buscabais en Marrakech?* Alicante: Editorial Cálamo, 2001.

———. *A vuelo de pájaro sobre Marruecos*. Alicante: Editorial Cálamo, 1995.

Lyotard, Jean-François. *The Differend: Phrases in Dispute*. Translated by Georges Van den Abbeele. Minneapolis: University of Minnesota Press, 1988.

MacCannell, Dean. *The Tourist: A New Theory of the Leisure Class*. 1976. Reprint, Berkeley: University of California Press, 1999.

MacKenzie, John. *Orientalism: History, Theory, and the Arts*. Manchester: Manchester University Press, 1995.

Mann, Vivian B., Thomas F. Glick, and Jerrilyn D. Dodds, eds. *Convivencia: Jews, Muslims, and Christians in Medieval Spain*. New York: George Braziller, Inc. 1992.

María Dueñas. Ediciones Planeta Madrid, S.A., 2020. Accessed April 26, 2020. www.mariaduenas.es.

Martín Gaite, Carmen. *Nubosidad variable*. Madrid: Anagrama, 1992.

Martínez Montávez, Pedro. Prologue to *¿Te acuerdas de Shahrazad?* By Montserrat Abumalham, 7–10. Madrid: Sial Ediciones, 2001.

Martínez de Pisón, Ignacio. *Una guerra africana*. Madrid: Ediciones SM, 2000.

Martin-Márquez, Susan. *Disorientations: Spanish Colonialism in Africa and the Performance of Identity*. New Haven: Yale University Press, 2008.

Marx, Karl. *Capital, Volume I*. New York: Penguin Books, 1990.

Mayrata, Ramón. *Alí Bey El Abasí: Un cristiano en La Meca*. Barcelona: Planeta, 1995.

———. "Aquel mendigo de la Plaza Esbehiheh." In *El imperio desierto*, 369–390. Madrid: Calamar Ediciones, 2008.

———. *Confín de la ciudad: El olivar de Castillejo*. Madrid: Los Libros de la Galera Sol, 1998.

———. *Una duda de Alicia*. Madrid: Frakson D. L., 1990.

———. *Estética de las serpientes*. Madrid: Azur, 1972.
———. "El esplendor de la Tierra Pura." *Album, letras, artes*, no. 53 (1997): 67–78.
———. "El hombre del ojo blanco y opaco." *Suplemento literario la nación* (1994): 8.
———. *El imperio desierto*. 1992. Reprint, Madrid: Calamar Ediciones, 2008.
———. *Miracielos*. Barcelona: Muchnik Editores, 2000.
———. *Miracielos: Adaptación Teatral de Carlos Rod*. Cádiz: XVII Festival Iberoamericano de Teatro de Cádiz, 2002.
———. *El ojo de la arbitrariedad*. Madrid: Ediciones Libertarias, 1986.
———. "La perplejidad del arte moderno." In *Los espectáculos del arte: Instituciones y funciones del arte contemporáneo*, edited by F. Calvo Serraller, 111–134. Barcelona: Tusquets, 1993.
———, editor. *Relatos del Sáhara*. Madrid: Clan, 2001.
———. *El sillón malva*. Barcelona: Planeta, 1994.
———. *Si me escuchas esta noche*. Madrid: Mondadori, 1991.
———. *Sin puertas: Poemas, 1990-1991*. Valencia: Pre-Textos, 1996.
Mayrata, Ramón, and Jesús Tablate. *Viaje por Egipto y Asia menor*. Madrid: Álbum letras artes, 1996.
Mazrui, Alia A. "The Re-invention of Africa: Edward Said, V. Y. Mudimbe, and Beyond." *Research in African Literatures* 36, no. 3 (Fall 2005): 68–82.
McDowell, Linda. "Place and Space." In *A Concise Companion to Feminist Theory*, edited by Mary Eagleton, 11–31. Blackwell Publishing, Ltd, 2003.
Mekuy, Guillermina. *El llanto de la perra*. Barcelona: Random House Mondadori, 2005.
———. *Tres almas para un corazón*. Madrid: Grupo Planeta, 2011.
———. *Las tres vírgenes de Santo Tomás*. Madrid: Suma de letras, 2008.
Melibea Obono, Trifonia. *La bastarda*. 2016. Reprint, Madrid: Flores raras, 2018.
———. *Las mujeres hablan mucho y mal*. Madrid: Sial Ediciones, 2018.
Memmi, Albert. *Colonizer and the Colonized*. New York: Orion Press, 1965.
Menocal, María Rosa. *The Ornament of the World: How Muslims, Jews, and Christians Created a Culture of Tolerance in Medieval Spain*. New York: Little, Brown and Company, 2002.
Merino, Ignacio. *Serrano Suñer: conciencia y poder*. Madrid: Algaba Ediciones, 2004.
Mernissi, Fatema. *Scheherazade Goes West: Different Cultures, Different Harems*. New York: Washington Square Press, 2001.
Mohanty, Chandra Talpade. *Feminism Without Borders: Decolonizing Theory, Practicing Solidarity*. Durham, North Carolina: Duke University Press, 2003.
Moreno Torregrosa, Pasqual and Mohamed El Ghreyb. *Dormir al raso*. Madrid: Ediciones Vosa, 1994.
Mota Ripeu, O'sírima. *El punto ciego de Cassandra*. Madrid: Sial Ediciones, 2017.
Mudimbe, V. Y. *The Idea of Africa*. Indianapolis: Indiana University Press, 1994.
———. *The Invention of Africa: Gnosis, Philosophy, and the Order of Knowledge*. Indianapolis: Indiana University Press, 1988.

Mundy, Jacob A. "Performing the Nation, Pre-Figuring the State: The Western Saharan Refugees, Thirty Years Later." *Journal of Modern African Studies* 45, no. 2 (2007): 275–297.
Mundy, Jacob A., and Stephen Zunes. *Western Sahara: War, Nationalism, and Conflict Resolution.* Syracuse: Syracuse University Press, 2010.
Muñoz Molina, Antonio. *La noche de los tiempos.* Barcelona: Seix Barral, 2009.
Ndongo-Bidyogo, Donato. *El metro.* Barcelona: El Cobre, 2007.
Ndongo-Bidyogo, Donato, and Alicia Campos Serrano. *De colonia a estado: Guinea Ecuatorial, 1955-1968.* Madrid: Centro de Estudios Políticos y Constitucionales, 2002.
Ndongo-Bidyogo, Donato, Alicia Campos Serrano, and Mariano L. de Castro Antolín. *España en Guinea: construcción del desencuentro: 1778-1968.* Madrid: Sequitur, 1998.
New Spanish Books. "Concha López Sarasúa." Accessed May 20, 2020. www.newspanishbooks.com/author/concha-l-pez-saras.
Nobile, Selena. "María Nsué Angüe y Guillermina Mekuy: De la escritura femenina en Guinea Ecuatorial a la construcción de una matria migrante." Proceedings of the XXXVIII Congreso Internacional del Instituto Internacional de Literatura Iberoamericana. Georgetown University, June 9–12, 2010.
Nonell, Carmen. *Zoco grande.* Madrid: Colenda, 1956.
Noticias jurídicas. "Ley 9/1968, de 5 de abril, sobre secretos oficiales." Accessed May 25, 2020. noticias.juridicas.com/base_datos/Admin/l9-1968.html.
Nsué Angüe, María. *Ekomo.* Madrid: Universidad Nacional de Educación a Distancia, 1985.
Nueva asociación de escritores marroquíes en lengua española. Facebook Group. Accessed May 15, 2020. www.facebook.com/NUEVAAEMLE.
Odartey-Wellington, Dorothy, ed. *Trans-afrohispanismos: Puentes culturales críticos entre África, Latinoamérica y España.* Boston: Brill Rodopi, 2018.
Okenve-Martínez, Enrique S. "Equatorial Guinea 1927-1979: A New African Tradition." PhD diss., School of Oriental and African Studies (SOAS), University of London, 2007.
Omar, M. Sidi. *Los estudios post-coloniales: Una introducción crítica.* Castellón: Universitat Jaume I, 2008.
Ong, Walter J. *Orality and Literacy: The Technologizing of the Word.* New York: Methuen, 1982.
Oropesa, Salvador A. "Todo por la patria: Lorenzo Silva y su contextualización en la novela policiaca española." *Espéculo: Revista de estudios literarios*, no. 22 (November 2002–February 2003). webs.ucm.es/info/especulo/numero22/silva.html.
Ortiz, Lourdes. *Fátima de los naufragios.* Barcelona: Planeta, 1998.
O'Shea, Stephen. *Sea of Faith: Islam and Christianity in the Medieval Mediterranean World.* New York: Walker & Company, 2006.
el-Ouahhabi, Mohamed Lemrini. "Viaje al pasado" In *La puerta de los vientos: Narradores marroquíes contemporáneos*, 217–223. Edited by Marta Cerezales, Miguel Ángel Moreta, and Lorenzo Silva. Barcelona: Destino, 2004.

Payne, Stanley G. *Franco and Hitler: Spain, Germany, and World War II.* New Haven: Yale University Press, 2008.
Prendergast, Ryan. *Reading, Writing, and Errant Subjects in Inquisitorial Spain.* New York: Routledge, 2016.
Pérez Beltrán, Carmelo, editor. *Entre las 2 Orillas: Literatura marroquí en lengua española.* Granada: Universidad de Granada y Fundación, 2007.
Pratt, Mary Louise. *Imperial Eyes: Travel Writing and Transculturation.* New York: Routledge, 1992.
Reverte, Javier. *El aroma del Copal (Trilogía de Centroamérica).* Madrid: Editorial Debate, 1989.
———. *Caminos perdidos de África (Trilogía de África).* Barcelona: DeBols!llo, 2004.
———. *La canción de Mbama.* Madrid: Plaza & Janés, 2011.
———. *Los dioses bajo la lluvia (Trilogía de Centroamérica).* 1986. Reprint, Madrid: Plaza & Janés Editores, 1986.
———. *El hombre de la guerra (Trilogía de Centroamérica).* Madrid: Editorial Bitácora, 1994.
———. *El médico de Ifni.* Barcelona: Random House Mondadori, 2005.
———. *Poemas africanos.* Madrid: Reino de Cordelia, 2011.
———. *El sueño de África: En busca de los mitos blancos del continente negro (Trilogía de África).* Barcelona: DeBols!llo, 2007.
———. *Vagabundo en África (Trilogía de África).* Barcelona: DeBols!llo, 2005.
Ricci, Cristián H. *¡Hay moros en la costa!: Literatura marroquí fronteriza en castellano y catalán.* Madrid: Iberoamericana Vervuert, 2014.
———. *Literatura periférica en castellano y catalán: El caso marroquí.* Madrid: Ediciones del Orto, 2010.
Rizo, Elisa G. "Entrevista a Guillermina Mekuy Mba Obono." *Revista Iberoamericana* LXXX, no. 248–249 (2014): 1133–1140.
Roldán, Concha. "diálogo interreligioso: hablamos con . . . Montserrat Abumalham." *Todos uno.* Accessed May 16, 2020. *www.todosuno.org/dimontserrat.htm.*
Rueda, Ana. *Cartas sin lacrar: La novela epistolar y la España ilustrada, 1789-1840.* Madrid: Iberoamericana Vervuert, 2001.
———. "El enemigo 'invisible' de la Guerra de África (1859-60) y el proyecto histórico del nacionalismo español: Del Castillo, Alarcón y Landa." *The Colorado Review of Hispanic Studies*, no. 4 (2006): 147–167.
———. "El poder de la carta privada: *La incógnita* y *la estafeta romántica.*" *Bulletin of Hispanic Studies* 77, no. 3 (2000): 375–391.
———. "Sender y otros novelistas de la guerra marroquí: humanismo social y vanguardia política." *Romance Quarterly* 52, no. 3 (2005): 175–196.
Rueda, Ana, and Sandra Martín, collab. *El retorno/el reencuentro: La inmigración en la literatura hispano-marroquí.* Madrid: Iberoamericana Vervuert, 2010.
Said, Edward W. *Orientalism.* 1978. Reprint, New York: Vintage Books, 1994.
Salvo, Jorge. "La formación de identidad en la novela hispano-africana: 1950-1990." PhD diss., Florida State University, 2003.

Sampedro Vizcaya, Benita. "Transiting Western Sahara." *Journal of Spanish Cultural Studies* 20, nos. 1–2 (2019): 17–38.
Santí, Enrico Mario. "Fernando Ortiz: Counterpoint and Transculturation." In *Ciphers of History: Latin American Readings for a Cultural Age*, 169–218. New York: Palgrave Macmillan, 2005.
Sender, Ramón. *Imán*. 1930. Reprint, Huesca: Instituto de Estudios Altoaragoneses, 1992.
Scott, James C. "Everyday Forms of Resistance." *The Copenhagen Journal of Asian Studies*, vol. 4 (1989): 33–62.
———. *Seeing Like a State: How Certain Schemes to Improve the Human Condition Have Failed*. New Haven: Yale University Press, 1998.
Silva, Lorenzo. *El alquimista impaciente*. Barcelona: Ediciones Destino, 2000.
———. *Carta blanca*. Madrid: Espasa, 2004.
———. *Del Rif al Yebala. Viaje al sueño y la pesadilla de Marruecos*. Barcelona: Ediciones Destino, 2001.
———. *La flaqueza del bolchevique*. Barcelona: Ediciones Destino, 1997.
———. *El lejano país de los estanques*. Barcelona: Ediciones Destino, 1998.
———. *Lorenzo Silva: Una página personal dedicada a los lectores*. Lorenzo Silva Web. Accessed May 20, 2020. www.lorenzo-silva.com/.
———. *El nombre de los nuestros*. Barcelona: Ediciones Destino, 2008.
———. *Noviembre sin violetas*. Barcelona: Ediciones Destino, 2003.
———. Prologue to *Imán*. By Ramón J. Sender. Barcelona: Ediciones Destino, 2001.
Silva, Lorenzo, and Luis Miguel Francisco. *Y al final, la guerra: La aventura de los soldados españoles en Irak*. Madrid: La Esfera de los Libros, 2006.
Silva, Lorenzo, and Manuel Martín Cuenca, writers. *La flaqueza del bolchevique*. Directed by Manuel Martín Cuenca, performances by Luis Tosar, Mar Regueras, and María Valverde. Taznia Media, 2005.
Soja, Edward W. *Thirdspace: Journeys to Los Angeles and Other Real-and-Imagined Places*. Malden: Blackwell Publishers, 1996.
Spellberg, Denise A. *Politics, Gender, and the Islamic Past: The Legacy of A'isha Bint Abi Bakr*. New York: Columbia University Press, 1994.
Spivak, Gayatri Chakravorty. "Can the Subaltern Speak?" *Marxism and the Interpretation of Culture*, edited by. C. Nelson and L. Grossberg, 271–314. Champaign: University of Illinois Press, 1988.
Tauchnitz, Juliane. "Identity Questions in *El diablo de Yudis* by Ahmed Daoudi." In *The World in Movement: Performative Identities and Diasporas*. Edited by Alfonso de Toro and Juliane Tauchnitz, 216–228. Leiden: Brill, 2018.
Thiong'o, Ngũgĩ wa. *Decolonising the Mind: The Politics of Language in African Literature*. 1986. Reprint, Nairobi: East African Educational Publishers.
———. "Decolonising the Mind." *Diogenes* 184, vol 46/4 (1998): 101–104.
Thompson, James, and David Scott. *The East Imagined, Experienced, and Remembered: Orientalist Nineteenth Century Paintings*. Dublin: National Gallery of Ireland, 1988.
Torbado, Jesús. *El imperio de arena*. Barcelona: Plaza & Janés, 1998.
Torres, Rafael. *Yo, Mohamed*. Madrid: Temas de Hoy, 1995.

Turner, Bryan. *Orientalism, Postmodernism, and Globalism*. Boston: Routledge, 1994.
Ugarte, Michael. *Africans in Europe: The Culture of Exile and Emigration from Equatorial Guinea to Spain*. Chicago: University of Illinois Press, 2010.
Valle-Inclán, Ramón del. *Luces de Bohemia*. 1920. Madrid: Espasa-Calpe, 1973.
Varisco, Daniel Martin. *Reading Orientalism: Said and the Unsaid*. Seattle: University of Washington Press, 2007.
Vázquez-Figueroa, Alberto. *África llora*. 1996. Reprint, Barcelona: DeBols!llo, 2004.
———. *Alberto Vázquez-Figueroa*. Official English-language website. Desperado Management, 2008. Accessed Dec 1, 2011. www.albertovazquezfigueroa.com.
———. *Arena y viento*. 1953. Reprint, Barcelona: Plaza & Janés Editores, 1992.
———. *Ébano: La ruta de los esclavos*. 1975. Reprint, Barcelona: Plaza & Janés Editores, 1983.
———. *Garoé*. Madrid: Mr Novela Histórica, 2010.
———. *Los ojos del Tuareg*. 2000. Barcelona: DeBols!llo, 2005.
———. *Tuareg*. 1980. Barcelona: DeBols!llo, 2004.
———, screenplay. *Tuareg: The Desert Warrior* [*Tuareg—Il guerriero del desierto*]. Directed Enzo G. Castellari, performances by Mark Harmon, Luis Prendes, and Ritza Brown. Aspa Producciones Cinematográficas, 1984.
Villanova, José Luis. *El Protectorado de España en Marruecos: Organización política y territorial*. Barcelona: Edicions Bellaterra, 2004.
Warraq, Ibn. *Defending the West: A Critique of Edward Said's* Orientalism. New York: Prometheus Books, 2007.
Young, Eric. "Bubi." In *The Encyclopedia of Africa, Vol. 1*, edited by Anthony Appiah and Henry Louis Gates, 206–207. Oxford: Oxford University Press, 2010.
———. "Fang." In *The Encyclopedia of Africa, Vol. 1*, edited by Anthony Appiah and Henry Louis Gates, 460. Oxford: Oxford University Press, 2010.
Young, Robert J. C. *White Mythologies: Writing, History, and the West*. New York: Routledge, 2004.

Index

Abbeele, Georges Van den, 75–76, 121–126, 129–130, 144–146, 165n14, 166n30
abóm, 95–96
Abrighach, Mohamed, x, 36, 38–40, 45
Abumalham Mas, Montserrat, 9–11, 13–14, 75–77, 99–108, 117n159, 177–178; *¿Te acuerdas de Shahrazad?*, 99–108
Abumalham, Nayib, 117n159
Afinoguénova, Eugenia, 136, 169n83
Africa, 1, 3–6, 8–15, 16n25, 17n28, 18nn50–52, 21–23, 25–27, 32, 34–38, 40–42, 44–45, 59n4, 60nn17–18, 66n121, 73–87, 94, 98, 101, 108n4, 118n169, 121–127, 130, 140–141, 148, 165n4, 166n23, 167n44, 169n76, 177–179; as a dark continent, 76, 98, 178; as virgin territory, 12, 73, 76, 98; as Other, 1, 3, 4, 9–15, 23–24; Spanish in, 7–9, 16n22, 16nn24–25
African authors, 1–2, 6–10, 97, 118nn168–169, 155
African literature, 7–8, 118n169. *See also* Hispano-African literature
Aixa, 74, 108n10
Alarcón, Pedro Antonio de, 2, 9, 26, 30, 62n43, 73–77

Aleixandre, Vicente, 46
aleya, 66n108
al-halqa. See halqa
alienation, 156, 160–161, 163, 173n172. *See also* colonial alienation
aljamía, 36, 65n98
Allan, Joanna, 16n25, 93–96, 98, 113n95
Almarcegui, Patricia, 61n25
alterity, 2–3, 5, 13, 24, 26–28, 45, 76, 122
Althusser, Louis, 126
Amaury Sport Organisation, 170n104
American Anthropological Association, 2; Statement on 'Race,' 2
Amine, Khalid, 124, 155–156, 161–163, 165, 174n183
Andrés-Gallego, José, 63n69
Anidjar, Gil, 11, 25–27, 49
animism, 94–95
Antón, Jacinto, 167n44
The Arabian Nights: Tales of 1,001 Nights, 76, 100–102, 104, 106, 118
archetype, 13, 30, 75, 87, 100–103, 105–107, 124, 147, 157, 163–164
Ascherson, Neal, 139
Aousserd, 128, 133, 135
Atxaga, Bernardo, 14, 60n17

Badía y Leblich, Domingo (Alí Bey), 14, 22–23, 46–47, 121
Balbontín, José Antonio, 25
Barea, Arturo, 25, 166n22
Beigbeder y Atienza, Juan Luis, 83–84, 111n53
Berhardt, Johannes, 111n50
Bey, Alí. *See* Badía y Leblich, Domingo
Bhabha, Homi, 6, 91
blocao, 66n16
Boampong, Joanna, 91, 97, 16n25
Bobbitt, Brian J., 154
Borm, Jan, 121, 165
Bouissef Rekab, Mohamed, 100
Bowen, Wayne H., 111n49
Brecht, Bertolt, 156–157, 159–160, 163–164, 173n172
Broeck, Paul Van Den, 61n32
Bubi, 98, 112n84
Butler, Judith, 92

Cadalso, José de, 121
Cairo, Heriberto, 41, 66n121
Calderwood, Eric, 16n25
Campos Serrano, Alicia, 60n18
Campoy-Cubillo, Adolfo, 6, 16n24–25, 154–156, 160, 162–163
Carlson, Marvin, 164
Carrasco González, Antonio, 17n28, 18n49, 62n46, 122–123, 165n4
Carreras Serra, Lluís, 69n172
Castillo, Rafael del, 26, 30, 62n43
Castro, Mariano L. de, 60n18
Census: in Equatorial Guinea, 21, 59n1; in Spanish Protectorate of Morocco, 21, 37; in Spanish Sahara, 21
Cerarols Ramírez, Rosa, 98
Cercas, Javier, 59n4
Cervantes Saavedra, Miguel de, 117n159, 128, 178
Chacón, Dulce, 59n4
Chakor, Mohamed, 173n165
Chamberlain, Muriel Evelyn, 60n17
Chavez, Leo, 124
Civil War. *See* Spanish Civil War

Cixous, Hélène, 3
Clarín, Leopoldo Alas, 78
colonial, 5, 8–13, 18n49, 18nn57–58, 21–24, 34–35, 39–42, 46–48, 51–52, 57–58, 60n17, 66n122, 73, 78–79, 82–83, 86–87, 89–90, 93–96, 98, 99, 110n34, 112n84, 122–123, 125, 128, 137, 156, 161, 165n4, 165n18, 178; alienation, 7, 161; encounter, 40; nostalgia, 41, 82, 86; rule, 93–95; subject, 47–48; tropes, 98
colonialism, 6, 8, 12, 23, 40, 46, 56, 73, 81, 90, 94, 126, 160
colonized, 51, 56
colonizer, 66n122, 82, 83, 110n34, 110n36, 146
contact zones, 40–44, 46, 126
Costa, Joaquín, 118n51
Craig-Odders, Renée, 61n32
cultural capital, 79–80, 85
cuota militar, 63n69

Dakar Rally, 170n104. *See also* Amaury Sport Organisation
Daoudi, Ahmed, 7, 9, 11, 14, 77, 117n156, 123–125, 127, 153–165, 177–179
Decolonization, 9, 12–13, 21, 47–48, 50, 52, 69n68, 87
Deleuze, Gilles, 8
Derrida, Jacques, 29, 70n193
Díaz Fernández, José, 23, 25, 60n16, 74, 76–77, 110n31, 166n22, 177
differend, 158
Disaster of Annual, 23, 25, 60n15
Disembarking of Alhuemas [El desembarco de Alhucemas], 62n46
Dodds, Jerrilyn D., 18n50
Dueñas, María, 8–9, 11, 14, 17n36, 22, 75–76, 77–87, 178; *El tiempo entre costuras*, 8–9, 13, 17, 18n48, 22, 59n4, 75, 77–87
Dumas, Alexandre, 18n51

Einfühlung (empathy), 156, 163

Ellison, Mahan L., 117n156
emigration, 17n38, 21–23, 40, 59n2, 60n121, 154–155
empathy. See *Einfühlung*
encounter, 22, 24, 30, 34, 57, 122, 126–127, 132–137, 140, 142–144, 150–153, 178
enemy, 13, 25, 26–31, 33–35, 49, 57, 63n57, 71n203, 149
epistolary: distance, 102; genre, 75, 100, 102, 103; novel, 13, 75, 102, 104, 107, 117n155
Equatorial Guinea, 7–7, 9–11, 13, 16n22, 16n25, 17n38, 19n58, 21, 23, 60n18, 77, 88–90, 93, 95, 112n84, 113n93, 113n95; Equatorial Guinean, 8–9, 75, 89, 95–96, 115n122. See *also* Spanish Guinea
esperpentic lens, 23, 60n20, 147
Esperpento, 60n20
Esquirol, Miguel, 61n32
Estévez Hernández, Pablo, 59n1
Evita Ika, Victoria, 113n93
exoticism, 79, 85, 87, 122

Fang, 88–90, 93–95, 98, 99, 112n84
Faszer-McMahon, Debra, 16n25
feminism, 81–82, 87–88, 110n43
feminist, 81, 87–88; theory, 80–81
Fernández Parrilla, Gonzalo, 5–6
Flaubert, Gustave, 3, 98–99, 169n71
Flores Morales, Ángel, 18nn50–51, 66n121, 116n141
Fornieles, Javier, 61n25
Fortuny i Marsal, Mariano, 73–74, 76–77, 108n4–5
Franco, Francisco, 15n7, 48, 62, 83, 111n49, 127, 167n45
Frente Polisario. See Polisario

Gahete, Manuel, 17n39, 117n160
Ganivet, Ángel, 18n52
García Figueras, Tomás, 60n18
García Jambrina, Luis, 61n32

gender, 2, 4, 11–13, 73, 75–77, 81–82, 89, 95, 100, 104, 106–107, 109n16, 133; gendered, 73–74, 75–77, 94–95, 101, 104, 108n5; gendering, 76–77
Generation of '98, 60n20
Gerling, David Ross, 61n25, 61n32
El Ghreyb, Mohamed, 155
Giménez Caballero, Ernesto, 2, 23
Glick, Thomas F., 18
Global Hispanophone, 6, 16n22
Gorton, Kristyn, 80
Goytisolo, Juan, 76–77
Gozálvez Pérez, Vicente, 37, 40, 65n102
Guattari, Félix, 8
Guirao, Olga, 100

al-Hakim, Taufiq, 100
Halstead, Charles R., 111n53
halqa, 154–158, 160–165, 174n183
Hamilos, Paul, 170n104
Harka, 28–31, 33–35, 63n60
el-Harti, Larbi, 100–101
Harvey, L. P., 18n50, 68n146, 68n149
Hispano-African, 6–10, 18n49, 88, 97, 122, 123; literature, 123; vs. Afro-Hispanic, 7; Wars, 74
hlayqi, 155–156, 159, 164
Hodges, Tony, 18n57, 60n19, 69n168, 69n171, 167n45
Hodgson, Barbara, 109n16
homeland, 80, 84, 131, 135; fatherland, 13, 45, 73, 130, 131; motherland, 58, 73; *patria*, 24, 73

Ifni, 18n56, 2–22, 60n18, 128, 130–131, 133–135
immigrant, 7, 10, 12–13, 16n25, 22, 40, 45, 88, 99, 124–125, 127, 154–155, 157, 166n25, 166n31
immigration, 9–11, 13, 15, 37, 65n102, 66n121, 82, 100, 122, 124, 155, 163, 173n165
International Court of Justice (ICJ), 47–49, 51, 69n170
Isabel la Católica, 15n7, 66n121

jaima, 135, 169n76
Jameson, Frederic, 164, 173n172

Kapuściński, Ryszard, 2, 26–27, 57, 126–127, 131, 139, 151, 172n142
Ketz, Victoria L., 16n25
kidnapping. *See abóm*
Krim, Abd el, 34

Lachica Garrido, Margarita, 67n143
Landa, Nicasio, 26, 30, 62n43
Landow, George P., 4, 15n13
Larequi, Eduardo-Martín, 61n25
Leante, Luis, 14, 22
legible, 48–54, 57, 108
legibility, 46–47, 49, 53
Leguineche, Manuel, 60n15
Levinas, Emmanuel, 3, 11, 26–27, 29–30, 126–127, 133, 140, 151
Lewis, Bernard, 4, 15n13
Lewis, Marvin A., 9, 88–89; Lewis, Reina, 109n16
Law of Official Secrets of 1968 [Ley 9/1968, de 5 de abril, sobre secretos oficiales], 48, 69n172, 70n184
Law of Recruitment [Ley de Reclutamiento], 63n69
López Rodríguez, Marta Sofía, 88, 90–91, 97, 113n89, 113n93, 115n122
López Sarasúa, Concha, 8–9, 11–14, 22–24, 35–46, 66n121, 177, 178; *La llamada del almuédano*, 8–9, 13, 22–24, 35–46, 57, 59
Lyotard, Jean-François, 159

MacCannell, Dean, 136, 169n83, 171n118
MacKenzie, John, 4, 15n13
Maghreb, 14, 16n22, 23, 44, 101–102, 118n169; Hispano-/Hispanophone Maghrebi, 75, 101; Maghrebi, 7, 107, 124, 155
Mann, Vivian B., 18n50,
Mare Nostrum, 36
Martín Gaite, Carmen, 100

Martin-Márquez, Susan, 5–6, 18n51, 108n5, 169n84
Martín, Sandra, 117n160, 124
Martínez de Pisón, Ignacio, 14, 22
Martínez Montávez, Pedro, 100
Martí-Olivella, Jaume, 136, 169n83
Marx, Karl, 33, 40, 64n75
Mauritania, 18n57, 47–48, 51, 167n45
Mayrata, Ramón, 9, 11–14, 17n42, 22–24, 36, 46–59, 123, 166n24, 177–179; *El imperio desierto*, 9, 13, 18n42, 22–24, 36, 46–59, 69n178, 166n24
Mazrui, Alia A., 5
McDowell, Linda, 80–81
Mekuy, Guillermina, 9–11, 13–14, 75–77, 88–99, 116n145, 177, 179; *Las tres vírgenes de Santo Tomás*, 9, 13, 75, 88–99, 116n145
Melibea Obono, Trifonia, 97, 113n93
Memmi, Albert, 66n122, 110n34, 110n36
Menocal, María Rosa, 18n50
Merino, Ignacio, 111n49,
Mernissi, Fatema, 11, 76, 100–101, 103–105, 118n161, 169n71; *Scheherazade Goes West: Different Cultures, Different Harems*, 11, 76, 100, 118n161, 169n71
mētis, 124, 132, 145–146, 153, 168n62, 171n127
mission civilisatrice, 42,
Modern Language Association, 6
Mohanty, Chandra Talpade, 80–81, 87, 106, 110n43
Moreno Torregrosa, Pasqual, 155
Moroccan Protectorate. *See* Spanish Protectorate of Morocco
Morocco, 5–7, 10–11, 13, 18n56, 21, 23, 25, 27, 35–38, 40–41, 43, 45, 47–49, 51, 57–58, 65nn102–103, 78–79, 81–86, 99–100, 108n4, 109n27, 111n53, 116n141, 117n159, 123, 128, 130, 134, 138, 153–155, 157–158, 167n45, 174n183

Mota Ripeu, O'sírima, 97, 113n93
Mudimbe, V. Y., 5, 11, 87
Mundy, Jacob A., 69n168, 69n171, 167n45
Muñoz Molina, Antonio, 59n4

Ndongo-Bidyogo, Donato, 6–8, 60n18, 173n165
Nistal Rosique, Gloria, 116n145
Nobile, Selena, 88
nomad, 12–13, 123–125, 127, 132, 140, 142–147, 151; nomadic, 49, 123–124, 130–132, 141, 145–147, 150–151, 166n31, 169n76, 170n103; nomadism, 49, 122, 166n24, 170n103
Nonell, Carmen, 18n51
nostalgia, 39, 41–42, 46, 78–79, 82, 86
nostalgic, 34, 54, 83
novelas moriscas, 128, 167n47, 178
Nsué Angüe, María, 88, 95, 115n122
Nueva asociación de escritores marroquíes en lengua española, 154

Odartey-Wellington, Dorothy, 16n25
oikos, 122–124, 129–133, 134–135, 139–140, 145–147
Okenve-Martínez, Enrique S., 95–96
Omar, M. Sidi, 6
Ong, Walter J., 70n193
Orient, 1, 3–5, 10, 30, 39–40, 53, 55, 73, 76, 82, 85–86, 103–104, 106–107, 109n16, 123, 126, 133, 142–143, 146–147, 152, 169n71
Orientalist: art, 108nn4–5; discourse, 1, 4–5, 10, 30–31, 33, 35, 43, 45, 50, 58, 75–77, 86, 87, 102, 104, 107–108, 122–123, 125, 127, 133–135, 140, 143, 147, 150, 152, 155, 163, 165, 177–179; gaze, 156, 163; legacy, 12; reflections, 6; stereotypes, 15, 23, 40, 43, 76–77, 84, 122, 124, 136, 143–144, 146; tendencies, 13, 74–75; theory, 11; tradition, 18n49, 140; tropes, 26, 30, 40, 43, 45, 84, 98, 99, 144, 146, 153. *See also* trope(s)
Orientalism, 1, 4–5, 9–13, 15, 15n13, 18n49, 30, 39–40, 45–47, 55–56, 74–75, 79, 80, 82, 85–87, 98–99, 104, 108, 109n16, 122–123, 126–128, 141, 143, 147, 152, 163–164, 169n71, 171n116, 177–179
Oriental woman, 3, 73
Oropesa, Salvador A., 61n32
Ortiz, Fernando, 66n112, 126, 166n34
Ortiz, Lourdes, 14
O'Shea, Stephen, 18n50
Other, 1–5, 8–13, 15, 23–36, 38–43, 45–46, 48, 50–51, 53, 55–59, 73–77, 79–81, 89, 99, 100–107, 121–128, 130–136, 138–144, 146–153, 177–179; Same and Other 3–4, 24, 32–35, 45, 76, 102, 123, 125–126, 128, 132–135, 138–140, 142–143
otherness, 1–2, 24–25, 27, 31, 34, 48, 74, 103–104, 123, 128, 131–133, 136, 138, 153, 161. *See also* alterity
el-Ouahhabi, Mohamed Lemrini, 173n165

patera 40, 157
patria. *See* homeland
patriarchy, 93, 95–96, 99
Payne, Stanley G., 111n50
Pérez Beltrán, Carmelo, 17n39, 173n165
Polisario, 48–50, 53, 55–56, 127, 128, 130, 167n45
positional superiority, 30–31, 35, 40, 43, 82, 87, 123, 125
postcolonial, 5, 8–9, 81, 89, 95, 161–164; identity, 155; subject, 160–161, 163–164
postcoloniality, 6, 154–155, 164
Pratt, Mary Louise, 39–40, 126
Prendergast, Ryan, 167n47
Protectorate of Morocco. *See* Spanish Protectorate of Morocco

resistance, 7, 13, 31, 48, 75, 77, 88–90, 93–99, 113n95, 149
Reverte, Javier, 9, 11, 13–14, 19n59, 22–23, 77, 121–125, 127–140, 166n23, 167n44, 178; *El médico de Ifni*, 9, 13–14, 22, 122–123, 125, 127–140, 167n46
Rif War, 24–25, 27, 60n15, 62n46, 63n57, 82
Rizo, Elisa G., 94, 98
Rueda, Ana, 26–27, 29–30, 34, 61n25, 61n29, 61n32, 62n43, 62n45, 79, 102, 117n155, 117n160, 124, 154, 163, 173n153

Saharawi, 6, 8, 9, 13, 24, 47–59, 69n178, 123, 127–132, 134, 136–138, 167n45; Refugee Camps, 48, 58, 128, 129, 131, 135, 167n45. *See also* Polisario
Said, Edward W., 1, 3–6, 9, 11, 12, 35, 39, 47, 53, 74, 85–87, 98, 123, 127, 146, 152–153, 163, 169n71, 171n116, 177–178; *Orientalism*, 1, 4, 5, 9, 11, 47, 74, 80, 86, 98, 104, 126, 141, 152, 163. *See also* Orientalism
Salvo, Jorge, 7
Sampedro Vizcaya, Benita, 6, 16nn23–24, 69n168, 69n171
Santí, Enrico Mario, 66n112, 166n34
Scheherazade. *See* Shahrazad
Scott, David, 108n4
Scott, James C., 11, 47, 49, 53, 95, 124, 131, 145, 168n62, 171n127
Scramble for Africa, 60n17
Sender, Ramón J., 23, 25–26, 60n16, 61n25, 61n29, 61n32, 62n45, 166n22, 177
Serrano Suñer, Ramón, 83–84, 111n49
sexuality, 13, 75–77, 89, 90–93, 97, 99
Shahrazad, 13, 75, 77, 99–108, 118n161, 118n164, 118n169, 154. *See also* Abumalham, Montserrat
Shahrayar, 104, 118n161
Sidi Ifni. *See* Ifni

Silva, Lorenzo, 9, 11–12, 14, 22–23, 24–35, 36, 39, 46, 59n4, 60n16, 61n29, 61n32, 173n165, 177–178; *El nombre de los nuestros*, 9, 12, 14, 22–23, 24–35, 36, 39, 59, 63n57, 71n203, 178
Soja, Edward W., 91
Spanish-American War, 11, 22
Spanish Civil War, 21, 37, 59n4, 80, 141
Spanish Guinea, 21, 89–90, 93–95, 98, 112n84. *See also* Equatorial Guinea
Spanish Protectorate of Morocco, 13, 21, 23, 25, 37–39, 41–42, 45, 47, 65n102, 66n121, 78–79, 81–84, 109n27, 117n159, 123
Spanish Sahara, 21–22, 47–50, 53, 54, 57, 127, 129, 137, 141, 167n45. *See also* Western Sahara
Spellberg, Denise A., 108n10
Spivak, Gayatri Chakravorty, 4, 6, substitute [sustituto], 32

Tangier, 37, 78–80, 84, 86
Tauchnitz, Juliane, 124, 154, 156–157, 163
techne, 124, 145–147, 149–150, 153, 171n127
Tétouan, 22, 78–84, 86, 99
Thiong'o, Ngũgĩ wa, 7, 8, 161,
Thompson, James, 108n4
Torbado, Jesús, 14, 22–23
Torres, Rafael, 155,
tourism, 88, 122–123, 128, 135, 169n83
tourist, 12–13, 86, 123, 125, 127, 131–132, 135–136, 140, 144–145, 160, 165n18, 169n83, 171n118
transculturation, 40, 66n112, 126, 152
travel, 11–14, 24–25, 36, 61n35, 75, 121–136, 139–140, 142, 143–147, 150, 152, 153, 165n5, 165n14, 165n18, 166n23, 166n30; metaphor of travel, 75, 121–122, 126, 139, 144, 166n30; traveler, 121–124, 126–127, 130, 134, 165n18; travel writing, 121, 126, 152, 165n5

trope(s), 12, 76, 128, 131; of Africa, 98, 76; of the veil, 74; of travel, 150; Orientalist, 10, 26, 30, 45, 74, 98–99, 108n5, 153. *See also* Orientalist, Orientalism
Tuareg, 13, 123, 141–142, 144–147, 149–152, 170n102–103, 171n131. *See also* Vázquez-Figueroa, Alberto
Turner, Bryan, 4

Ugarte, Michael, 17n38
Unamuno, Miguel de, 18n52

Valle-Inclán, Ramón del, 60n20
Varisco, Daniel Martin, 4, 11, 80, 86, 106
Vázquez-Figueroa, Alberto, 9–11, 13–14, 122–125, 127, 140–153, 170n96, 171n117–118, 177, 179; *Los ojos del Tuareg*, 9, 13, 122, 124–125, 140–153, 170n102, 170n104, 170n105
Verfremdungseffekt, 156, 159–160, 162–164, 173n172
V-effect. *See Verfremdungseffekt*
Villanova, José Luis, 109n27
virgin, 90, 92, 118n161; *See also* Africa as virgin territory
virginity, 88–92, 95–99

voyage, 40, 110n36, 121, 127, 129–130, 140, 145, 165n14, 166n30

war, 9–13, 21–28, 30–39, 46, 59n4, 60nn15–17, 61n32, 62n46, 63n57, 69n168, 74, 80, 82, 84, 108n4, 111nn49–50, 123, 141, 149, 152, 167n45, 177; enemy in, 11–13, 25–31, 33, 34–35, 49, 57, 63n57, 71n203, 130, 136, 149; other in, 24–35, 71n203. *See also* Hispano-African Wars, Rif War, Spanish-American War, Spanish Civil War, War of Africa, World War II
War of Africa (first African War), 22, 27, 59n4, 60n17, 74, 108n4, 123
Warraq, Ibn, 4, 15n13
Western Sahara, 6, 10, 11, 13, 16n22, 16n25, 18n57, 47, 60n19, 69n168, 69n170, 127, 135, 167n45. *See also* Spanish Sahara
"Western Sahara: Advisory Opinion of 16 October 1975," 69n170
World War II, 36–37, 80, 111n49–50

Young, Eric, 112n84
Young, Robert J. C., 4, 15n13

Zunes, Stephen, 69n168, 69n171

About the Author

Mahan L. Ellison, PhD, is associate professor of Spanish at Bridgewater College. His research focuses on the literary and historical connections between Spain and Africa. He has published articles in *Research in African Literatures*, *CELAAN* (*Review of the Center for the Study of Literatures and Arts of North Africa*), the *Vanderbilt e-Journal of Luso-Hispanic Studies*, *Confluencia*, and other journals. He is a 2020–2021 Fulbright Scholar, and his research has been supported by grants from the National Endowment for the Humanities and the Virginia Foundation for Independent Colleges Mednick Memorial Fellowship. More information can be found at www.mahanellison.com.

www.ingramcontent.com/pod-product-compliance
Lightning Source LLC
Chambersburg PA
CBHW020120010526
44115CB00008B/899